The Reference Shelf

Representative American Speeches 2018-2019

The Reference Shelf
Volume 91 • Number 6
H.W. Wilson
A Division of EBSCO Information Services, Inc.

Published by
GREY HOUSE PUBLISHING
Amenia, New York
2019

The Reference Shelf

Cover image: Lionel Bonaventure/AFP via Getty Images

The books in this series contain reprints of articles, excerpts from books, addresses on current issues, and studies of social trends in the United States and other countries. There are six separately bound numbers in each volume, all of which are usually published in the same calendar year. Numbers one through five are each devoted to a single subject, providing background information and discussion from various points of view and concluding with an index and comprehensive bibliography that lists books, pamphlets, and articles on the subject. The final number of each volume is a collection of recent speeches. Books in the series may be purchased individually or on subscription.

Copyright © 2019 by Grey House Publishing, Inc. All rights reserved. No part of this work may be used or reproduced in any manner whatsoever or transmitted in any form or by any means, electronic or mechanical, including photocopy, recording, or any information storage and retrieval system, without written permission from the copyright owner. For subscription information and permissions requests, contact Grey House Publishing, 4919 Route 22, PO Box 56, Amenia, NY 12501.

Publisher's Cataloging-In-Publication Data
(Prepared by The Donohue Group, Inc.)

Names: Grey House Publishing, Inc., publisher.
Title: Representative American speeches.
Other Titles: Representative American speeches (2015)
Description: Amenia, N.Y. : Grey House Publishing, 2015- | Series: The reference shelf / H.W. Wilson
Identifiers: ISSN 2639-9016
Subjects: LCSH: Speeches, addresses, etc., American--21st century--Periodicals. | LCGFT: Speeches. | Serial publications.
Classification: LCC PS668 .B3 | DDC 815--dc23

Printed in Canada

Contents

Preface ix

1

To the Graduating Class

Commencement Address to the Reed School of Media Class of 2019 3
Hilde Kate Lysiak

You Need to Know What You Believe 11
Stacey Adams

Your Perspective Is Unique 18
Glenn Close

Commencement Address to the 2019 Harvard Business School Graduates 23
Michael R. Bloomberg

Take Charge of Earth: Turn Your Fear into Excitement 30
Bill Nye

Letting Go of the Old Is Part of a New Beginning 36
Angela Merkel

2

Politics and Policies

Oval Office Address on Immigration and Border Security 43
Donald Trump

Solving Illegal Immigration [for Real] 47
Sonia Nazario

Remarks by President Trump at the National Rifle Association Leadership Forum:
    Law & Justice 53
Donald Trump

You Can Hear the People in Power Shaking 60
David Hogg

A Call for Action on Gun Control Legislation (Excerpt) 62
Cory Booker

Trump Impeachment Statement 68
Nancy Pelosi

Now Is the Time to Act 71
John Lewis

Remarks by President Trump on America's Environmental Leadership:
    Energy & Environment 73
Donald Trump

3

Responses in Controversial Political Times

Opening Statement to the Senate Judiciary Committee Christine Blasey Ford	89
Vote to Confirm Brett Kavanaugh Susan Collins	94
I'll Be the Bad Guy Alexandria Ocasio-Cortez	103
Harris Kicks Off Her Presidential Campaign Kamala Harris	106
New York City Campaign Rally Elizabeth Warren	113
Exploring a 2020 Run Against Donald Trump Bill Weld	122
Hearing of Former Attorney to President Donald Trump Michael Cohen	128
Analyzing Trump's Comments on the Whistle-Blower in a Private Meeting By Gregory Korte, Jennifer Jacobs, and Nick Wadhams	136

4

Scientists and Activists

SACNAS: National Diversity in STEM Conference Keynote Address Ellen Ochoa	147
Scientific Integrity in Federal Agencies (Excerpt) Michael Halpern	155
You Have Stolen My Dreams and My Childhood Greta Thunberg	160
Science Activation: How Do We Get Our Science Used by Those in Power? (Excerpt) Lucy Jones	162
Speech on the 50th Anniversary of the *Apollo 11* Moon Landing Mike Pence	169

5

Health Issues

Remarks on the HEAL Initiative Alex M. Azar II	177
Remarks on Individual Health Insurance Market Rates Alex M. Azar II	180
State Relief and Empowerment Waivers: Affordable Care Act Seema Verma	182
The Cost of Health Care Lamar Alexander	189
SAMSHSA's 2018 National Survey on Drug Use and Health (Excerpt) Elinore F. McCance-Katz	196
Time for Physicians to Create History Together Patrice A. Harris	206
Advancing Health Care through the Lens of History: Health Equity James L. Madara	210
Index	215

Preface

What words will stay with us from 2018–2019? Speeches in the past year have been dominated by politics, but climate change, health care, the opioid crisis, immigration, the gun debate, and scientific advances have also generated discussion. Impeachment proceedings against President Donald Trump highlight our controversial political landscape. Rising costs and access to health care have impacted opioid addiction and suicide rates, while weather-related disasters and species extinctions have brought scientists into public and government policy discussions. Civil rights, free speech, and the First and Second Amendments have all been common themes in the forum of this past year's public discussion. No less than six women announced presidential campaigns for 2020, and women in leadership roles are speaking out in hopes of inspiring future generations. This has also been a year for young speakers to make their mark, such as 16-year-old Greta Thunberg's call to action at the United Nations and 12-year-old Hilde Kate Lysiak's journalism commencement speech at West Virginia University.

Messages and Inspiration Not Just for the Graduating Class

Speeches to the graduating class continue to inspire those going out into the world to distinguish themselves. Many touched on values of honesty, integrity, trust, kindness, and empathy. A common thread was to trust yourself and follow your passion. Hilde Kate Lysiak, the youngest commencement speaker at age 12, stated, "We are the generation that can restore the peoples trust." Stacey Abrams urged graduates to set aside their labels at American University's School of Public Affairs, stating that "too often, adherence to conservative or progressive, to liberal or moderate, to Democrat or Republican or Independent, to being pro this or anti that, becomes an excuse for lazy thinking. It becomes an excuse for hostile action." Mike Bloomberg, addressing graduates at Harvard University, emphasized the importance of rejecting dishonesty over partisan politics: "No party has a monopoly on good ideas or good people. But I believe all of us have an obligation to reject those who traffic in dishonesty and deceit." Glenn Close spoke of the importance of embracing a unique identity to the graduating class of William & Mary, saying, "What each of you have, and what you must believe in from this day forward, is your inherent uniqueness. Your singular point of view. No one looks out onto the world through your eyes. Your perspective is unique. It's important and it counts. Try not to compare it to anyone else. Accept it. Believe in it. Nurture it." Angela Merkel, also at Harvard, urged belief in the seemingly impossible, noting the value of change: "But if we tear down the walls that restrict us, if we open the door and embrace new beginnings, then everything is possible. Walls can collapse. Dictatorships can disappear. We can stop global warming. We can overcome hunger. We can eradicate diseases. We can give people, especially girls, access to education. We can fight the causes of displacement and forced migration. We can do all this."

Guns, Immigration, and Impeachment

Political speeches, campaign and otherwise, continue to be a forum for policy debate. The Constitution and its amendments have become common topics in the media and give us reason to consider their intent at the time they were written. Modern interpretations vary—are free speech and the right to bear arms absolute? Mass shootings in schools and domestic terrorist attacks have made gun control one of the most divisive issues in the United States. The latest statistics from the Centers for Disease Control (CDC) list almost 40,000 gun deaths in 2017.[1] Donald Trump defended an absolute right to bear arms at an NRA convention, stating, "Every day, we are up against those who would restrict our liberties, and even those who want to abolish the Second Amendment." Gun control advocates, among them Senator Cory Booker, argue for a common-sense approach to the Second Amendment and for universal background checks. Booker goes on to warn against what is commonly referred to as the "gunshow loophole"—which allows the sale or transfer of guns without a background check under certain circumstances. And high school students affected by gun violence, such as David Hogg, who survived the Marjory Stoneman Douglas High School shooting in 2018, continue to crusade for stricter gun control laws in movements like Never Again MSD and March for Our Lives. Denouncing the influential gun manufacturer lobby, Hogg comments: "First off, I'm gonna start off by putting this price tag right here as a reminder for you guys to know how much Marco Rubio took for every student's life in Florida. One dollar and five cents."

President Trump's stance on immigration has been another polarizing element in American society. Trump is adamant that a border wall is necessary to keep illegal immigrants, drugs, and violent gang members out of the United States. His critics contend that the majority of those arriving at our southern border are fleeing untenable situations. Award-winning journalist Sonia Nazario, who in the course of reporting on immigrant children made the dangerous journey from Honduras to Mexico, talks about the gang-related violence and desperation faced by many people attempting to enter the United States from South America. While praising some U.S.-led efforts to curb violence in Latin American cities, Nazario points out that neither Republicans nor Democrats have presented a workable solution to the problem of immigration, stating, "We need to rip up this playbook and try something new."

Impeachment proceedings always deepen partisanship and hostility, and the September announcement to move ahead against Donald Trump was no exception. In her impeachment statement, House Speaker Nancy Pelosi says, "No one is above the law." Representative John Lewis says, "There comes a time when you have to be moved by the spirit of history to take action to protect and preserve the integrity of our nation." The impeachment question has produced some surprising opinions on both sides of the divide. *New York Times* columnist and Trump critic David Brooks writes:

> This is completely elitist. We're in the middle of an election campaign. If Democrats proceed with the impeachment process, it will happen amid candidate debates, primaries and caucuses. Elections give millions and millions of Americans a voice in selecting the president. This process gives 100 mostly millionaire senators a voice in selecting the president.
>
> As these two processes unfold simultaneously, the contrast will be obvious. People will conclude that Democrats are going ahead with impeachment in an election year because they don't trust the democratic process to yield the right outcome. Democratic elites to voters: *We don't trust you. Too many of you are racists!*[2]

Meanwhile, hardcore Republican and former Trump supporter John Kasich has come out in favor of impeaching the president:

> But if you are asking me if I was sitting in the House of Representatives today and you were to ask me how do I feel, do I think impeachment should move forward and should go for a full examination and a trial in the United States Senate, my vote would be yes.[3]

Responses in Controversial Political Times

The 116th Congress is one of the most racially and ethnically diverse in history, with record numbers of women, LGBTQ individuals, and people of color, many of whom have run in reaction to President Trump. Senator Booker criticized the "silence" and "amnesia" of former Department of Homeland Security head Kirstjen Nielsen, saying, "When ignorance and bigotry is allied with power, it's a dangerous force in our country." Representative Alexandria Ocasio-Cortez spoke against corporate lobbyists' influence with the executive branch in a House hearing, commenting, "I'm gonna be the bad guy, which I'm sure half the room would agree anyway, and I want to get away with as much bad things as possible, ideally to enrich myself and advance my interests, even if that means putting my interests ahead of the American people." In her presidential campaign kickoff speech, Senator Kamala Harris spoke of the importance of American identity: "We are here because the American Dream and our American democracy are under attack and on the line like never before. We are here at this moment in time because we must answer a fundamental question. Who are we? Who are we as Americans?" Senator Elizabeth Warren spoke of the need for the government to battle corruption: "Now, Americans disagree on many things, but we don't want each other's homes burned down by wildfires. We don't want each other's children murdered at school and we don't want each other's families bankrupted by medical bills. What we want is for our government to do something. And yet, our federal government is unable to act, unable to take even the most basic steps to protect the American people. . . . Corruption has put our planet at risk. Corruption has broken our economy, and corruption is breaking our democracy." Former Trump attorney Michael Cohen, sentenced to three years in federal prison for lying to the Senate, said of the president during his latest Senate testimony, "He is a racist. He is a conman. He is a cheat."

The Senate Judiciary Committee testimony of Christine Blasey Ford accusing Supreme Court Justice nominee Brett Kavanaugh of sexual assault riveted the nation. Ford stated that, although she was "terrified," she believed it was her "civic duty" to tell the nation of the assault. After careful consideration of Ford's claims, Maine Senator Susan Collins voted to confirm Kavanaugh's nomination based on what she felt was a lack of evidence. Collins expressed concern about such factors as political and media manipulation, claiming that "we have come to the conclusion of a confirmation process that has become so dysfunctional, it looks more like a caricature of a gutter-level political campaign than a solemn occasion." She went on to point out that "the politically charged atmosphere surrounding this nomination has reached a fever pitch even before these allegations were known, and it has been challenging even then to separate fact from fiction. We live in a time of such great disunity, as the bitter fight over this nomination both in the Senate and among the public clearly demonstrates. It is not merely a case of differing groups having different opinions. It is a case of people bearing extreme ill will toward those who disagree with them."

Activists and Scientists

Climate change and the role of scientists in society have played a major role in the forum of public discussion. Solutions are being demanded of those in authority, while scientists speak of the challenges of getting policymakers to implement their recommendations. Those in the path of natural disasters, while not having a background in meteorology or climatology, are nevertheless faced with taking a position. Michael Halpern, the deputy director of the Center for Science and Democracy, testified in a House hearing that "sometimes presidential administrations want to sideline, manipulate, misrepresent, or suppress information that comes out of federal agencies—especially if it doesn't support the policies they want to put forward. When that happens, valuable information is kept from the public, and it becomes easier for politicians to justify ill-advised public health and environmental protection decisions." California Institute of Technology researcher Dr. Lucy Jones addresses the difficulty in getting scientific ideas across to both the public and policymakers. Calling this "science activation," she talks of the need for nonscientists to have a basic understanding of the scientific method and of how to evaluate data. She states, "Believe it because you understand for yourself how it works out or how the logical reasoning works. . . . With this future we are all in this together."

Calls for action regarding climate change have become a perennial subject for public speaking. Most of us, regardless of our political affiliations, will not forget teenager Greta Thunberg's accusation, delivered at the United Nations: "You have stolen my dreams and my childhood with your empty words."

Diversity in the sciences continues to be an important issue, and pioneers who have crossed the gender and racial divide are speaking out to inspire others. Dr. Ellen Ochoa, the first Latina director of the Johnson Space Center and the first selected to go into space, talks of borderlands, real and metaphorical, at the Society for Advancement of Chicanos/Hispanics and Native Americans in Science (SACNAS)-sponsored National Diversity in science, technology, engineering, and mathematics (STEM) Conference: "A frontier is a place, it's often an actual place, where explorers come and pioneers settle. But sometimes it's more of a metaphor, and I think it's something that we all can relate to because a frontier is a place where boundaries are pushed. And certainly I've had the opportunity in my career to live and work on the frontier."

Vice president Mike Pence honored the astronauts of the first moon landing in a speech commemorating the 5oth anniversary of *Apollo 11* while also affirming American commitment to the National Aeronautics and Space Administration (NASA), with planned journeys to the moon and beyond.

Health Issues

Skyrocketing medical and insurance costs, the opioid crisis, and health equity have drawn public attention over the past year. The battle over Barack Obama's Affordable Care Act (ACA) is ongoing, as the Trump administration attempts to change provisions they deem unworkable. U.S. Secretary of Health and Human Services Alex M. Azar II remarks: "This administration has made no secret about it: We believe the Affordable Care Act simply doesn't work. It is still unaffordable for far too many." Seema Verma, administrator for the Centers for Medicare and Medicaid Services, argues for greater state control over health care issues and against the current "Medicare for All" proposals from Congress: "I came to this job with a belief that Washington doesn't have all the answers when it comes to our health care needs . . . that states are the testing grounds of innovation and reform . . . and that care decisions centralized in Washington too often come at the expense of patients." Dr. Patrice A. Harris, the first African American president of the American Medical Association (AMA), offers a different view: "While the Affordable Care Act brought coverage to millions of Americans, millions still lack coverage, and we know there are those who want to roll back the gains we've made." Harris goes on to list the things she hopes to be remembered for: "We moved the needle on health equity. We reformed prior authorization so that more patients could get the right care at the right time. And we saw the end to the opioid epidemic on the horizon and furthered alliances in Washington and across every state to remove barriers to treatment for those diagnosed with substance use disorders." AMA chief executive officer and executive vice president James L. Madara uses Chicago's neighborhoods to illustrate the unequal access to health care faced by many Americans. "Here in downtown Chicago, it's 2019, and life expectancy for those living here is 82 years. But if we hop on the train and ride just 20 minutes south to Fuller Park . . . life expectancy is only 65 years—that's less by 17 years. That's right . . . just a few miles south, a person loses 17 years of life. How far back in time would we have to travel for the average American to lose this much life expectancy—to expect to die at age 65? The answer is from the 1930s to the 1940s . . . a period overlapping with the Great Depression . . . Prohibition . . . the infamous Chicago Stockyards."

While HHS Secretary Azar announced $1 billion in grants for the National Institute of Health's HEAL initiative combating the opioid crisis, the 2018 Substance Abuse and Mental Health Services Administration's National Survey on Drug Use and Health, presented by Dr. Elinore F. McCance-Katz, detailed a lack of treatment for many with substance abuse and mental health issues:

> The treatment gaps remain vast. . . . Nearly 90 percent of those with substance use disorders get no treatment; nearly 57 percent of those with mental illnesses get no treatment; 36 percent with serious mental illness, no treatment; over ninety percent with co-occurring disorders, no treatment; and over 58 percent of our adolescents with major depression will get no treatment. Use of one substance . . . is strongly correlated with poly substance use and with serious mental health conditions. . . . This underscores the need to screen for all substances as well as mental disorders when evaluating a person.

The words of this year's public speakers leave us much to consider. Oliver Sacks, physician and author of *Seeing Voices*, states, "We speak not only to tell other people what we think, but to tell ourselves what we think. Speech is a part of thought."[4] While we have unprecedented access to information—and misinformation—through the internet and social media, "fake news" and media bias mean that we often need to fact-check or extensively research an issue in order to make an educated decision. American poet Robert Frost believed that the spoken word needed careful evaluation: "Half the world is composed of people who have something to say and can't, and the other half who have nothing to say and keep on saying it."[5] The best speeches are the most memorable, resonating with an audience and inspiring high ideals. The words that stay with us will be different for each of us.

Notes

1. Mahita Gajanan, "Gun Deaths in the U.S. Are at Their Highest Rates in Decades, CDC Says." *Time*. December 14, 2018. https://time.com/5479993/gun-deaths-us-cdc/.
2. Brooks, David. "Yes, Trump Is Guilty, but Impeachment Is a Mistake." *New York Times*. September 26, 2019. https://www.nytimes.com/2019/09/26/opinion/impeachment-trump-mistake.html,
3. Iyer, Kaanita, "Former Republican Ohio Gov. John Kasich Says He's Now for Impeaching Trump." CNN. October 18, 2019. https://www.cnn.com/2019/10/18/politics/kasich-calls-for-trump-impeachment/index.html.
4. Sacks, Oliver. *Seeing Voices*. https://www.goodreads.com/quotes/527827-we-speak-not-only-to-tell-other-people-what-we.
5. Frost, Robert. https://www.goodreads.com/quotes/31532-half-the-world-is-composed-of-people-who-have-something.

1
To the Graduating Class

Photo by Jessica McGowan/Getty Images.

Stacey Abrams urged graduates at American University's School of Public Affairs to look beyond the easy labels of party and ideology to deeply held convictions.

Commencement Address to the Reed School of Media Class of 2019

By Hilde Kate Lysiak

American journalist, founder, and publisher of Orange Street News *in Selinsgrove, Pennsylvania in 2014, Lysiak is an author with a seven-series book deal from Scholastic. A TV mystery series based on her life is in process. She is also a recipient of the 2019 Zenger Award for Press Freedom and she is the youngest member of the Society of Professional Journalists. At twelve years of age, Hilde Kate Lysiak is also the youngest person to give a college commencement speech, with this one at West Virginia University on May 10, 2019.*

Thank you, Dean Reed, members of the Faculty, family and friends, and most importantly, the class of 2019.

It is an amazing honor for me to be here today.

But first, let me address the thoughts I am sure are going through many of your heads right now—

I'm in $80,000 dollars in debt and my school can't even afford a full grown human to give the commencement speech.

Is this some kind of scam or what!

No, but seriously…

I'd like to begin by repeating a few things I'm sure you've already heard…

Your education has been one big, huge, waste of time.

That you are all going into a dying industry!

Or how about this one— journalism is dead!

You've heard all of this, right?

And seriously, how can you blame people for thinking these things?

Everywhere we turn we see bad news about the news: like how people don't buy newspapers anymore. It seems like everyday we are reading about another newspaper that had to close

And how the ones that have stayed open have had to slash their staffs.

And how the reporters who are left standing are all hacks.

Or Fake News.

A week doesn't go by where someone doesn't tell me I should find another job.

You know, one with a future.

Delivered on May 20, 2019, at the Reed School of Media, West Virginia University, Morgantown, WV.

And I'm only twelve—what does this mean for all of you old washed up twenty-somethings?

To the 2019 Graduating Class, you face a daunting task.

There will be those out there waiting for you to fail.

And others who believe you were doomed before even earning your first byline…

Ignore them.

They are wrong.

Look..

There is another path…

But getting there won't be easy.

As someone who has written hundreds of stories, exposed countless cases of corruption, and developed a devoted readership that spans all across the world—I have some ideas on how we can create a bridge to THAT future.

And if it's okay I'd like to dispense a few of these little nuggets of reporting wisdom I've learned along the way now..

1. Keep Your Ledes Tight

If you are going to ask the people to dedicate even a sliver of their life to staring on their screen at the words you've written, you need to respect your reader.

See—words on screens are usually in shades of black on white, but life if full of bright colors.

There are amazing mysteries and stories all around us.

Life isn't boring. Don't let your writing be.

People are busy. And they don't have a huge attention spans.

Get to the point. Let the facts tell the story. And most importantly, keep your ledes short.

Remember, if it is taking you two hundred words to get to the meat of your story—then no one, and I mean no one, is going to get to the desert, much less the main course.

2. Talk to Real People

Politicians and law enforcement can be great sources of information.

But my best stories never came from a press release—they came from biking down my main street, knocking on doors, and talking to the real people.

Who are the real people?

These are the small business owners. That group of old people who hang out at the coffee shop. Or just that nice neighbor man who is raking leaves.

It is here, buried in the nosey lady next door or at the church dinner, where the real nuggets of gold can be found.

Real people have real stories.

And if you take the time to listen, you would be amazed at what the real everyday people know.

3. Trust No One

Sometimes when working on a story you'll confront two people telling you two different versions of the same event and you will be asking yourself, which person should I trust?

The answer; Don't trust either of the people.

Everyone lies.

Even good people.

And sometimes without knowing it.

Sometimes cops lie.

Sometimes government officials lie.

And yes, sometimes even the everyday people lie.

That's why it is important to have your loyalty NOT to any personalities but to the truth.

And only the truth.

Trust no one.

Follow the facts.

4. Get Away from Your Desk

So many reporters just sit at desks all day refreshing their emails or checking social media.

That sounds like death to me.

The best reporters I know aren't waiting for the story to hit their inbox. They go find the story.

As publisher, editor, and the only reporter of the *Orange Street News*, I don't have an assignment editor. I have to generate my own story ideas.

That is why after waking up everyday at 4:30 in morning the first thing I do is to go outside and run a mile.

I also try to be part of my community. I go to the local restaurants and shop at the local stores. I'm out there.

How can you report on a community from an office? That sounds like a fraud to me.

Don't sit at a desk waiting for email tips or press releases. Get out into your community.

And I promise, the more time you spend exploring the world around you, the more the stories will find you.

5. Bring Pencils
Pens stop working when it gets cold outside.

I learned this one the hard way.

6. Remember YOUR Boss
After I was first to break the story of a murder in my hometown I was told by another reporter that they had the story too, but the police told them not to report it.

So they didn't.

I was only nine—but seriously, I think I almost threw up in my mouth when I heard that.

I knew even at that age that a reporter doesn't work for the police.

A reporter works for the people.

You are reporters.

You don't work for the police.

You don't work for the government.

You work for the people. And if you recognize that, the people will work for you.

7. Don't Read the Comments
I admit, this one is hard.

We all want to see what people are saying about our work.

And I understand that most of you are going to ignore this advice, at least at first.

But trust me—Don't read the comments.

They will only make you feel bad about yourself.

And bad about the world.

8. Don't Forget Your Super Power
Reporting is about getting the truth to the people.

How do we get to the truth?

This isn't complicated.

It's the same way reporters have gotten to the truth for years.

By answering the six sacred questions of journalism—Who? What? Where? When? Why? How?

Look—everybody wants to change the world.

And a reporter is armed with the most persuasive tool in the world—the facts.

That is why a fair reporter can inspire far more change than even the best opinion columnist in the world.

Look—readers are smart. More often than not when given the right facts they will come to the right conclusions.

That's the power of the truth. The power of facts.

And THAT is the REAL super power of a reporter.

Which leads me to my next point—

9. Don't Mix Politics and Reporting

Look—I believe the future has never been brighter for reporters.

Think about it. Has there ever been a time when more people wanted or needed the news more than at THIS very moment right now?

Because of the internet, people from all around the world can access information anytime and anywhere and all from the screen of their smartphone.

This isn't a good thing.

This is a great thing.

Each one of these people is a potential subscriber to the *Orange Street News*.

Oh but I know what the skeptics all say, that newspapers might get online readers, but they don't make money anymore.

To answer that claim, I'd like to point them to the only newspaper that exclusively serves the people of Selinsgrove, Pennsylvania.

I'm proud to say that the newspaper I'm the publisher of, the *Orange Street News*, DOES make a profit. And I do this while also publishing all my stories online for free and without accepting paid a single dollar in advertising. In fact, my print subscribers are enough for me to pay for all of my expenses including printing along with a few upgrades.

How?

First, I keep my expenses low.

But most importantly, I never stop working to get good stories, and good scoops leads to new subscribers.

It isn't complicated. I know that as soon as the *Orange Street News* stops getting exclusive stories that are important to the people, the people will stop buying the *Orange Street News*.

And I think that is how it should be.

But the skeptics aren't all wrong.

See—there IS a crisis in media.

But it isn't the shrinking newsrooms or losses in revenue.

The crisis we are facing, is one of trust.

See—too many people just don't trust what they are reading anymore.

And if you are wondering how we got to this point, just look no further than the current generation of reporters.

Too many of them have strayed from the basics I knew by age six—that reporting was about finding answers to those six sacred questions.

Instead, too many of today's reporters made a decision to start mixing their reporting with a kind of theater, a disgusting sort of political based entertainment that seeks to divide people along political party lines to fulfill whatever bias they might feel or maybe to generate page clicks or whatever.

Don't believe me?

Pull up your favorite reporter's Twitter account, spend two minutes going through their feed, and then ask yourself if the other fifty percent of the country who don't agree with their political opinions are going to believe A SINGLE WORD of their reporting.

These so-called reporters spend so much time trying to persuade other people to think just like they do, but what they never understood is that by doing so they've become nothing but more noise.

See—by mixing their political opinions with their news they've created two different medias.

As a result, YOU are inheriting a world where people are increasingly only talking to themselves, or to those who already think the exact same way that they do.

And without new information, how can people grow?

That's why I keep my political opinions to myself and am careful to report only facts.

I know that if I lose the trust of my readers, I might as well find another job.

But as long as I have that trust, I can keep growing.

And if you take this advice, so will you.

But these reporters who spent their time dividing us and not reporting facts aren't the future.

They are about to be the past.

See—they are dinosaurs.

And they are all going extinct.

I say good riddance.

They've had their time. Its over.

WE are the generation that can restore the people's trust.

See—we aren't the pro-Trump reporters.

We aren't the anti-Trump reporters.

We aren't the left-wing reporters.

We aren't the right-wing reporters.

We are the generation that will be known simply as............REPORTERS.

That is a trust I guard with my life.

You should too.

And as you move forward, it will be your most important currency.

To the Class of 2019—

Today is supposed to mark the beginning of a new life in the world, the beginning of your professional life…

It is up to each and every one of you to change that narrative.

To declare that we are the generation of reporters who will choose to have our loyalty to one thing and one thing only—to the truth.

To the facts.

To uncovering corruption—where ever we find it.

In just a few moments you will be graduating.

You are moments away from beginning this journey.

Moments away from embarking on the most noble of professions—that of reporter.

It will not be easy.

You will not make a lot of money.

And if you are good at your job, you will be despised by more people than you can possibly imagine.

But if you keep your ledes short, talk to real people, trust no one, get away from your desk, always bring a pencil, remember who you work for, ignore the comments, rise above the temptation to infuse your writing with politics, and most importantly of all, stay laser focused on the truth…

If you do these things, then I believe history will look back on this moment—not as the dark last days before the profession of journalism died—

But as new beginning…

When this generation…

Your generation…

The class of 2019, didn't just save the news…but ushered in a new golden age of fact-based information that shined a light so bright it touched every corner of the globe.

A media based on truth.

On those six timeless questions…Who?, What?, Where?, When?, Why?, and How?

Thank you.

Print Citations

CMS: Lysiak, Hilde Kate. "Commencement Address to the Reed School of Media Class of 2019." Commencement Address for Reed School of Media, West Virginia University, Morgantown, WV, May 10, 2019. In *The Reference Shelf: Representative American Speeches, 2018–2019,* edited by Sophie Zyla, 3-10. Amenia, NY: Grey House Publishing, 2019.

MLA: Lysiak, Hilde Kate. "Commencement Address to the Reed School of Media Class of 2019." Reed School of Media, 10 May 2019, West Virginia University, Morgantown, WV. Commencement Address. *The Reference Shelf: Representative American Speeches, 2018–2019,* edited by Sophie Zyla, Grey House Publishing, 2019, pp. 3-10.

APA: Lysiak, H.K. (2019, May 10). Commencement Address to the Reed School of Media class of 2019. West Virginia University, Morgantown, WV. In Sophie Zyla (Ed.), *The reference shelf: Representative American speeches, 2018–2019* (pp. 3-10). Amenia, NY: Grey House Publishing.

You Need to Know What You Believe

By Stacey Adams

Stacey Abrams is the first woman to lead in the Georgia General Assembly and the first African American to lead in the Georgia House of Representatives (2007–2017). Abrams also served on the Appropriations, Ethics, Judiciary, Non-Civil, Rules and Ways & Means committees. Abrams is a Harry S. Truman Scholar, and her numerous awards include the John F. Kennedy New Frontier Award, the Elmer Staats Award for Public Service, and the Stevens Award for Outstanding Legal Contributions. After a narrow defeat in her bid to become governor of Georgia in 2018, Abrams founded Fair Fight Action to address the issue of voter suppression. Abrams received her BA in Interdisciplinary Studies from Spelman College, a master's degree in public affairs from the University of Texas at Austin, and a JD from Yale Law School.

Thank you. You guys are too nice to me. I may not go home. To President Burwell, to Provost Meyers, Dean Wilkins, trustees, faculty administration, family, friends, and the graduating class of 2019, thank you for having me here today. As a—you're welcome! As a fellow graduate, in the work of public affairs, I've had more than 20 years to think about what I intended to do with my degree. And where I am today. And to cut to the chase: I had no idea this is what was going to happen.

I didn't imagine any of the outcomes of the last six months, and I knew precious little about the preceding 20 years, and that's entirely okay. I certainly thought I knew what was to come. Some of you may know from my book *Lead from the Outside*, when I was 18, I had a very bad breakup with a very mean boy. He said nasty things about me and how I was not going to find love. Because I was too committed to doing other things. I . . . possibly said inappropriate things about him. I don't remember that part of the conversation.

But what I do remember, was the sense that I was going to show him. I was going to accomplish many things and I was going to control the world and make his life very, very difficult. So I took myself to the computer lab at Spelman College, and—Thank you!—this is back in 1992, so when I turned on the computer, I did not log onto the internet, I logged into Lotus, 123. I began to type out all of the things I intended to accomplish for the next 40 years. I wanted to be mayor of Atlanta. I wanted to be somewhere near Oprah. . . . I wanted to be writer. And I knew that the way I could get those things done was to write it down. And over the last 20 years, I have tended my spreadsheet like Gollum tends his Precious. I have looked at it and cultivated it and made changes and edits. I've erased things and ignored others, and

---

Delivered on May 11, 2019, at the School of Public Affairs, American University, Washington, DC.

along the way I realized I had no idea what I was talking about. Because you see I made a plan for my life, but what I was trying to do, was prepare to succeed. And that's what I want to talk to you about today. Because you don't have to plan your life the way I did. But in the process, we have to prepare to succeed, and we do that by knowing what we believe, knowing what we want, and knowing that sometimes it might not work.

First, you need to know what you believe. Our ambitions, our decisions, our responses are shaped by what we hold to be true. Beyond the easy labels of party and ideology are the deeply held convictions that shape those labels. But too often, adherence to conservative or progressive, to liberal or moderate, to Democrat or Republican or Independent, to being pro this or anti that, becomes an excuse for lazy thinking. It becomes an excuse for hostile action. And for today, at least, I urge you to set aside your labels, and explore what your principles say about the world you wish to serve. Because beliefs are anchors, if they aren't we run the risk of opportunism, making choices because others do so, not because we should. But those anchors should never weigh us down. They shouldn't weigh down our capacity for thoughtful engagement and reasonable compromise. For seven years, I served as the Democratic leader in the House of Representatives, and they told me about my ability to be successful because my title was Minority Leader. There was to be no confusion that I was going to get there by myself. What they wanted me to understand, what the system is designed to do, is force compromise, and force our beliefs to be lived. And that's why I was able to work with a Republican governor to push forward the strongest package of criminal justice reform in Georgia history. And, I would argue, in American history.

Because my belief said—Thank you—because my belief said I had to set aside labels for the work that we were going to do together. And it worked!

We also have to understand that it's critical to know what you believe, because public policy is complicated. We're balancing the needs and desires and the arguments of many—a cacophony of demands that all seem to have merit. And as leaders you represent not only those who share you core values, but people who despise all that you hold dear.

Therefore, your beliefs, your principles, must be concrete, and fundamental, and you have to know what they are. Be willing to distinguish between a core belief and an idea you just like a lot, or it sounded good when you read it on Twitter. As public servants, you will impose your beliefs, through policy and through action. So take the time to deeply examine those notions that you would call your own. Be certain you would ask others not only to share those principles, but as leaders that you would deny access or restrict someone's freedom to enforce that belief because fundamentally that's what we do. And, no, ancestral teachings or religious tendencies are not sufficient cause for belief. You clap for that. That's okay. As Provost Meyers pointed out I'm the daughter of not one, but two, United Methodist ministers, and one of the darkest days of my life was when my parents said they weren't taking us to heaven with them. It was really harsh. We were coming back from church and we made some comment and my mom said, "Look, you got to figure out what you believe because we can't take you with us." She was telling us, what my father said even less kindly, was that we had to examine what we wanted to be true and how we were going to live our lives, that they were there as guide posts but they were never going to be able to make our decisions for us. They wanted us to understand that we needed to hold our core beliefs, because our beliefs would shape the world we would bring forth.

So if you believe something, make sure you mean it. Once you know what you believe, try not to believe in too much. I am loathe to follow folks who are absolutely certain they know everything. The ones who have a definite opinion about every headline, every decision, and they can give you the answer before you ask the question. And if you can't figure out who in your circle is that person, it might be you.

But you see, beliefs shouldn't be on everything. Public policy usually isn't good or evil. Sometimes it's not even that interesting. It's mundane and routine, and it cuts across neighborhoods and nations and ideologies. But when your lens only allows for a single myopic focus, when you've already made your decision before you know the question, then you do not have the capacity to be a leader. Because you leave no room for debate and you miss the true role of government and public policy and miss the chance to learn and become a better public servant.

Now I do have core beliefs, but I don't have an unshakeable position on every issue. I do not believe that taxes are good or evil. I do believe that poverty is an abomination and that freedom of speech must be held sacrosanct and we have the right to restore justice to criminal justice.

I believe climate change is real but I don't believe there's one answer to solving the problem. And I understand most of all that I have to accept that I may not know enough about an issue to actually render judgment. Which is why I have to study, and read everything I can, especially counterarguments to my own position. That's why we must always seek to understand what others believe. Why?

I had a good friend in the state legislature, Bobby Franklin. Bobby and I both agreed that we were from Georgia, that was about it. Bobby introduced legislation every year that I would have opposed every year, but we sat together and we talked together and we learned about one another. And in the process we were able to aid one another and work together on a bill. It was about civil asset forfeiture, which is [a] deeply scintillating topic. But when Bobby and I introduced an amendment together it was so surprising and startling to the body that the Speaker actually called it out without following the process, and we think it passed just because people were too stunned to say no. But it was because I listened to Bobby's concerns and he listened to mine. We were able to figure out how to address an issue that affected his rural white community and my urban black community. We were able to move beyond our positions, and hear each other's arguments, and find a solution together.

The truest road to good decision making is acknowledging that the other guy might have a point. Even if it's not yours. And if it turns out that the new information alters your thinking, the terrifying reality may be that you are accused of flip-flopping. I know that's the death sentence to any ambition. But as a society that seeks to champion knowledge, we must accept that a person can change what he or she believes as long as that change is authentic, and grounded in true examination of philosophy, and reality. Changing who you are to accommodate others, or to advance your career, that is craven and not worthy of real leaders, not ever.

But hear me clearly: in this day and age, when evolution is based on investigation and interrogation, when people are willing to admit they made a mistake and are willing to right their wrongs, then that should be celebrated and welcomed. It makes us smarter, it makes us better, it makes us stronger.

As you enter the world of public affairs for the first time, or on a return ticket, be careful to know if you are evolving, or caving in. Because the internet will never let you forget. And whether you leave here destined to be an administrator or a policy maker or an active citizen—always keep clear in your mind the difference between principle and policy, between belief and behavior. Policy is what we should do. Principle, belief is why we do it. So know what you believe, know why you believe it, and be willing to understand the other side. So know what you believe, and then next know what you want.

Some of you may have heard that in 2018, I ran for governor of Georgia. And the first few weeks after I announced my candidacy I did what you're supposed to do in politics, which is to reach out to your friends and family to raise the absurd amount of money it takes to become an elected official. My family has no money, so I was mostly calling friends, and in the course of this process, I raised over 42 million dollars, the most raised by any candidate in Georgia history.

But it didn't start out that way. You see, I started calling friends, people who had invested in me when I ran for [the] legislature in 2006, people who invested in me when I stood to become Minority Leader, people who supported the New Georgia Project and the organization I started to register more than 300,000 people of color in the state of Georgia, people who stood with me, at every turn.

But over and over, I would call and I would hear, "Stacey, we think you're so talented. Stacey I think you're so qualified. But you're a black woman."

I was like, "I know."

But they whispered it to me as if they were giving me a terminal diagnosis, because you see, they had decided what I was capable of, based on what they saw. Not based on what they knew. People I had known for years, kept telling me that I wasn't ready for this. In fact, it was suggested that I support the other person running, and just ask for a role in her administration. That didn't work for me then, and it doesn't work for me now!

I was told that I needed to wait until Georgia was ready for me. I was told to wait my turn. And after a while, listening to people who had supported me for so many years, I started to wonder if they were correct. If maybe I was pushing too far, too fast. If maybe what I wanted wasn't real or possible. I listened to their doubts and I started to internalize their dimunition of my capacity. Until I reminded myself that I knew what I wanted and I had a plan to get it. Because when you aim high, when you stretch beyond your easiest conceptions, the temptation to pare back your ambitions will be strong. Especially when there are those who don't share them.

Hear me clearly: Do not edit your desires.

You are here in the space, you are entering this world, to want what you want, regardless of how big the dream. You may have to get there in stages, you may stumble along the way, but the journey is worth the work. And do not allow logic to be an excuse for setting low expectations. This occurs when we allow ourselves to be less because we think, if it were possible, someone would have done it before. But the fact is, no one—the fact is, no one can tell you who you are. And the fact that no one has done it before doesn't mean it can't be done. I became the first black woman to be a major party nominee for governor in our nation's 242-year history.

Let's be clear: I realize I am not the governor.

That's a topic for another day. But what I do not ask is why hasn't anyone else done it? What I ask is how do I get it? Because if we have the ambition to save our world, we have to ask how we do it, not why it hasn't been done before. That's why you're here. That's what you're going forth to do! How—How? By writing it down and making a plan. If it's simply an idea in your head it's easy to forget, easy to let it float away, an ephemeral idea that doesn't have any concrete meaning and doesn't have any concrete action. If you just see a title on a roster but you don't make a plan to get there, you'll be regretting it for the rest of your life. If you know what you want, force the question, by plotting how you get there. By knowing what you believe you have the reason, and by knowing what you want, you can start to draw the map. But if you know what you believe, and you know what you want, you need to be prepared, to know it might not work. Otherwise known as Stacey 2019.

Because the thing is, our beliefs may close off avenues that are available to others, our ambitions may be too audacious or too different for traditional paths, and our very persons may challenge the status quo more than the quo is read to accommodate. Plus, you might just screw it up and have to try again. But opportunity is not a straight road. And to take full advantage we must be prepared to fail, to stumble, or to win in a way that looks nothing like you imagined. For those of us who are not guaranteed access, we must realize that not all worlds operate the same. We are required to discover the hidden formulas to success. And too often opportunity looks nothing like we expected. But to have this very real possibility, look for unusual points of entry. I began my career by learning how to do the various jobs it would take to get me to my ultimate goals. I needed to know how to manage a team, how to raise money, how to make tough choices. So I volunteered to fundraise when no one else wanted to. I showed up in places I wasn't expected. And I asked to do the jobs that others avoided. Each of you harbors a dream that seems outsized. Maybe even too big to admit to yourself. You see, I've talked about my dreams publicly. And I've been discouraged for doing so. That I wanted to be the governor of Georgia, that one day I intend to be the president of the United States, and that in between, but in between my responsibility is to do the work, to make those things real, not only for myself, but for the person who is sitting there thinking, "I want that, too," but they're afraid to say it aloud. We lead not only for ourselves, we lead for others, and our stumbles are opportunities to lay a path for others to follow. And we have to understand that knowing what we believe and knowing what we want means that sometimes there are going to be obstacles to us getting there.

But I will tell you, that if you are willing to put in the effort, to accept the grunt work that lets you prove your ground, it will come. It may not be in the form, in the shape, that you expected. But sometimes it leads you to standing on a stage, addressing a group of people you didn't know you would have a chance to meet. Because your stumble led you into falling into new opportunities.

To get there, I need you to utilize your networks. You are joining an extraordinary community of graduates from the American University. While you may not know everyone, most of the help you need is only a few degrees away. Ask for it, and if you don't get what you need, ask for it again. Broaden your understanding of who knows whom, and who can help, and broaden your understanding of where power actually lies. Don't ignore the IT guy or the administrative assistant, the housekeeping staff. Or that mid-level associate you haven't quite figured out what they do. Because the thing of it is, it's the administrative assistant who can squeeze you on the calendar when you're trying to get to see someone, it's the janitor who can open that office when you forgot to do something that needs to be done before anyone notices, and it's the person, the intern that you ignore who can help you finish the last-minute project. Regardless of status, those who share our space are a part of our networks. Show them respect, and they can show you the way.

But when you learn that it might not work, embrace the fail and search for new opportunities. In the wake of my campaign for governor for about ten days I wallowed in my despair and then I reminded myself of why I got into this in the first place. I grew up in poverty in Mississippi. A working-class poverty my mom called the genteel corps, we had no money but we watched PBS and read books. I grew up in a family where my parents would wake us up on Saturdays to go and serve, to take us to soup kitchens and homeless shelters, to juvenile justice facilities and nursing homes. And we would point out that the lights were off at home, that we didn't have running water. My mother would remind us that no matter how little we had there was someone with less, and our job was to serve that person. My dad would just say having nothing is not an excuse for doing nothing.

I ran for governor of Georgia because I believe in a better world. I believe that we can educate our children, guarantee economic security. I believe that we can provide access to justice and a clean environment. I believe more is possible, for all of us. I believe you can center communities of color and acknowledge the marginalized, and not exclude those who have opportunity and access. I believe that we can be an inclusive society without relegating ourselves to notions of identity as a bad thing, but instead, using identity to say we see one another. We see your obstacles and we will make you better and stronger because of it. This is why I ran.

And so, in the wake of not becoming governor of Georgia, I had the opportunity to sit back, and wallow, to worry and to fret. Or to simply be angry. But instead, I decided to found Fair Fight Action, because I believe voter suppression is real and a threat to our democracy, and we will fight for voter rights and for electoral integrity because I believe in the United States of America; that is what we are going to do!

I also launched Fair Count because I know the 2020 census is the story of America for the next decade, and we have to make certain that everyone is counted, because if they're not they will not count; that is our opportunity!

Neither role is where I expected to be today, and there are other roles that wait for me. Maybe before 2020, and maybe after. But for me, the responsibility is to act as though today is the last day. To do the work I know needs to be done, not because of the position I hold, but because of the work that awaits us. And that is your charge, that is your calling. That is your obligation. When life doesn't work, when the fail seems permanent, acknowledge the pain, but reject the conclusion. Our principles, our beliefs, exist to sustain us.

Our ambitions are there to drive us. And our stumbles exist to remind us that the work endures.

Public service is a passion play. It's the drama of how we shape the lives of those around us, how we allocate resources and raise hopes, and ground our dreams and robust reality. You stand as the architects of our better lives. Those who don't fret, and worry, who don't stand on the sidelines and watch but get into the scrum and make it work. You are here because you believe that more is possible. And you have been trained to make more a reality.

You are here today because you have accepted your destiny. As public servants, as leaders, for our current age. Our nation is grappling with existential questions and our allies and our enemies watch to see how we respond. The tension of elections pull against the urgency of governance, and we cannot forget that they are not the same thing. You might be tempted to harden yourself, to cast your lot with what you know, and to wall yourself off from people and ideas that challenge your direction. But you are here in this school because you understand the deeper calling of our obligations to serve the grace that is our social contract, to build a better, stronger, more resilient world. And you are the embodiment of the most deeply held belief of everyone here—that American University, that the School of Public Affairs, that your friends and your family and your classmates and I all hold today—a singular belief that shall illuminate us today and going forward. We believe in you. Thank you and congratulations.

Print Citations

CMS: Abrams, Stacey. "You Need to Know What You Believe." Commencement Address at the School of Public Affairs, American University, Washington, DC, May 11, 2019. In *The Reference Shelf: Representative American Speeches, 2018–2019,* edited by Sophie Zyla, 11-17. Amenia, NY: Grey House Publishing, 2019.

MLA: Abrams, Stacey. "You Need to Know What You Believe." School of Public Affairs, 11 May 2019, American University, Washington, DC. Commencement Address. *The Reference Shelf: Representative American Speeches, 2018–2019,* edited by Sophie Zyla, Grey House Publishing, 2019, pp. 11-17.

APA: Abrams, S. (2019, May 11). Commencement Address on you need to know what you believe. The School of Public Affairs. American University, Washington, DC. In Sophie Zyla (Ed.), *The reference shelf: Representative American speeches, 2018–2019* (pp. 11-17). Amenia, NY: Grey House Publishing.

Your Perspective Is Unique

By Glenn Close

Glenn Close was the first woman in her family to graduate from college and did so at the College of William & Mary in 1974. Her younger days were divided between the Democratic Republic of the Congo and boarding school in Switzerland before she entered prep school at Rosemary Hall. After college Close moved to New York, where she made her Broadway debut in Love for Love *(1974), won her first Tony Award in 1984 for* The Real Thing, *an Academy Award nomination for* The World According to Garp, *and Oscar nominations for* Fatal Attraction *and* Dangerous Liaisons. *During a high school singing trip Close found "kindred souls" at William & Mary and ultimately enrolled against her parents' wishes. Her message to the graduates includes questioning and assessing your beliefs, maintaining your individuality, and believing in your uniqueness.*

Thank you Chancellor Gates, Rector Littel and President Rowe for this great, great honor. I am humbled and deeply moved to receive this from a community that had everything to do with who I am today. A community that challenged me, prepared me and inspired me. A community whose passions and philosophies became part of my DNA, giving me strength and resilience, as I stepped out into the world. Thank you. Thank you. I will treasure this always.

To the distinguished faculty, guests, families and—most importantly—to the graduating class of 2019, I'm proud to be here to help celebrate the women who have worked, taught and studied at this incredible institution. And I am particularly proud to be on this stage with President *Katherine* Rowe. I'm pretty sure King William is spinning in his grave. God bless 'im!

But I *know* the dust of Queen Mary has been fist-pumping in the nether world for the past 100 years. At a time when being part of a tribe can have negative, divisive connotations, I am deeply and forever proud to be a part of the mighty tribe of William & Mary graduates—past, present and future.

When I graduated, 45 years ago, I was the first woman in my family to earn a college degree. My mother never finished high school. She got married at 18 and had her first child two years later. Neither of my grandmothers, or great-grandmothers, went to college. In their society, at the time, it just wasn't done. My paternal grandmother, however, did run away from Texas and worked in a bank in order to put her *sister* through college. *My* two sisters never went to college. So being here today has an extra special significance for me.

Delivered on May 11, 2019, at the College of William & Mary, Williamsburg, VA.

I just want to mention briefly *why* I happened to end up at William & Mary. I won't go into the complexities of the story, but suffice it to say that the first time I saw this campus was in the late 60's when I sprinted off the girls' bus, in my cheery travel uniform, as a member of a singing group for which I wrote songs and performed for five years after high school. The show was the offshoot of a cult-like group that my parents fell prey to when I was 7-years-old. Once off the bus, we enthusiastically set up our mics and speakers in the old Student Rec Center on Dog Street, and proceeded to sing our hearts out for whatever students paused to listen.

As I sang the simplistic songs and did the regimented choreography, I studied the students who were lounging on the furniture or leaning against the walls and there came a moment when I knew that I had to somehow *leave* the group and come get my education *here*. And you want to know why? It was because, almost to a person, they were looking at us like this … as if they were thinking—"*Really?*" That's what I'd been secretly feeling for a long, long time, but I hadn't had the courage to *face* it and *do* something about it. "*Really? Is this who I really am?*"

Somehow, in spite of my ignorance, I sensed that on this campus, I would find kindred souls. So eventually, against their wishes, and with no encouragement, whatsoever, I left the group and, 49 years ago, I entered The College of William & Mary in Virginia, a 22 year-old clueless freshman, with an essentially empty toolbox and a passionate determination to get a liberal arts education and become an actress. That fateful September, I walked into Phi Beta Kappa Hall and auditioned for the first play being staged that season—*Twelfth Night*. Professor Howard Scammon, head of the Theater Department, cast me in one of the principal roles: Olivia. He eventually understood the seriousness of my intent and was my mentor for the four years I was here. Meanwhile, I soaked up everything I could learn and, like a desert when the rains come, for the first time in my life I started to bloom. The rest is history.

I wanted to tell you about why I ended up here because I have learned how important it is to have a healthy dose of skepticism. I don't mean cynicism or contempt, I mean the crucial ability to question and assess—from a dispassionate, objective point of view—whatever beliefs or tribes you eventually choose to espouse. It doesn't come to me naturally. I had been raised to be a total believer, to *not* question. But for me, coming into this ideas-rich community, having had all my beliefs and behaviors dictated to me from the age of 7, it was vital that I learn how to question. You have a much harder time of it now than I ever had. When I graduated, there was no Internet. You wrote your papers on typewriters! There was no Facebook, Twitter or Instagram. I didn't have the added, enormous pressure of social media against which to develop as an adult. I think my mind would have exploded. I didn't have that insistent, seductive noise in my pocket and at my fingertips. Even now, I try to question, but how do I maintain my individuality without thinking that I am somehow not relevant, not hip enough, rich enough, not posting enough, that I don't have enough followers?

What each of you have, and what you must believe in from this day forward, is your inherent uniqueness. Your singular point of view. No one looks out onto the world through your eyes. Your perspective is unique. It's important and it counts. Try not to compare it to anyone else. Accept it. Believe in it. Nurture it. Stay fiercely, joyously connected to the friends you have made here, to those you love and trust. You will have each other's backs for the rest of your lives.

I wish I were funny like Robin Williams. I wish I could make you laugh so hard you'd fall off your chairs. I'm not wise. I have had the lucky chance to learn by *doing*. After being in my profession for 45 years, though, I *have* learned a few things that I want to briefly share with you today.

In order to inhabit a character I have had to find where we share a common humanity. I can't do characters justice if I am judging them. I have to find a way to love them. The exploration into each character I play has made me a more tolerant and empathetic person. I have had to literally imagine myself in someone else's shoes, looking out of someone else's eyes. I urge you to learn how to do that. You can with practice. Start by being curious about the "whys" of someone's behavior. Before you judge someone, before you write them off, take the time to put yourself in their shoes and see how it feels.

I have been a part of collaborative companies of actors and directors for 45 years. Companies are like living organisms, extremely sensitive to the chemistry, to the contributions of all those involved. When I was in a Broadway musical early in my career, my dressing room was right next to the stage door. I wasn't *the* star, but I was a co-star and I was working my ass off every night to squeeze all there was to squeeze out of what was a pretty thankless role. It was hard work. The play was a big hit, which was fabulous, but *every performance* I would empty myself out, emotionally and physically, onstage and *every night* I could hear the producers come in the Stage Door and pass by my dressing room, on their way up to schmooze the star. It really hurt that they never knocked on my door, not to schmooze or hang out, but to simply say thank you for the hard work—eight shows a week—for which they were reaping huge benefits.

I remember that hurt and because of it, when I am the member of a company, especially if I am leading that company, I am careful to notice everyone on the team, learn about what they do and thank them. People like the craft-service guy on a movie set, who gets up earlier than everyone else and leaves the set after everyone else, who hauls heavy urns of coffee and food from location to location, rain or shine. To be aware of and to sincerely appreciate the contributions of everyone on a team makes a palpable difference.

Then there is kindness. My nephew, Calen, lives with schizophrenia. He had his first psychotic break when he was 17. My sister, Jessie, Calen's mom, lives with bipolar disorder. Ten years ago, we founded an organization called *Bring Change to Mind* to fight against the stigma around mental illness because they found that stigma is as hard—sometimes harder—than the diseases themselves. We decided to talk about mental illness and stigma on a national platform. Jessie and Calen were inconceivably courageous, because 10 years ago, not many people were talking about it.

The fact is that, conservatively, one in six of us in this room is touched in some way by mental illness. It makes absolutely no sense to me that we don't talk about it like any other chronic illness. Starting the conversation is the first step. Two days ago, I was with Calen, in front of 2,000 people, listening to him talk about living with something as scary as schizophrenia. I am astounded by how he has willed himself to manage his illness. He spoke, albeit sometimes hesitantly, searching for words without losing his train of thought, talking with grace and knowledge. Someone from the audience asked him what they should do when confronted with someone who is struggling with mental health issues and Calen simply said, "Be kind."

Kindness. It's a simple word, but it is essential if we are to survive as a species on this planet. So I come to another thing I've learned. I learned, from reading the writings of the great Edward O. Wilson, that one of the core reasons we have been so successful as a species is that we evolved the capacity to empathize. That means that the tribes who *espoused* empathy were more successful at survival than the ones who didn't. In order for the community, the tribe, to survive and thrive, we humans had to evolve the ability to register the emotions, the plight, the fears and the needs of other members of our tribe and to respond to them with empathy. We die without connection. Nothing is worse for us humans than to be bereft of community. Empathy evolved because two eyes looked into two eyes. It's the most immediate and powerful way we humans communicate. Empathy evolved because we looked at each other, face to face, not on a screen. Studies have shown that the farther away we get from two eyes looking into two eyes, the harder it is to empathize. What I have learned is that if we are to remain a free and viable society, we need to spend less time looking at screens and more time looking into each other's eyes.

To end, I thought I'd share with you bits of a letter that somehow got to me from an old William & Mary friend. I wrote it to him 42 years ago, when I had been out in the world for three years. Reading it from where I am now in my life and in my career was quite moving. I wrote:

> *My mind has been all over the place because of a very erratic rehearsal schedule. I did get the part of Estelle in the Rose Tattoo and am right now of the frame of mind that I should never have taken it. The scene is over before it starts. There is no time to really make any kind of statement. ... any kind of progression. So one has to enter as a totally interesting and real person, be on for five minutes and leave. I really hate it, but I suppose it's a good exercise of sorts. I'm just at the despairing stage and am feeling totally untalented. ... Oh, well.*
>
> *To maintain any semblance of wit and equilibrium seems to be a major feat. As life unfolds before me, I have more and more respect for anyone who survives and prevails. Just to endure is impressive enough, but to endure and to triumph—on your own terms—is the feat of a lifetime. Everyone needs so much gentleness and love. I don't mean that idealistically; I mean it as a major means of survival. There is just too much working against sanity and civilization. ... from within ourselves, to the differences between people and sexes ... to the whole human comedy. Gentleness and love. I can forget so easily, but it's always a great comfort to come back to.*
>
> *I'm going to cook a hamburger and some zucchini.*

Thank you.

Print Citations

CMS: Close, Glenn. "Your Perspective Is Unique." Commencement Address at the College of William & Mary, Williamsburg, VA, May 11, 2019. In *The Reference Shelf: Representative American Speeches, 2018–2019,* edited by Sophie Zyla, 18-22. Amenia, NY: Grey House Publishing, 2019.

MLA: Close, Glenn. "Your Perspective Is Unique." College of William & Mary, 11 May 2019, Williamsburg, VA. Commencement Address. *The Reference Shelf: Representative American Speeches, 2018–2019,* edited by Sophie Zyla, Grey House Publishing, 2019, pp. 18-22.

APA: Close, G. (2019, May 11). Commencement Address on your perspective is unique. The College of William & Mary, Williamsburg, VA. In Sophie Zyla (Ed.), *The reference shelf: Representative American speeches, 2018–2019* (pp. 18-22). Amenia, NY: Grey House Publishing.

Commencement Address to the 2019 Harvard Business School Graduates

By Michael R. Bloomberg

Michael Bloomberg is a three-term mayor of New York City, a billionaire businessman and philanthropist, and a graduate of Johns Hopkins University and Harvard University. While Mayor he established a 311 calling system for reporting crimes and other city problems. Active in the arenas of climate change and global health, Bloomberg works with the World Health Organization to assist medical efforts in impoverished countries and launched Beyond Carbon in an effort to retire coal-fired power plants and oil and gas and move the country toward clean energy. Bloomberg Philanthropies has been a large financial supporter to the Paris Climate Agreement. In his remarks to the 2019 Harvard graduating class, Bloomberg spoke of his days at Harvard, his career changes, and workplace ethics, and what he believes to be the present ethical crisis corroding our society.

Well good afternoon. Thank you, Dan for the introduction—and you really don't have to call me Mayor Bloomberg. Mr. Bloomberg would be just fine, thank you.

Let me also thank Nitin for the honor of addressing you. I didn't have much choice when he called—he didn't ask me to come, he told me I was coming.

Let me begin with the most important words I can say today: congratulations to the distinguished graduates of the great class of 2019.

It was only 53 years ago that I was in your shoes, so I know you've had an amazing experience here. You have mastered the case method during your time on campus—and the art of asking tough questions, like why don't the printers ever work here? Why on earth do they use the case method to teach accounting? Who thought of that?

And the toughest question of all: how many people does it take to finish a Scorpion Bowl at Hong Kong? For the record, the correct answer there is more than one.

HBS really does have a special place in my heart. Not only did I graduate from here, but so did my daughter, Emma.

My foundation teamed up with the B-School and K-School to create a mayoral leadership program run by Professor Abdelal.

And my father—who died a year before I was accepted to HBS—has his name on the building that stands behind Baker, an honor that would have thrilled him.

Delivered on May 29, 2019, at Harvard University Business School, Cambridge, MA.

He and my mother raised my sister and me just five miles from here in Medford, Massachusetts. That was convenient, because I never would have made it through the B-School without my mother nearby—she typed all my papers. Five decades later I still can't type—or spell. But I do have the good sense to have someone proof my tweets.

As you can imagine, I also had the good sense to keep my Boston connections to myself when I was Mayor of New York City, especially when the Red Sox, Celtics, Bruins or Patriots came to town. I will just note that during my time in City Hall, the Giants beat the Patriots in two Super Bowls. I did my job.

We moved to Medford from Brookline a few miles from here when I was four-years-old. And I can still remember my first day in our new home. A boy from up the street clunked me over the head with a rock and I went in bleeding to my mother, which is to say I learned about Boston hospitality at a young age. I guess I had a hard head even back then.

Even though I grew up just a trolley car ride away, when I first arrived on campus I felt like I'd entered a whole new world. Suddenly, I was in classes with friends whose families had built major companies and had famous last names. That was a pretty radical change from my childhood. My mother once told me: we never knew anybody whose name was in the newspaper, unless it was in the crime or the obit section.

I can't say I spent a lot of time across this lawn in Baker Library. My transcript is evidence of that. I was always one of those who made the top half of the class possible. I was more likely to be over the bridge at what is now the Russell House Tavern. Back then, it was a German beer hall called The Wursthaus. It's where I first learned that it's better not to watch sausage being made.

Now, I'm sure many of you have already lined up a job. But for those who haven't, don't worry. I was a month away from graduating from the B-School and I still had no idea what I wanted to do. I asked a classmate for advice. He said, "Go to Wall Street." I said, "I don't know anything about finance." He said, "Just apply for jobs at Salomon Brothers & Hutzler, and a firm named Goldman Sachs." And I said, "Who are they? What do they do?"

Yes, I was a B-School kid who had never heard of Goldman Sachs. A lot has changed since then.

Goldman, I remember, flew me down to New York and offered me a job starting at $14,000 a year—not bad pay for 1966. Salomon Brothers sent me a train ticket and offered me a job for only $9,000. After the interviews, I thought I would fit much better into Salomon. But I told the senior partner, John Gutfreund, I couldn't afford to pay the rent on that salary. Rent in New York was really expensive back then—120 bucks a month, as I remember.

He said, "how much do you need?" I didn't want to be piggy about it, so I said on the spur of the moment $11,500. He said, "OK, $9,000 in salary and a $2,500 loan." And he walked out of the room. This is a true story, I didn't know what to do.

So I showed up two months later and I just started working. So much for my negotiating skills.

For the record, my first year bonus was $500 loan forgiveness, and my second year bonus was forgiveness for the other two grand. Just remember that when you think you are getting stiffed on a bonus negotiation.

But seriously, when you weigh a job offer my message to you is, even later in life when you're considering a career change, leave salary out of the equation. Make decisions based on the quality of the opportunity, and where you'll have the most fun and the most room for growth.

What's important for your career is not your starting salary. It's your development and happiness. The cash will come later on.

I learned a lot about finance at Salomon, but the most valuable lesson I learned had nothing to do with stocks and bonds. They were lessons on how to apply what I had learned—not only here at HBS, but also from my parents, and from my time as an Eagle Scout.

The head of Salomon Brothers, Billy Salomon, never went to college, no less business school. He never took a class in corporate responsibility—and he didn't need to. Being ethical does not require a Masters degree. It requires having a conscience—and following it. It requires being honest and truthful, and never lying or cheating.

Let me give you a quick example: there was a rule at Salomon against giving gifts to clients to win more business. When Billy caught someone sending a case of wine to a major client, he fired him on the spot. Period, end of story. It didn't matter that he was perhaps the most productive salesman in the company.

"You can say Billy over-reacted—but I don't think so. The rules he asked us to follow he followed himself—no exceptions. And when it came to ethics, there was no compromising.

Billy treated everyone the same—from senior partners to the custodial staff. No one was better than anyone else. And Billy believed if you were lucky enough to make some money, you had an obligation to give a percentage of it away to help others. In fact, he didn't ask you what the percentage should be, he told you and you did it.

I've been very lucky in my career. But my luckiest break wasn't getting fired—although that was pretty lucky it turned out. My luckiest break was taking a job where I got to see the ethics I learned growing up put into practice in the workplace. And I'd like to think the principles that I learned at Salomon have guided my life ever since.

But when we look at today's world, it's not clear that everyone with a degree in business has those principles. And that's one reason, I believe, that this great country of ours is suffering from an ethical crisis that is corroding our society.

Today, Americans are questioning whether those in the private sector—and in Washington—can provide the moral leadership our country needs, both economically and politically. They see the rewards of the economy increasingly concentrated at the top. They see wealthy parents scamming the college admissions process. They see families unable to afford health care and housing in the world's richest country.

They see decades of discrimination based on race and ethnicity trapping another generation into poverty. And they wonder: is our economic system breaking down?

At the same time, if they are not blinded by partisanship when they look at Washington, D.C., they see truth and science being trampled with reckless abandon. They see the rule of law being attacked and undermined. They see a chorus of enablers who defend every lie and abuse of power. And they wonder: is our political system breaking down, too?

Now, as you may know, I've never been much for party politics. I've supported Democrats, Republicans, and Independents. Hell, I've actually been a Democrat, Republican, and independent.

No party has a monopoly on good ideas or good people. But I believe all of us have an obligation to reject those who traffic in dishonesty and deceit. That is not a partisan position. That is a patriotic position.

For full disclosure, back in 2016 at the Democratic National Convention in Philadelphia when the Republican nominee was promising to run our country like he ran his business, I said, "God help us." And not just because he went to Wharton. Actually I wish I hadn't been right.

But unfortunately, when we elect people to public office who have no interest in ethics, that depravity trickles down and it seeps into our culture.

Thirty years ago, New York Senator Daniel Patrick Moynihan—a Harvard professor I should note—described society's growing tolerance for illicit behavior as "defining deviancy down."

Today, we face the same problem—only the bad behavior is not on city streets but in the halls of power in Washington. And as our political culture degenerates, so does our ability to address all the big challenges that we face.

Now, the good news is there is a solution. In fact, I believe that the solution to our political problems is also the solution to our economic problems. And I can sum it up in one word: integrity.

In Econ 101, you were probably taught that markets are based on supply and demand. But for capitalism to really function, people need to have faith that they will be entering into generally fair exchanges—that one side won't cheat on the other.

Of course, not every person can be trusted to act with integrity, so we do have laws and regulations that are intended to guarantee it. Those legal controls don't always work—and periodically, we do need to update them.

For example, a century ago, Teddy Roosevelt took on the largest corporations that were destroying competition. Twenty five years later, Franklin D. Roosevelt's New Deal provided relief from a Great Depression that some thought would lead to the downfall of capitalism.

For their leadership, T.R. and F.D.R. were reviled by many in the business world—and considered traitors to their class. But their actions preserved the integrity of markets—by restoring people's faith in them.

Now, I'm as much of a capitalist as you will ever find, but anyone who believes that unfettered capitalism works hasn't read history.

Today, we hear echoes of the challenges the Roosevelts faced. Industry consolidation has reached record levels, and is suppressing competition and choice. And more and more Americans—especially in your generation—are questioning whether capitalism is capable of creating a just society. Their faith in America—and all that we represent—is being shaken.

If we do not act to restore it, the turmoil in our politics today will be only a prelude of what's to come, and that could shake the very foundations of our society.

Graduates, we cannot allow those issues to fester. We must address them now. We must find new ways to build a capitalist society that is more dynamic and more secure, more affluent and more equal.

So think of this as your next case study. And it's the ultimate case study for our country, because it's based on the ultimate question: how do we restore faith in the promise of America and the future of the American dream?

There are no silver bullets, but I believe all of you have a critical role to play. So let me offer you a few ideas on how you can help lead the way.

First, start with yourself. Wherever your career leads you, be honest with your colleagues, clients and contractors. Don't ever try to take advantage of them. Don't hesitate to speak up when someone else does.

Public faith in private markets rests on individual actions. Billy Salomon understood that. And I hope you will seek out organizations that are led by people who understand it, as well.

Second, when applying for a job, align yourself with companies that are engaged in philanthropy. I tell job applicants all the time, if you want the fruits of your labor—the company's profits—spent on education, public health, the arts, government innovation, and the environment, come to work at Bloomberg. If that's not what you want, you're not the right person for us.

Philanthropy gives us a competitive advantage, we think, in recruiting and retaining talent. And I can tell you from personal experience it is also good for the bottom line, as good a thing a company can do.

Third, give back on your own and don't wait. I'll never forget watching my father write a check for 50 bucks to the NAACP—which was a lot of money for us when I was a kid. I asked him, "Daddy, why?" And he said, "Because discrimination against anyone is a threat to everyone."

And I can just tell you after 50-plus years in business and government, people have a hell of a lot more respect for those who make a difference in society than they do for people who just make money. And the networks that you will make through philanthropy will open up lots of new opportunities for your career.

Gordon Gekko was wrong: greed ain't good.

All of you have spent two years studying how to run and manage organizations. There are so many groups that could benefit from your expertise. So volunteer, serve, go into government. Just remember the difference between business and government: business is a dog-eat-dog world. And government is exactly the reverse. So you can do it.

Fourth, if and when you end up in an executive position, don't make one of the fundamental mistakes that I see businesses and boards make all the time: undervaluing their labor force, and over-compensating their CEOs.

Management often treats workers like widgets—which they're not. And boards treat CEOs like irreplaceable geniuses, which they rarely are.

At Bloomberg, we pay employees very well, we invest in their training and education, and we offer industry-leading benefits. In return, our employees pay us back ten-fold with their dedication and loyalty.

Doing right by your employees pays. It really does. And there is no better way to strengthen capitalism than to give people a greater stake in its success.

Fifth and finally, never self-deal. Ever. And avoid even the slightest perception of a conflict of interest.

After I was elected mayor, I decided to refuse a $15 million city tax break that Bloomberg had already qualified for. And I waived the fees for the Bloomberg Terminals that the city agencies had under contract. And I certainly never charged taxpayers $300,000 in golf cart fees for my security team. I would've thought Wharton would teach its students not to do that, but who knew?

But really, your reputation is everything. Don't sell it or trade it for anything.

Finally, after following all of these principles, insist on no less from the people who ask for the most precious commodity you will ever own, and that is your vote.

Elect people who understand that it's their obligation to make capitalism work for everyone, and not be so naive to think other systems will be better. That means picking up where Teddy Roosevelt and Franklin Roosevelt left off, and modernizing capitalism for our time.

America must always be a place where it's possible to get rich through perspiration and innovation. But it must never be a place where the middle class steadily loses ground—and where many of those feel trapped at the bottom.

Unfortunately, that is the path we are on. And the further we go down that path, the more likely that the most extreme voices on both the left and right will attract large followings, win power, and do real harm to our country.

Now, I'm an optimist, and we will change direction I think, partly because of how business leaders are already taking on one of the biggest challenges that we face: climate change.

Today, I'm glad to announce that HBS will hold an alumni conference next year, on investing in the age of climate change—with Bloomberg Philanthropies' support. It's another example of where doing right and doing good are aligned.

Investors are demanding that businesses disclose the climate risks they face—because it affects their bottom line. I've helped spearhead a push for more transparency, through the Task Force on Climate-related Financial Disclosures. And next year here at HBS, we will bring government and business leaders together to discuss how we can harness the power of the market to protect the environment.

Market forces are among the most powerful tools in the world. But whether it's climate change, or income inequality, or gun violence, or any other issue, those forces must be guided by ethical leaders, or else the market's invisible hand can turn into a clenched fist.

And when society's most defenseless take it on the chin, I can promise you they will fight back with unpredictable consequences—and demand a better deal, as they should.

Graduates, restoring the faith that Americans have been losing in our economic and political systems is a big job. If you won't lead it, who will?

You've been fortunate to spend two years on this pristine campus—where even the squirrels seem to have come from the spa. But as you know, the real world can be dirty, unfair, and unjust, unless you insist otherwise. And capitalism can run amok, unless you steer it back on course.

As graduates of the Harvard Business School you have the ability to help our nation do all of that and much more—and I sincerely hope that you will.

So tonight, have one last Scorpion Bowl, and tomorrow start helping to restore and renew our national sense of integrity.

Our country needs you, and you can do it.

Congratulations and best of luck.

Print Citations

CMS: Bloomberg, Michael. "Commencement Address to the 2019 Harvard Business School Graduates." Commence Address at Harvard Business School, Cambridge, MA, May 29, 2019. In *The Reference Shelf: Representative American Speeches, 2018–2019*, edited by Sophie Zyla, 23-29. Amenia, NY: Grey House Publishing, 2019.

MLA: Bloomberg, Michael. "Commencement Address to the 2019 Harvard Business School Graduates." Harvard Business School, 29 May 2019, Cambridge, MA. Commencement Address. *The Reference Shelf: Representative American Speeches, 2018–2019*, edited by Sophie Zyla, Grey House Publishing, 2019, pp. 23-29.

APA: Bloomberg, M. (2019, May 29). Commencement Address to the 2019 Harvard Business School graduates. Harvard Business School, Cambridge, MA. In Sophie Zyla (Ed.), *The reference shelf: Representative American speeches, 2018–2019* (pp. 23-29). Amenia, NY: Grey House Publishing.

Take Charge of Earth: Turn Your Fear into Excitement

By Bill Nye

Bill Nye the Science Guy is an educator, a mechanical engineer at Boeing, a Cornell University graduate, a comedy show writer, author, and performer, and a voice for the science community. The Bill Nye the Science Guy *show won 19 Emmy Awards during its five-year run, and Nye personally won seven for writing, performing, and producing. Nye has many accomplishments, including his children's books, movies, talk show appearances, and the development of a hydraulic pressure resonance suppressor for the Boeing 74 and of sundials for Mars Rover missions. Nye was awarded an honorary doctorate from Rensselaer Polytechnic Institute, Johns Hopkins University, and Goucher College, where he spoke to the 2019 graduating class, advocating that graduates turn their fear about climate change into excitement, enabling them to change the world.*

Thank you all so much, thank you so much for including me today. Ladies and gentlemen, distinguished faculty, distinguished speakers, alumni, parents, boys, girls, kids of all ages, and especially graduates. Congratulations, you made it. Nicely done. Yes. Now, you might be thinking, those parents and all those older adults, they can't get me now. Well, it's too late people, they already did.

Now, we want you to go out there and, dare I say it, change the world. As you may have heard a moment ago, I was awarded an honorary doctorate from Goucher 20 years ago. So when I'm here at Goucher especially, you can trust me, because I'm a doctor.

For your entire life, I imagine, you've heard people say you are the future. And there's a reason for that. Trust me, you are the future. And right now in the spring of 2019, your future looks both exciting, full of astonishing promise, and, trust me, it also looks terrifying for everyone on Earth.

You have access to more human knowledge, more computing power, and more fun, in your electric phone machines than your ancestors could imagine, let alone make use of. And it sure looks like information, transportation, and agricultural technologies are going to get better and better. The future is full of astonishing promise.

But our world is changing. There are now so many of us living increasingly energy-intensive lives and burning ancient plants to get that energy that we are changing

---

Delivered on May 24, 2019, at Goucher College, Baltimore, MD.

the climate of a whole planet. You might say the world is on fire, and these are scary times for everyone on Earth.

Speaking of scary times for everyone on Earth, as you may have heard a moment ago, my mother graduated from Goucher in 1942, and in the winter of 1941 and 1942, everyone around here, in the United States, was terrified. They could see the troubles in Europe and Asia were about to become troubles for everyone on Earth. The first such conflict, the first big war to end all wars—which it didn't—was rekindled and the U.S. was once again going to be dragged into the deadliest war ever, or maybe just so far: the Second World War.

That winter, my mother's boyfriend disappeared, captured by the Japanese navy from Wake Island, a tiny atoll 5,000 nautical miles west of Pearl Harbor. That spring, my mother, along with several other Goucher women, class of 1942, became cryptanalysts, the codebreakers. They all went on to have remarkable careers; they all helped win the war. But back then, so did everyone. Everyone in the U.S., most people everywhere, went to work to solve a global conflict. I mean, win the war and get back to work—and they did. It was an extraordinary time because everyone was scared. Everyone pitched in, and in five short years, they got 'er done.

Now all of you aren't facing a global war, or, at least, not yet. Instead, you're facing a global change of life itself. Our world is warming, and the living things around us are changing and dying at an unprecedented rate. So you are going to have to make big changes in the way you and your kids live. At the start of the Industrial Revolution, after James Watt came up with a very practical steam engine, we had about 280 parts per million of carbon dioxide in Earth's atmosphere. Today, we have nearly 415, a change by a factor of one and a half in just two-and-a-half centuries. We're not talking about two million years; we're talking about 200 years. The only other times climates have changed this fast here on Earth are associated with the occasional asteroid impact. There's never been anything like it in all of human history.

When my grandmother, who grew up in Washington, DC, went to see the Wright Brothers aeroplane fly in College Park, MD, in 1909, there were a few more than one-and-a-half billion people on Earth. Today, there are almost six times that many. We are burning and breathing an atmosphere that's so thin...how thin is it? It's so thin, if you can drive straight up, you'd be in outer space in an hour. On 695, it would be two and a half hours.

With every passing second, there are four more people born on Earth. By the time you all reach your billionth second on this planet, a little over halfway into your 31st year, we will have nine billion people, we may have close to 10 billion people, on Earth.

We, by that I mean you, are going to find ways to feed us all. And you will, with technology derived from science, and with policies that support innovation investment in the greater good, policies based on facts. It is no longer a matter of only keeping the air and water clean, curtailing the accidental creation of plastic trash, like straws, and hoping that will be OK. No. Nowadays we, by that I mean you, are going to have to steer our spaceship, take charge of Earth. It's no longer a matter of just being good stewards. From now on, we humans will have to deliberately control what we do to our atmosphere, the land and sea, to ensure that we maintain as much biodiversity as possible, while taking care of all of us.

Now when it comes to changing the world, don't be scared. Don't freak out. When you have to perform doing anything, be it a final exam, dressing for a date, winning a world war, or managing a planet, you might be nervous. You might be scared. And that fear can stop you cold. But don't let it. As we say in the theater, and on television, take that fear and turn it into excitement. You're Goucher graduates, for crying out loud. You can do this, people! Take a chance, make a difference. It's what everyone here wants you to do in every challenge you face—turn your fear into excitement and change the world.

If you could, in Harry-Potter-magic-wand-ical fashion, make one sweeping change to the world that would address climate change, it would be this. You would raise the standard of living for girls and women worldwide. That's a fact. My mom was a woman, for example. Now instead of a magic wand, let us provide these three things for everyone on Earth. And women of the world, they'll be educated, they'll have fewer kids, and the kids they do have will be educated, healthy, and productive, so here we go.

First, we want clean water for every citizen in the world. Water enables us to be healthy. It enables us to have agriculture, feed our populations. Second, we want energy for everybody. In general, when we say energy, we mean renewably produced reliable electricity for everyone on Earth. Electricity is magical. You can use it to light a room, navigate by satellite, produce TV shows, make instant-grams, or you can use it to make toast. It's versatile, it's transmittable, it's efficient. Third, we want access to the internet, or whatever you kids call internet in the coming decades, to provide global information for everyone in the world. By connecting everybody electronically, landline or a constellation of low-orbiting satellites, we can change things.

When I think about those three big, big ideas, I sense some tough challenges. But I'm filled with optimism. This is as good a moment as any in our time together to talk about advice. Just regular advice. It's a good idea, for example, to always wear shoes in a factory where they make thumbtacks. When crossing a highway in a car or especially on foot, it's a good idea to look up from your phone once in a while. Once in a while! And it's good to read the label on a can of paint—before you drink it. You see, you should be paying attention. It's just what I'm talking about.

Now when I was in college, and for twenty more years in the workforce, if I wanted to know something fun, like the atomic number of rubidium, or if I wanted to know something important, like the score of the Orioles game, I had to look it up in a printed source, a newspaper, a journal, a chemical handbook. But now, facts like those are available in a few milliseconds from several generally very reliable sources. I mean, it's not that likely that someone is going to create a website on which they deliberately state that rubidium has 38 protons instead of 37. Ha, that would be funny. Oh, man.

But people do make up a lot of misleading and just plain wrong things and post them on the internet. The skill we all need now is that of critical thinking. It's what we used to call reasoning or logic, the ability to reason, whether or not something is reasonable, and then to find a way to check it, to verify it.

Now here's something else I hope you'll carry with you as long as you live. Everyone you'll ever meet knows something you don't. Everyone. Farmers know things about plants that most of us, even botanists, never will. Bricklayers have an intimate knowledge of what it takes to lay bricks. Cooks know how to use copper bowls to control egg proteins, and that's cool. Respect that knowledge and learn from others. It will bring out the best in them, and it will bring out the best in you.

Keep in mind, everyone, that if you couldn't choose where to be born on Earth, but you could choose when, this would be the time to be born. This is the most exciting time in human history. Life is better now, for more of us, than ever before in history. As strange as it may seem, this really is the best time. The opportunities before us are amazing. No matter what else is going on, everyone, please be optimistic. People who are not optimistic don't get very much done. They get spun up and worn down by their own self-doubt, and they'll bring you down with them.

When my grandparents joined our merry band here on Earth, no one had any idea what relativity was or is. They saw the creation of nuclear weapons and nuclear power. My grandmother was alive when the first Wright Brothers' flight took place, which would later fit in the cargo version of a 747 airplane that I worked on. The whole flight would fit inside, height and distance.

Your mobile phone uses both special and general relativities so that it can tell you what side of the street you're standing on. And speaking of relativistic physics, you were all in college when gravitational waves were proven to exist. You were in first grade or so when the universe was shown to be not only expanding but accelerating outward. And dark matter and dark energy are responsible. And you know what dark matter and dark energy are? Nobody knows!

Understanding those currently mysterious forces may lead to everyday technology like a mobile phone and will be in your lifetime. And by the way, I'm predicting right now that gravitons, particles of gravity, will be measured or even isolated. So will darkons. Darkons—particles of dark. It's just a word I kind of made up there. Mark my words, or my word. Darkon, well, they'll be dark.

And what I'm saying is, as troublesome as some of our global problems seem to be, you are all up to the challenges. You know more physics than Isaac Newton or Copernicus, you know more about evolution, biology, and genetics than Darwin or Wallace did, or even could. Those guys didn't even know there was DNA.

And speaking of biological acronyms (who isn't?), Clustered Regularly Interspaced Short Palindromic Repeats, or CRISPR, is going to change the way we farm, treat diseases, and give birth. In your lifetime, we may discover evidence of life on Mars or the ocean moon of Jupiter, Europa. The future, your future, is going to be extraordinary.

As graduates, I imagine more than a few of you are concerned about what's next. What you're going to do for a living. What you're going to do for the rest of your life.

My advice: Just get started. Just get started. As you may know, I worked on a TV show intended to get young viewers excited about science so in the future we'd have a more scientifically literate society and, of course, more scientists and engineers. But please, keep in mind, I'm not advocating for everyone to become a scientist, and I'm certainly not asking that everyone become an engineer. The fashion consequences alone would be very troubling.

I got here today by taking a good job in the aerospace industry. I started writing jokes for a local comedy show. I left my full-time regular engineering job October 3, 1986 roughly, to pursue a career in television. I just got started and one thing led to some other pretty good things. So turn any concern you have, any time you have it, about your future into excitement.

Wait, wait, there's one more thing that's not really advice, people. I guess it's the closest thing I can provide to a command. Vote! You have to vote. Thank you! I'm glad this is not controversial. Hang on, there's just a little more! Voting is how we influence policymakers, it's how we make big changes, it's how we get things done. If you don't want to vote, will you please just shut up, so the rest of us can get on with changing things for the better.

To me, the Founding Fathers, the people who wrote the U.S. Constitution, were nerds. They were trying to come up with a system that would always work for people who, for some reason, don't always get along. And built in is change. That's the key, and for me, the key to the progress—to the process—of science. And I remind you, Article 1 Section 8 of the U.S. Constitution refers to the progress of science and useful arts. And that, to me, reflects this insight that our Founding Fathers had. Change is what you have to have in order to adapt. And that's what you all are going to do as you go out to, dare I say it, change the world.

As Bruno Mars remarked, before we leave, I'd like to tell you a little something. Take a moment and consider what you have accomplished here at Goucher, and what you'll be able to accomplish on account of your Goucher days. Whatever it cost, it's priceless. Your diploma will be worth more tomorrow than it is today. It'll be worth even more, far more, ten years from now. You have a liberal arts education. This enables you to understand the world in ways that many other people choose not to. So class of 2019, here's wishing you excitement, optimism, and joy in what you do. Use your knowledge and your abilities to bring out the best in those around you, and let them bring out the best in you. We are all excited about your future because you can, and you will, dare I say it, change the world! This has been an honor. Thank you, thank you so much. Thank you. Woo!

Print Citations

CMS: Nye, Bill. "Take Charge of Earth: Turn Your Fear into Excitement." Commencement Address at Goucher College, Baltimore, MD, May 24, 2019. In *The Reference Shelf: Representative American Speeches, 2018–2019,* edited by Sophie Zyla, 30-35. Amenia, NY: Grey House Publishing, 2019.

MLA: Nye, Bill. "Take Charge of Earth: Turn Your Fear into Excitement." Goucher College, 24 May 2019, Baltimore, DC. Commencement Address. *The Reference Shelf: Representative American Speeches, 2018–2019,* edited by Sophie Zyla, Grey House Publishing, 2019, pp. 30-35.

APA: Nye, B. (2019, May 24). Commencement Address on take charge of Earth: Turn your fear into excitement. Goucher College, Baltimore, MD. In Sophie Zyla (Ed.), *The reference shelf: Representative American speeches, 2018–2019* (pp. 30-35). Amenia, NY: Grey House Publishing.

Letting Go of the Old Is Part of a New Beginning

By Angela Merkel

Angela Merkel is the first female chancellor of Germany and a leading figure of the European Union. Merkel was trained as a physicist and entered politics after the fall of the Berlin Wall. Joining the Christian Democratic Union, she served as Helmut Kohl's minister for women and youth, and later for environment and nuclear safety. Merkel was at the top of the Forbes' *list of most powerful women in the world for twelve years, seven of those consecutive. Merkel talked to Harvard graduates about her youth during the Cold War in a divided Germany, dictatorship, and living with the divisions created by the Berlin Wall. She also spoke of believing in the impossible—like the fall of the Berlin Wall— peaceful order based on common values, and the importance of working together.*

Thank you. And, I think, let's start.

President Bacow, Fellows of the Corporation, Members of the Board of Overseers, Members of the Alumni Board, Members of the Faculty, Proud Parents, and Graduates:

Today is a day of joy. It's your day. Many congratulations. I am delighted to be here today and would like to tell you about some of my own experiences. This ceremony marks the end of an intensive and, probably also, hard chapter in your lives. Now the door to a new life is opening. That's exciting and inspiring.

The German writer Hermann Hesse had some wonderful words for such a situation in life. I'd like to quote him and then continue in my native language. Hermann Hesse wrote:

In all beginnings dwells a magic force
For guarding us and helping us to live.[1]

These words by Hermann Hesse inspired me when I completed my physics degree at the age of 24. That was back in the year 1978.

The world was divided into East and West. It was during of the Cold War. I grew up in East Germany, in the GDR, at a time when that part of my homeland was not free, in a dictatorship. People were oppressed and monitored by the state. Political opponents were persecuted. The government of the GDR was afraid that the people would run away to freedom. And that's why the Berlin Wall was built. It was made of concrete and steel. Anyone who was discovered trying to overcome it was arrested

---

Delivered on May 30, 2019, at Harvard University, Cambridge, MA.

or shot. This wall in the middle of Berlin divided a people—and it divided families. My family was divided too.

My first job after graduation was as a physicist in East Berlin at the Academy of Sciences. I lived near the Berlin Wall. On the way home from my institute I walked past it every day. Behind it lay West Berlin, freedom. And every day, when I was very close to the wall, I had to turn away at the last moment—and head towards my apartment. Every day I had to turn away from freedom at the last minute. I don't know how many times I thought, I couldn't stand it anymore. It was really frustrating.

I was not a dissident. I did not run up and bang against the wall, but neither did I deny its existence because I did not want to lie to myself. The Berlin Wall limited my possibilities. It was literally in my way. But one thing that this wall could not do in all these years: It could not impose limits on my own inner thoughts. My personality, my imagination, my yearnings—these could not be limited by prohibitions and coercion.

Then came the year 1989. Throughout Europe, the shared will for freedom unleashed incredible powers. Hundreds of thousands took to the streets in Poland, Hungary, Czechoslovakia, and the GDR. The people demonstrated and brought down the wall. What many people had not thought possible—even me—became reality. Where once there had been a dark wall, a door suddenly opened. The moment had come for me, too, to step through that door. I did not have to turn away from freedom at the last minute any longer. I could cross that line and venture out into the great, wide open.

During these months, 30 years ago, I personally experienced that nothing has to remain as it is. This experience, dear graduates, is the first thought I would like to share with you today for your future: What seems fixed and unchanging can in fact change.

And in matters both large and small, every change begins in the mind. The generation of my parents had to learn this most painfully. My father and mother were born in 1926 and 1928. When they were as old as most of you here today, the rupture of civilization that was the Shoa [Holocaust] and the Second World War had just ended. My country, Germany, had brought unimaginable suffering upon Europe and the world. How likely would it have been for the victors and the vanquished to remain irreconcilable for many years? But instead, Europe overcame centuries of conflict. The result was a peaceful order based on common values rather than supposed national strength.

Notwithstanding all the discussions and temporary setbacks, I am firmly convinced that we Europeans have united for the better. And the relationship between Germans and Americans shows how former enemies in war can become friends.

It was George Marshall who gave a significant contribution to this with the plan which he proclaimed in this very place at a Commencement Address in 1947. The transatlantic partnership with our values of democracy and human rights has given us a time of peace and prosperity to the benefit of all that has lasted for over 70 years. And today? It will not be long now before the politicians of my generation are no longer subject to the program of "Exercising Leadership," but at most will be dealt with in "Leadership in History."

Dear Harvard Class of 2019: Your generation will face the challenges of the 21st century in the coming decades. You are among those who will lead us into the future. Protectionism and trade conflicts endanger free world trade and thus the foundations of our prosperity. The digital transformation covers all areas of our lives. Wars and terrorism lead to displacement and forced migration. Climate change threatens our planet's natural resources. It and the resulting crises are caused by humans. So we can and must do everything humanly possible to really get this challenge to humanity under control. This is still possible. But everyone has to do their part and—I say this self-critically—get better. Therefore, I will do my utmost to ensure that Germany, my country, will reach the goal of climate neutrality by 2050.

Change for the better is possible if we tackle it together. Going it alone, we will not succeed. And so this is my second thought for you: More than ever we have to think and act multilaterally instead of unilaterally, global instead of national, cosmopolitan rather than isolationist. In short, together instead of alone.

You, dear graduates, will in the future have quite different opportunities for this than my generation did. After all, your smartphone probably has far more computing power than the IBM mainframe replicated by the Soviet Union, which I was allowed to use in 1986 for my dissertation in the GDR.

Today, we use Artificial Intelligence to scan millions of images for symptoms of disease—for example, to better diagnose cancer. In the future, empathic robots could help doctors and caregivers to focus on the individual needs of individual patients. We can not say what applications will be possible, but the opportunities that come with [AI] are truly breathtaking.

Class of 2019, it is essentially up to you as to how we will take advantage of these opportunities. It will be you who will decide how our way of working, communicating, moving, and even developing our way of life will evolve.

As Federal Chancellor, I often have to ask myself: Am I doing the right thing? Am I doing something because it is right, or just because it's possible? You should ask yourself that again and again—and that is my third thought for you today: Do we set the rules of technology or does technology determine how we interact? Do we focus on people with their dignity in all its many facets, or do we only see the customer, the data sources, the objects of surveillance?

These are difficult questions. I have learned that answers to difficult questions can be found if we always see the world through the eyes of others; if we respect the history, tradition, religion, and identity of others; if we firmly stand by our inalienable values and act accordingly; and if we do not always follow our initial impulses, even with all the pressure to make snap decisions, but instead stop for a moment, keep quiet, think, take a break.

Of course, that takes a lot of courage. Above all, it requires being truthful to others and perhaps most importantly to ourselves. Where better to begin with it than here, in this place, where so many young people from all over the world come to learn under the motto of Truth—to do research, and discuss the questions of our time? This implies that we do not describe lies as truth and truth as lies.[2] As well, it implies that we do not accept grievances as our normality.

But what, dear graduates, could stop you—what could hinder us from doing that? Again, there are walls: walls in the mind, walls of ignorance and narrow-mindedness. They exist between members of a family as well as between social groups, between those of different skin colors, peoples, religions.[3] I would like us to break down these walls—walls that repeatedly prevent us from communicating about the world in which we want to live together.

Whether we succeed is up to us. Therefore, dear graduates, my fourth thought is this: Take nothing for granted. Our individual freedoms are not self-evident; democracy is not self-evident; neither is peace nor prosperity.

But if we tear down the walls[4] that restrict us, if we open the door and embrace new beginnings, then everything is possible. Walls can collapse. Dictatorships can disappear. We can stop global warming. We can overcome hunger. We can eradicate diseases. We can give people, especially girls, access to education. We can fight the causes of displacement and forced migration. We can do all this.

So let us not ask first what is wrong or what has always been. Let us first ask what is possible and look for something that has never been done before.[5]

It was these exact words I spoke in 2005 during my very first policy statement, as the newly elected Federal Chancellor of the Federal Republic of Germany, as the first woman in this office, in the German Bundestag, the German Parliament.

And with these words I would like to share with you my fifth thought: Let us surprise ourselves with what is possible—let us surprise ourselves with what we can do.

In my own life, it was the fall of the Berlin Wall that allowed me to step out into the open almost 30 years ago. At that time, I left behind my work as a scientist and went into politics. It was an exciting and magical time, just as your lives will be exciting and full of magic. But I also had moments of doubt and worry. For we all knew what lay behind us, but not what might lie ahead. Perhaps you're feeling a bit like that today amidst all the joy of the occasion.

Therefore, as my sixth thought, I can also tell you this: The moment you stand out in the open is also a moment of risk. Letting go of the old is part of a new beginning. There is no beginning without an end, no day without night, no life without death. Our whole life consists of this difference, the space between the beginning and the ending. What's in between, we call life and experience.

I believe that we must always be ready to finish things to feel the magic of beginnings and to make the most of our opportunities. That was my experience in study, in science, and it's what I have experienced in politics. And who knows what's in store for me after life as a politician? It is completely open. Only one thing is clear: It will again be something different and something new.

That's why I want to leave this wish with you: It's six things [to remember]:
1. Tear down walls of ignorance and narrow-mindedness, for nothing has to stay as it is.
2. Take joint action in the interests of a multilateral global world.

3. Keep asking yourselves: Am I doing something because it is right or simply because it's possible?
4. Don't forget that freedom is never something that can be taken for granted.
5. Surprise yourself with what is possible.
6. Remember that openness always involves risks. Letting go of the old is part of the new beginning.

And above all, nothing can be taken for granted; everything is possible.

Thank you!

Notes

1. Hesse, H. Stages. In *The Glass Bead Game* (Magister Ludi). New York: Henry Holt, Available online at: http://hesse.projects.gss.ucsb.edu/works/stages.html.
2. Timely antimetabole.
3. Thoughtful asyndeton.
4. Allusion to President Reagan's famous words during his Brandenburg Gate Address.
5. Merkel, A. (2005). *Regierungserklärung von Bundeskanzlerin Dr. Angela Merkel vor dem Deutschen Bundestag am 30. November 2005 in Berlin*. https://www.bundesregierung.de/breg-de/service/bulletin/regierungserklaerung-von-bundeskanzlerin-dr-angela-merkel-795782.

Print Citations

CMS: Merkel, Angela. "Letting Go of the Old Is Part of a New Beginning." Commencement Address at Harvard University, May 30, 2019, Cambridge, MA. In *The Reference Shelf: Representative American Speeches, 2018–2019*, edited by Sophie Zyla, 36-40. Amenia, NY: Grey House Publishing, 2019.

MLA: Merkel, Angela. "Letting Go of the Old Is Part of a New Beginning." Harvard University, 30 May 2019, Cambridge, MA. Commencement Address. *The Reference Shelf: Representative American Speeches, 2018–2019*, edited by Sophie Zyla, Grey House Publishing, 2019, pp. 36-40.

APA: Merkel, A. (2019, May 30). Commencement Address on letting go of the old is part of a new beginning. Harvard University, Cambridge, MA. In Sophie Zyla (Ed.), *The reference shelf: Representative American speeches, 2018–2019* (pp. 36-40). Amenia, NY: Grey House Publishing.

2
Politics and Policies

By US Department of Labor, via Wikimedia.

House Speaker Nancy Pelosi announced impeachment proceedings against President Donald Trump in September 2019, stating "No one is above the law."

Oval Office Address on Immigration and Border Security

By Donald Trump

Donald John Trump is the 45th and current president of the United States. Born on June 14, 1946, in Queens, New York, he attended the New York Military Academy. After graduation, he began his career as a real estate developer, eventually taking over his father's business and expanding into other arenas, such as his role as a reality TV star. He has been married three times; wife Ivana with children Donald Jr., Ivanka, and Eric; wife Marla Maples with daughter Tiffany; and wife Melania, with son Barron. Trump graduated from the University of Pennsylvania in 1968 with an economics degree. In this Oval Office Address, President Trump tells the audience that America welcomes millions of legal immigrants that improve our nation. At the same time, there is a vast quantity of drugs flowing across our southern border, along with hundreds of thousands of criminal aliens. His proposal to end this crisis includes technology and a border wall.

My fellow Americans,

Tonight I am speaking to you because there is a growing humanitarian and security crisis at our southern border. Everyday, Customs and Border Patrol agents encounter thousands of illegal immigrants trying to enter our country. We are out of space to hold them, and we have no way to promptly return them back home to their country.

America proudly welcomes millions of lawful immigrants who enrich our society and contribute to our nation, but all Americans are hurt by uncontrolled illegal migration. It strains public resources and drives down jobs and wages.

Among those hardest hit are African-Americans and Hispanic Americans.

Our southern border is a pipeline for vast quantities of illegal drugs, including meth, heroin, cocaine, and fentanyl. Every week 300 of our citizens are killed by heroin alone, 90% of which floods across from our southern border. More Americans will die from drugs this year than were killed in the entire Vietnam War.

In the last two years, ICE officers made 266,000 arrests of aliens with criminal records, including those charged or convicted of 100,000 assaults, 30,000 sex crimes, and 4000 violent killings. Over the years, thousands of Americans have been brutally killed by those who illegally entered our country and thousands more lives will be lost if we don't act right now.

Delivered on January 8, 2019, at the White House, Washington, DC.

This is a humanitarian crisis, a crisis of the heart and a crisis of the soul.

Last month, 20,000 migrant children were illegally brought into the United States, a dramatic increase. These children are used as human pawns by vicious coyotes and ruthless gangs. One in three women are sexually assaulted on the dangerous trek up through Mexico. Women [and] children are the biggest victims by far of our broken system.

This is the tragic reality of illegal immigration on our southern border. This is the cycle of human suffering that I am determined to end.

My Administration has presented Congress with a detailed proposal to secure the border and stop the criminal gangs, drug smugglers, and human traffickers. It's a tremendous problem. Our proposal was developed by law enforcement professionals and border agents at the Department of Homeland Security. These are the resources they have requested to properly perform their mission and keep America safe—in fact, safer than ever before.

The proposal from Homeland Security includes cutting-edge technology for detecting drugs, weapons, illegal contraband, and many other things. We have requested more agents, immigration judges, and bed space to process the sharp rise in lawful immigration fueled by our very strong economy. Our plan also contains an urgent request for humanitarian assistance and medical support. Furthermore, we have asked Congress to close border security loopholes so that illegal immigrant children can be safely and humanely returned back home.

Finally, as part of an overall approach to border security, law enforcement professionals have requested 5.7 billion dollars for a physical barrier. At the request of Democrats, it will be a steel barrier rather than a concrete wall. This barrier is absolutely critical to border security. It's also what our professionals at the border want and need.

This is just common sense.

The border wall would very quickly pay for itself. The cost of illegal drugs exceeds 500 billion dollars a year—vastly more than the 5.7 billion dollars we have requested from Congress. The wall will also be paid for indirectly by the great new trade deal we have made with Mexico.

Senator Chuck Schumer, who you will be hearing from later tonight, has repeatedly supported a physical barrier in the past, along with many other Democrats. They changed their mind only after I was elected President.

Democrats in Congress have refused to acknowledge the crisis. And they have refused to provide our brave border agents with the tools they desperately need to protect our families and our nation.

The Federal Government remains shut down for one reason, and one reason only: because Democrats will not fund border security. My Administration is doing everything in our power to help those impacted by the situation. But the only solution is for Democrats to pass a spending bill that defends our borders and reopens the government.

This situation could be solved in a 45 minute meeting. I have invited Congressional leadership to the White House tomorrow to get this done. Hopefully, we can rise above partisan politics in order to support national security.

Some have suggested a barrier is immoral. Then why do wealthy politicians build walls, fences, and gates around their homes? They don't build walls because they hate the people on the outside, but because they love the people on the inside. The only thing that is immoral is the politicians to do nothing and continue to allow more innocent people to be so horribly victimized.

America's heart broke the day after Christmas when a young police officer in California was savagely murdered in cold blood by an illegal alien who just came across the border. The life of an American hero was stolen by someone who had no right to be in our country.

Day after day, precious lives are cut short by those who have violated our borders. In California, an Air Force veteran was raped, murdered, and beaten to death with a hammer by an illegal alien with a long criminal history. In Georgia, an illegal alien was recently charged with murder for killing, beheading, and dismembering his neighbor. In Maryland, MS-13 gang members who arrived in the United States as unaccompanied minors were arrested and charged last year after viciously stabbing and beating a 16-year-old girl.

Over the last several years, I've met with dozens of families whose loved ones were stolen by illegal immigration. I've held the hands of the weeping mothers and embraced the grief stricken fathers. So sad; so terrible. I will never forget the pain in their eyes, the tremble in their voices, and the sadness gripping their souls.

How much more American blood must we shed before Congress does its job?

To those who refuse to compromise in the name of border security, I would ask: Imagine if it was your child, your husband, or your wife whose life was so cruelly shattered and totally broken?

To every member of Congress: Pass a bill that ends this crisis.

To every citizen: Call Congress and tell them to finally, after all of these decades, secure our border.

This is a choice between right and wrong, justice and injustice. This is about whether we fulfill our sacred duty to the American citizens we serve.

When I took the Oath of Office, I swore to protect our country, and that is what I will always do so help me God.

Thank you and good night.

Print Citations

CMS: Trump, Donald. "Oval Office Address on Immigration and Border Security." Presentation at the White House, Washington, DC, January 8, 2019. In *The Reference Shelf: Representative American Speeches, 2018–2019,* edited by Sophie Zyla, 43-46. Amenia, NY: Grey House Publishing, 2019.

MLA: Trump, Donald. "Oval Office Address on Immigration and Border Security." The White House, 8 January 2019, Washington, DC. Presentation. *The Reference Shelf: Representative American Speeches, 2018–2019,* edited by Sophie Zyla, Grey House Publishing, 2019, pp. 43-46.

APA: Trump, D. (2019, January 8). Oval Office Address on immigration and border security. The White House, Washington, DC. In Sophie Zyla (Ed.), *The reference shelf: Representative American speeches, 2018–2019* (pp. 43-46). Amenia, NY: Grey House Publishing.

Solving Illegal Immigration [for Real]

By Sonia Nazario

Sonia Nazario is a journalist with two Pulitzer Prizes and she is a finalist for a third in public service. Nazario is best known for her story of a young Honduran boy's search for his mother in Enrique's Journey. *She is a contributing writer for the* New York Times. *Nazario has an undergraduate degree from Williams College and a master's from the University of California. Her work has been recognized by numerous awards, including, Champion of Children by First Focus, Golden Door by HIAS Pennsylvania, American Heritage Award by the American Immigration Council, and the National Peacemaker Award by Houston Peace and Justice Center. Nazario addresses issues of drugs, gangs, violence, and migrants with thoughts of lawful solutions.*

People have always called me a rabble rouser.

When I was three years old, my nickname was "la granuja," Spanish for "troublemaker." That year, in my very first drawing, I was clutching two glasses of whiskey. When I drank the first, I told my mom, well, then, I'd drink the second one.

As a Jew, my mother fled Poland before World War II to go to Argentina. My father was born in Argentina, right after his Christian family fled persecution in Syria. Seeking opportunity, my parents came as newlyweds to the U.S. where I was born. When I was 13 years old, my father died suddenly, and my mom took us back to live in Argentina. Her timing was terrible; the military was taking power. I lived in fear every single day. Officers would roam the streets in unmarked cars, picking people up who disappeared, tens of thousands of people.

One day, walking down the street, I saw a puddle of blood on the sidewalk. The military had killed two journalists. "Why?" I asked my mom. "Because they're trying to tell the truth about what's going on here."

I decided that very instant—some of you would have made a different career choice staring at blood—to become a journalist. In the U.S. as a reporter, I became known for throwing myself right in the middle of the action on the front lines so I could take my readers there and they could see, smell, feel the big social issues that I wrote about up close.

The ride of my life started two decades ago in my kitchen when I asked my house cleaner: "Carmen, are you thinking about having any more children?" It was an innocent question; I thought she just had one young boy. Sobbing, Carmen told me about four children she had left behind in Guatemala. She could only feed them

---

Delivered on February 9, 2017, at TEDx, Pennsylvania Avenue.

once a day. And at night when they cried out with hunger, she would tell them: "Sleep face down so your stomach doesn't growl so much."

I could not fathom the desperation that it took to leave your children and go to a strange land 2,000 miles away. Carmen hadn't seen her children in 12 years. I soon discovered that there were millions of single mothers who had come to the U.S. in recent years, unlawfully, from Mexico, from Central America, and they had left children behind. These separations, they often stretched to a decade. And each year tens of thousands of these kids would despair and set off on their own to come and find these mothers. Most of them are teenagers like this boy I met traveling north through Mexico, but I learned of kids as young as seven years old crossing four countries alone. They were hitchhiking, walking hundreds of miles, and they were gripping on mostly to the tops and sides of freight trains that go through Mexico, that go north.

Often these children are robbed, raped, beaten. Many times they are killed by bandits along the rails, by corrupt cops in Mexico, and by gangsters who control the tops of these trains. And they hurl them off, and children lose legs, arms, fingers. I met Enrique when he had made it all the way north to northern Mexico. He told me he was just five years old—this is his kindergarten mug shot—when his mama left him in Honduras to go to the United States. Eleven years later, this is what he looked like. He set off to go and find her, and all he had on him was this tiny scrap of paper with his mother's telephone number inked on it. He was on his eighth attempt to get through Mexico; seven times Mexico had deported him.

I wanted to truly grasp the hell he told me he had already been through. So, I went back to his starting line in Honduras, and I did this journey step by step, the exact route, just as he had done it a few weeks before. I would travel on top of seven freight trains. I almost got swept off the top of one train; that branch that hit me swiped off a boy on the car behind mine. He probably died. A gangster, he tried to rape me on the train. Every day for three months, I felt filthy, thirsty, hungry; I feared the worst, and yet I knew because of the advantages I had I wasn't going through, facing, 1% of what these children endure.

I chronicled this odyssey children make in a newspaper series and later a book, called *Enrique's Journey*. Back in 2002, 6,800 children were arriving alone on our southern border and being apprehended. But by 2014 that number had risen tenfold: 68,000 Enriques. Honduras had the number one homicide rate in the world of countries not at war. And together with El Salvador and Guatemala, these had become among the most dangerous countries in the world.

Children understood that the danger of dying traveling north, it was less than the danger of dying if they stayed. Honduras's Rivera Hernandes neighborhood was the most lethal place in the city of San Pedro Sula, which itself for four years running was dubbed "the murder capital" of the world. I mean parents, they didn't let their kids go outside during broad daylight. Six gangs controlled this neighborhood, and they enforced a six P.M. curfew.

Bodies would litter the streets in the morning. One day these gangsters were casually playing soccer out in the street with the decapitated head of someone they had just executed. One thousand families had fled this neighborhood. Gangsters took over their homes, stripped them, sold anything they could, leaving whole blocks in rubble. Children, refugees, were fleeing for their very lives.

Last summer in Rivera Hernandes, I met Kevin Rodriguez. When he was seven years old, Kevin started collecting cans in the neighborhood to recycle. When he was eight, the gangsters started pressuring him: "You must join." They wanted him to use his bag to deliver drugs and guns throughout the neighborhood for the gang. They pressured Kevin every day. He always answered, "No."

When he was 10 years old, three gangsters barged into his hut when his mom was out working. They held him down, the three gangsters, and they took turns raping this boy. When he was 11 years old, he was at a soccer game in the neighborhood when gangsters showed up, and they massacred 15 spectators and referees in front of him. And when he was walking to middle school one day, he had to sidestep a body hacked to bits that had been stuffed in a black, plastic bag.

Kids like Kevin, they get the dicey odds of making it in one piece through Mexico. The bloodthirsty narco cartels and gangsters, they are kidnapping 18,000 Central Americans every single year. These are the faces of the disappeared, migrating through Mexico. They enslave children; they put girls to work as prostitutes. They will kill you and harvest your organs. Recently, the last two-three years, the U.S. has made matters much worse. We gave Mexico tens of millions of dollars to fund a ferocious crackdown aimed at keeping these children from arriving at our border and begging for asylum, which, by the way, they are legally entitled to do.

Despite all these mounting obstacles, today, just as many children are fleeing these countries than ever before. In the U.S., the largest wave of immigration in our nation's history, it produced winners and losers. Businesses, well they got cheap, compliant workers, and this fueled our economy. But the losers are the folks who can least afford it in this country: the one in 14 Americans who do not have a high school degree. They were forced to compete with migrants in certain industries and that drove down their wages.

Migration hurts migrants, too: something we don't talk about very much. Children feel abandoned by the very person who's supposed to love them the most in this world, their mothers. There's no happy ending. The truth? Most migrants, they don't want to actually be here. Imagine if you had to leave everything that you know and love; your family, friends, culture, language, to fling yourself out into an unknown, often hostile environment.

I want to be very clear: I am not an open borders gal. I want a policy that actually works. Our politicians, both on the left and on the right, have been promoting, pushing, three immigration solutions for the last 40 years: border enforcement; guest worker programs; and legalization.

All three have failed to permanently stem the flow of migrants coming here unlawfully, and keep more children and families safe back in their home countries. We build walls, and we're probably going to do more of this. We spend $18 billion a year at this, at last count. And yet, studies show 97% of those who try repeatedly get in. In 1986, we legalized millions of people. But then they sent, often illegally, for friends and family to come from back home.

We need to rip up this playbook and try something new. The good news, and there is good news, the U.S. is helping bring a new strategy that cuts violence in Central America. In Latin America cities, four out of every five homicides, they happen in fewer than 2% of all street addresses. Usually, it's just a few people, a handful that are doing most of the killing. In taking what's worked in L.A. and in Boston, the U.S.-trained Honduran police are using data to increasingly target where are those violent hot spots, the neighborhoods, and even the very corners within neighborhoods where murders take place.

Like in Rivera Hernandes, where Kevin lives, where the U.S. is helping courageous residents who are putting their lives on the line to try to jumpstart change in this neighborhood. We organize community leaders, the U.S. And we funded partly outreach centers where kids can go and get mentors, vocational training, help get jobs so we can dry up the lifeblood of gangs, new recruits. We have another program that zeroes in on kids in schools in this neighborhood who have some of the nine risk factors of going into gangs, and we get them a year of family counseling, making them 77% less likely to commit crimes or abuse drugs or alcohol. And in a country where 96% of all homicides in Honduras get no conviction—you can shoot someone in broad daylight and totally get away with it—we are helping bring criminals to justice.

Witnesses understand that if you step forward in Honduras to testify today, you're going to be dead tomorrow. But the U.S. is funding a Honduran nonprofit that goes into the most violent neighborhoods and resolves to investigate all homicides in that neighborhood. And they are also coaxing reluctant witnesses to step forward, anonymously, covered in a black burqa. . . . Now, more than half of homicides in this neighborhood and in seven pilot neighborhoods in Honduras, they are getting guilty verdicts. In two years in Rivera Hernandes, a 62% drop in homicides. They have cut the number of kids fleeing this neighborhood in half. Kevin, who was determined that other children not face what he faced at the hands of the gangs, he's volunteering in one of these outreach centers, and just last month at the age of 17, he started U.S.-sponsored studies to become a stronger community organizer to try to reweave the tattered fabric of his neighborhood.

Just to be clear, Rivera Hernandes is still crazy violent. And the U.S. approach, it has huge flaws. The State Department doesn't even do what most studies show works best: work with active gangsters. They're the ones doing the shooting. We need to leverage community leaders with sway over these guys. We need clergy or ex-cons gone straight to drive home a message delivered by the police: If one person in your gang shoots someone, we will immediately come down on your whole gang like a ton of bricks.

We must scrap Treasury Department rules that don't even allow us to work with one of the two main gangs in the region, MS-13. Still, something incredibly promising is happening here. Honduras is the country where the U.S. has most aggressively pushed these violence prevention programs. Three years ago, 18,000 Honduran kids showed up at our southern border alone. Last year, that number was cut almost in half. Meanwhile, kids leaving El Salvador, Guatemala, the numbers keep going up. If a politician swears to you they can solve illegal immigration by driving down on the same three policies of the past, don't buy it.

Let's invest in violence prevention programs that actually work. Let's replicate these in other countries. And let's get corrupt governments, like Honduras, to put some skin in the game as well; after all it's their country, right?

I know many Americans do not want to spend one red cent in foreign lands. I get that. But this is smart policy. It is a rare win-win for us. We can keep spending billions of dollars once these children arrive at our doorstep. And by the way, that doesn't even include the fact that we don't give these kids government lawyers when they arrive in our country to go before immigration court. Half of these kids are going before judges alone to argue their asylum cases. I witnessed a seven-year-old boy. He was shaking with fear standing before that court. Toddlers pee their pants. They clutch teddy bears because anything they tell that judge can send them hurtling back to danger. This is a sham that we are doing in our courts, and we should remedy it. But we can spend billions here, or we can spend $100 million in Honduras, which is what we're spending on these violence prevention programs each year there, and we can cut migration.

The solutions are there; they are not here. Mexico, for years, promoted family planning, and the average Mexican family went from seven kids per family, nearly, to just over two. Today, more Mexicans, they're leaving the United States than actually coming here illegally. In one decade experts believe that in Latin America—it has a tenth of the world's population but a third of all of its homicides—with the right programs, we can cut this carnage in half. And we can see more children happily playing out in the streets, like they're doing here in Rivera Hernandes.

We can keep screaming across the political divide. Or we can do something that actually works on the immigration issue. We can do the right thing. If a vulnerable child is running from danger and that child knocks at our door, a nation like ours, we should always open that door. We should also help ensure that child never has to run north in the first place.

Thank you.

(Applause)

Print Citations

CMS: Nazario, Sonia. "Solving Illegal Immigration, for Real." Keynote Address at TEDx, Pennsylvania Avenue, March 15, 2017. In *The Reference Shelf: Representative American Speeches, 2018–2019,* edited by Sophie Zyla, 47-52. Amenia, NY: Grey House Publishing, 2019.

MLA: Nazario, Sonia. "Solving Illegal Immigration, for Real." TEDx, Pennsylvania Avenue, 15 March 2017. Keynote Address. *The Reference Shelf: Representative American Speeches, 2018–2019,* edited by Sophie Zyla, Grey House Publishing, 2019, pp. 47-52.

APA: Nazario, D. (2017, March 15). Keynote Address on solving illegal immigration, for real. TEDx, Pennsylvania Avenue. In Sophie Zyla (Ed.), *The reference shelf: Representative American speeches, 2018–2019* (pp. 47-52). Amenia, NY: Grey House Publishing.

Remarks by President Trump at the National Rifle Association Leadership Forum: Law & Justice

By Donald Trump

President Trump sends a message that our country is a great country, and doing better every day. Despite what others may try, we will stand to protect Second Amendment rights. We are protecting our border, reducing violent crime, and removing government regulation.

Thank you, Chris, for that kind introduction and for your tremendous work on behalf of our Second Amendment. Thank you very much. (Applause.) I want to also thank Wayne LaPierre for his unflinching leadership in the fight for freedom. Wayne, thank you very much. Great. (Applause.)

I'd also like to congratulate Karen Handel on her incredible fight in Georgia 6. (Applause.) The election takes place on June 20th. And, by the way, on primaries, let's not have 11 Republicans running for the same position, okay? (Laughter.) It's too nerve-shattering. She's totally for the NRA and she's totally for the Second Amendment. So get out and vote. She's running against someone who's going to raise your taxes to the sky, destroy your healthcare, and he's for open borders—lots of crime, and he's not even able to vote in the district that he's running in. Other than that, I think he's doing a fantastic job, right? (Laughter.) So get out and vote for Karen.

Also, my friend—he's become a friend, because there's nobody that does it like Lee Greenwood. Wow. (Applause.) Lee's anthem is the perfect description of the renewed spirit sweeping across our country. And it really is, indeed, sweeping across our country. So, Lee, I know I speak for everyone in this arena when I say, we are all very proud indeed to be an American. Thank you very much, Lee. (Applause.)

No one was more proud to be American than the beloved patriot — and you know who I'm talking about—we remember on gatherings like today, your former five-term President, the late Charlton Heston. How good was Charlton? (Applause.)

And I remember Charlton, he was out there fighting when maybe a lot of people didn't want to be fighting. He was out there for a long time. He was a great guy.

And it's truly wonderful to be back in Atlanta, and back with my friends at the NRA. You are my friends, believe me. (Applause.) Perhaps some of you remember the last time we were all together. Remember that? We had a big crowd then, too.

Delivered on April 26, 2017, at the National Rifle Association Leadership Forum, Georgia World Congress Center, Atlanta, GA.

So we knew something was happening. But it was in the middle of a historic political year, and in the middle of a truly historic election. What fun that was—November 8. Wasn't that a great evening? Do you remember that evening? (Applause.)

Remember that? (Applause.)

Remember they were saying, "We have breaking news: Donald Trump has won the state of Michigan." They go, "Michigan? How did that"—"Donald Trump has won the state of Wisconsin, whoa." But earlier in the evening, remember, Florida, North Carolina, South Carolina, Pennsylvania, all the way up—we ran up the East Coast. And, you know, the Republicans have a tremendous disadvantage in the Electoral College, you know that. Tremendous disadvantage. And to run the whole East Coast, and then you go with Iowa and Ohio, and all of the different states. It was a great evening, one that a lot people will never forget—a lot of people. (Applause.) Not going to forget that evening.

And remember they said, "There is no path to 270." For months I was hearing that. You know, they're trying to suppress the vote. So they keep saying it, so people say, you know, I really like Trump, he loves the Second Amendment, he loves the NRA; I love him, but let's go to the movie because he can't win. Because they're trying to suppress the vote.

But they'd say—I mean, hundreds of times I heard, there is no—there's no route. They'd say it, "There is no route to 270." And we ended up with 306. So they were right: Not 270, 306. (Applause.) That was some evening. Big sports fans said that was the single-most exciting event they've ever seen. That includes Super Bowls and World Series and boxing matches. That was an exciting evening for all of us, and it meant a lot.

Only one candidate in the General Election came to speak to you, and that candidate is now the President of the United States, standing before you again. (Applause.) I have a feeling that in the next election you're going to be swamped with candidates, but you're not going to be wasting your time. You'll have plenty of those Democrats coming over and you're going to say, no, sir, no thank you—no, ma'am. Perhaps ma'am. It may be Pocahontas, remember that. (Laughter and applause.) And she is not big for the NRA, that I can tell you.

But you came through for me, and I am going to come through for you.

(Applause.) I was proud to receive the NRA's earliest endorsement in the history of the organization. And today, I am also proud to be the first sitting President to address the NRA Leadership Forum since our wonderful Ronald Reagan in 1983. (Applause.) And I want to thank each and every one of you not only for your help electing true friends of the Second Amendment, but for everything you do to defend our flag and our freedom.

With your activism, you helped to safeguard the freedoms of our soldiers who have bled and died for us on the battlefields. And I know we have many veterans in the audience today, and we want to give them a big, big beautiful round of applause. (Applause.)

And, like I promised, we are doing a really top job already—99 days—but already with the Veterans Administration, people are seeing a big difference. We are working really hard at the VA, and you're going to see it, and you're already seeing it. And it's my honor. I've been telling you we're going to do it, and we're doing it. (Applause.) Thank you.

The NRA protects in our capitols and legislative houses the freedoms that our servicemembers have won for us on those incredible battlefields. And it's been a tough fight against those who would go so far as to ban private gun ownership entirely. But I am here to deliver you good news. And I can tell you that Wayne and Chris have been fighting with me long and hard to make sure that we were with you today, not somebody else with an empty podium. Because believe me, the podium would have been empty. They fought long and hard, and I think you folks cannot thank them enough. They were with us all the way, right from the beginning. (Applause.)

But we have news that you've been waiting for for a long time: The eight-year assault on your Second Amendment freedoms has come to a crashing end. (Applause.) You have a true friend and champion in the White House. No longer will federal agencies be coming after law-abiding gun owners. (Applause.) No longer will the government be trying to undermine your rights and your freedoms as Americans. Instead, we will work with you, by your side. We will work with the NRA to promote responsible gun ownership, to protect our wonderful hunters and their access to the very beautiful outdoors. You met my son—I can tell you, both sons, they love the outdoors. Frankly, I think they love the outdoors more than they love, by a long shot, Fifth Avenue. But that's okay. And we want to ensure you of the sacred right of self-defense for all of our citizens. (Applause.)

When I spoke to this forum last year, our nation was still mourning the loss of a giant, a great defender of the Constitution: Justice Antonin Scalia. (Applause.) I promised that if elected, I would nominate a justice who would be faithful and loyal to the Constitution. I even went one step further and publicly presented a list of 20 judges from which I would make my selection, and that's exactly what we did.

And, by the way, I want to thank, really, Heritage. And I want to thank also all of the people that worked with us. Where's Leo? Is Leo around here? Where is he? He's got to be here. Where is he? He has been so good. And also from Heritage, Jim DeMint. It's been amazing. I mean, those people have been fantastic. They've been real friends. (Applause.) The Federalist people—where are they? Are they around here someplace? They really helped us out.

I kept my promise, and now, with your help, our brand-new Justice—and he is really something very special—Neil Gorsuch, sits on the bench of the United States Supreme Court. (Applause.) For the first time in the modern political era, we have confirmed a new justice in the first 100 days. (Applause.) The last time that happened was 136 years ago, in 1881. Now, we won't get any credit for this, but don't worry about it, the credit is in the audience, right? The credit is in the audience. (Applause.) All of those people. They won't give us credit, but it's been a long time, and we're very honored.

We've also taken action to stand up for America's sportsmen. On their very last full day in office, the previous administration issued an 11th-hour rule to restrict the use of lead ammunition on certain federal lands. Have you heard about that, folks? I'm shocked to hear that. You've all heard about that. You've heard about that. On his first day as Secretary of the Interior, Ryan Zinke eliminated the previous administration's ammunition ban. (Applause.) He's going to be great. Ryan is going to be great.

We've also moved very quickly to restore something gun owners care about very, very much. It's called the rule of law. (Applause.) We have made clear that our administration will always stand with the incredible men and women of law enforcement. (Applause.) In fact, countless members of law enforcement are also members of the NRA, because our police know that responsible gun ownership saves lives, and that the right of self-defense is essential to public safety. Do we all agree with that? (Applause.)

Our police and sheriffs also know that when you ban guns, only the criminals will be armed. (Applause.) For too long, Washington has gone after law-abiding gun owners while making life easier for criminals, drug dealers, traffickers and gang members. MS-13—you know about MS-13? It's not pleasant for them anymore, folks. It's not pleasant for them anymore. That's a bad group. (Applause.) Not pleasant for MS-13. Get them the hell out of here, right? Get them out.

(Applause.)

We are protecting the freedoms of law-abiding Americans, and we are going after the criminal gangs and cartels that prey on our innocent citizens. And we are really going after them. (Applause.)

As members of the NRA know well, some of the most important decisions a President can make are appointments—and I've appointed people who believe in law, order, and justice. (Applause.)

That is why I have selected as your Attorney General, number one, a really fine person, a really good man, a man who has spent his career fighting crime, supporting the police, and defending the Second Amendment. For the first time in a long time, you now have a pro-Second-Amendment, tough-on-crime Attorney General, and his name is Jeff Sessions. (Applause.)

And Attorney General Sessions is putting our priorities into action. He's going after the drug dealers who are peddling their poison all over our streets and destroying our youth. He's going after the gang members who threaten our children. And he's fully enforcing our immigration laws in all 50 states. And you know what? It's about time. (Applause.)

Heading up the effort to secure America's borders is a great military general, a man of action: Homeland Security Director [sic], John Kelly. (Applause.)

Secretary Kelly, who used to be General Kelly, is following through on my pledge to protect the borders, remove criminal aliens, and stop the drugs from pouring into our country. We've already seen—listen to this; it never happened before, people can't even believe it. And, by the way, we will build the wall no matter how low this number gets or how this goes. Don't even think about it. Don't even think about it. (Applause.)

You know, they're trying to use this number against us because we've done so unbelievably at the borders already. They're trying to use it against us. But you need that wall to stop the human trafficking, to stop the drugs, to stop the wrong people. You need the wall. But listen to this: We've already seen a 73 percent decrease—never happened before—in illegal immigration on the southern border since my election—73 percent. (Applause.)

You see what they're doing, right? So why do you need a wall? We need a wall.

AUDIENCE MEMBER: Build the wall!

THE PRESIDENT: We'll build the wall. Don't even think about it. Don't even think about it. Don't even think about it. That's an easy one. We're going to build the wall. We need the wall.

I said to General Kelly, how important is it? He said, very important. It's that final element. We need the wall. And it's a wall in certain areas. Obviously, where you have these massive physical structures you don't need, and we have certain big rivers and all. But we need a wall, and we're going to get that wall. (Applause.)

And the world is getting the message. They know that our border is no longer open to illegal immigration, and that if you try to break in, you'll be caught and you'll be returned to your home. You're not staying any longer. And if you keep coming back illegally after deportation, you will be arrested, prosecuted, and you will put behind bars. Otherwise it will never end. (Applause.)

Let's also remember that immigration security is national security. We've seen the attacks from 9/11 to Boston to San Bernardino. Hundreds of individuals from other countries have been charged with terrorism-related offenses in the United States.

We spend billions and billions of dollars on security all over the world, but then we allow radical Islamic terrorists to enter right through our front door. That's not going to happen anymore. (Applause.) It's time to get tough. It's time we finally got smart. And yes, it's also time to put America first. (Applause.)

And perhaps—I see all of those beautiful red and white hats—but we will never forget our favorite slogan of them all: Make America Great Again. All right? (Applause.)

Keeping our communities safe and protecting our freedoms also requires the cooperation of our state leaders. We have some incredible pro-Second Amendment governors here at the NRA conference, including Governor Scott of Florida. Where is Governor Scott? Great guy doing a great job. Governor Bryant of Mississippi. What a wonderful place. Governor Bryant is here. Thank you. Governor Deal of Georgia. (Applause.) And we're also joined by two people that—well, one I loved right from the beginning; the other one I really liked, didn't like, and now like a lot again. (Laughter.) Does that make sense? Senator David Perdue—he was from the beginning—and Senator Ted Cruz—like, dislike, like. (Applause.) Where are they? Good guys. Good guys. Smart cookies.

Each of these leaders knows that public officials must serve under the Constitution, not above it. We all took an oath to preserve, protect, and defend the Constitution of the United States—and that means defending the Second Amendment. (Applause.)

So let me make a simple promise to every one of the freedom-loving Americans in the audience today: As your President, I will never, ever infringe on the right of the people to keep and bear arms. Never ever. (Applause.) Freedom is not a gift from government. Freedom is a gift from God. (Applause.)

It was this conviction that stirred the heart of a great American patriot on that day, April, 242 years ago. It was the day that Paul Revere spread his Lexington alarm—the famous warning that "the British are coming, the British are coming." Right? You've all heard that, right? The British are coming.

Now we have other people trying to come, but believe me, they're not going to be successful. That I can tell you. (Applause.) Nothing changes, right, folks? Nothing changes. They are not going to be successful. There will be serious hurt on them, not on us.

Next, came the shot heard around the world, and then a rag-tag army of God-fearing farmers, frontiersmen, shopkeepers, merchants that stood up to the most powerful army at that time on Earth. The most powerful army on Earth. But we sometimes forget what inspired those everyday farmers and workers in that great war for independence.

Many years after the war, a young man asked Captain Levi Preston, aged 91, why he'd fought alongside his neighbors at Concord. Was it the Stamp Act? Was it the Tea Tax? Was it a work of philosophy? "No," the old veteran replied. "Then why?" he was asked. "Young man," the Captain said, "what we meant in going for those Redcoats was this: We always had governed ourselves, and we always meant to" govern ourselves. (Applause.)

Captain Preston's words are a reminder of what this organization and my administration are all about: the right of a sovereign people to govern their own affairs, and govern them properly. (Applause.) We don't want any longer to be ruled by the bureaucrats in Washington, or in any other country for that matter. In America, we are ruled by our citizens. We are ruled by each and every one of you.

But we can't be complacent. These are dangerous times. These are horrible times for certain obvious reasons. But we're going to make them great times again. Every day, we are up against those who would take away our freedoms, restrict our liberties, and even those who want to abolish the Second Amendment. We must be vigilant. And I know you are all up to the task.

Since the first generation of Americans stood strong at Concord, each generation to follow has answered the call to defend freedom in their time. That is why we are here today: To defend freedom for our children. To defend the liberty of all Americans. And to defend the right of a free and sovereign people to keep and bear arms.

I greatly appreciated your support on November 8th, in what will hopefully be one of the most important and positive elections for the United States of all time. And to the NRA, I can proudly say I will never, ever let you down.

Thank you. God Bless you. God Bless our Constitution, and god bless America. Thank you very much. Thank you. Thank you. (Applause.)

Print Citations

CMS: Trump, Donald. "Remarks by President Trump at the National Rifle Association Leadership Forum: Law & Justice." Keynote Address at the National Rifle Association Leadership Forum, Georgia World Congress Center, Atlanta, GA, April 26, 2017. In *The Reference Shelf: Representative American Speeches, 2018–2019,* edited by Sophie Zyla, 53-59. Amenia, NY: Grey House Publishing, 2019.

MLA: Trump, Donald. "Remarks by President Trump at the National Rifle Association Leadership Forum: Law & Justice." National Rifle Association Leadership Forum, 26 April 2017, Georgia World Congress Center, Atlanta, GA. Keynote Address. *The Reference Shelf: Representative American Speeches, 2018–2019,* edited by Sophie Zyla, Grey House Publishing, 2019, pp. 53-59.

APA: Trump, D. (2017, April 26). Remarks by President Trump at the National Rifle Association leadership forum: Law & justice. National Rifle Association Leadership Forum, Georgia World Congress Center, Atlanta, GA. In Sophie Zyla (Ed.), *The reference shelf: Representative American speeches, 2018–2019* (pp. 53-59). Amenia, NY: Grey House Publishing.

You Can Hear the People in Power Shaking

By David Hogg

David Hogg went from student at Marjory Stoneman Douglas High School to American gun control activist after he survived the February 14, 2018 shooting that killed 17 and left many injured. Hogg is a founding member of the student-led group Never Again MSD and March For Our Lives movement. Hog is studying political science at Harvard University.

First off, I'm gonna start off by putting this price tag right here as a reminder for you guys to know how much Marco Rubio took for every student's life in Florida. One dollar and five cents.

The cold grasp of corruption shackles the District of Columbia. The winter is over. Change is here. The sun shines on a new day, and the day is ours. First-time voters show up 18 percent of the time at midterm elections. Not anymore. Now, who here is gonna vote in the 2018 election? If you listen real close, you can hear the people in power shaking. They've gotten used to being protective of their position, the safety of inaction. Inaction is no longer safe. And to that, we say: No more.

Ninety-six people die every day from guns in our country, yet most representatives have no public stance on guns. And to that, we say: No more. We are going to make this the voting issue. We are going to take this to every election, to every state, in every city. We are going to make sure the best people get in our elections to run, not as politicians, but as Americans. Because this—this is not cutting it. When people try to suppress your vote, and there are people who stand against you because you're too young, we say: No more.

When politicians say that your voice doesn't matter because the NRA owns them, we say: No more. When politicians send their thoughts and prayers with no action, we say: No more. And to those politicians supported by the NRA, that allow the continued slaughter of our children and our future, I say: Get your résumés ready.

Today is the beginning of spring, and tomorrow is the beginning of democracy. Now is the time to come together, not as Democrats, not as Republicans, but as Americans. Americans of the same flesh and blood, that care about one thing and one thing only, and that's the future of this country and the children that are going to lead it.

Now, they will try to separate us in demographics. They will try to separate us by religion, race, congressional district and class. They will fail. We will come together.

Delivered on March 24, 2018, at the March for Our Lives, Washington, DC.

We will get rid of these public servants that only serve the gun lobby, and we will save lives. You are those heroes.

Lastly, let's put the USA over the NRA. This is the start of the spring and the blossoming of our democracy. So let's take this to our local legislators, and let's take this to midterm elections, because without the persistence—heat—without the persistence of voters and Americans everywhere, getting out to every election, democracy will not flourish. But it can, and it will. So, I say to those politicians that say change will not come, I say: We will not stop until every man, every woman, every child, and every American can live without fear of gun violence. And to that, I say: No more.

Thank you, I love you all, God bless all of you, and God bless America. We can, and we will, change the world.

Print Citations

CMS: Hogg, David. "You Can Hear the People in Power Shaking." Keynote Address at March for Our Lives, Washington, DC, March 24, 2018. In *The Reference Shelf: Representative American Speeches, 2018–2019,* edited by Sophie Zyla, 60-61. Amenia, NY: Grey House Publishing, 2019.

MLA: Hogg, David. "You Can Hear the People in Power Shaking." March for Our Lives, 24 March 2018, Washington, DC. Keynote Address. *The Reference Shelf: Representative American Speeches, 2018–2019,* edited by Sophie Zyla, Grey House Publishing, 2019, pp. 60-61.

APA: Hogg, D. (2018, March 24). Keynote Address on you can hear the people in power shaking. March of Our Lives, Washington, DC. In Sophie Zyla (Ed.), *The reference shelf: Representative American speeches, 2018–2019* (pp. 60-61). Amenia, NY: Grey House Publishing.

A Call for Action on Gun Control Legislation (Excerpt)

By Cory Booker

Cory Booker has been the junior United States Senator from New Jersey since 2013. A member of the Democratic Party, Booker is the first African-American U.S. Senator from New Jersey. He previously served as the 36th Mayor of Newark, from 2006 to 2013. Booker announced his 2020 presidential campaign on February 1, 2019, with a video entitled "We Will Rise," which was posted on his YouTube channel. He intentionally chose the first day of Black History Month to announce his candidacy.

You have not only been on your feet, not only have not left the floor to use the facilities, but you have stood in the saddle and have been for this entire time, as your colleagues have flowed through this chamber, you have been answering question after question after question after question on a topic that you are passionate about, on a topic that you feel deeply and personally. And I just want to thank you for your leadership because it's captured the attention of our nation. This filibuster right here—I know a little bit about social media. This filibuster right here has been the focus, trending on Twitter, the focus of Facebook. It has created a media attention on a problem because in a sense you're giving hope. Your very intention of coming here has met the need, the urgent need that the public has seen that this body here, this auspicious body, this greatest deliberative body on the planet earth, that this Senate, designed by the Constitution to deal with the biggest problems of our land, that this body would not just go on as business as usual. What you chose to do is to say enough. Stop.

We are going to have a discussion about an issue that is not just on the minds of the American public, but it is grievously affecting the hearts and the spirit of our nation. Tens of thousands of people since Sunday have been standing around our country in vigils, in solidarity, expressing their pain and expressing their sorrow but expressing the feelings that they have that we should be better than to allow such grievous, terroristic hateful acts to happen on our soil. And so while the American public has been stepping up, this body that had a different plan, to move on a piece of legislation, to barely acknowledge this. And so before I want to really refrain this, Senator, I just want to say thank you to you for the courage that you have put forth to say enough is enough. No business as usual. That we are going to stop. And that we are going to push for two commonsense, sensible—commonsense amendments

---

Delivered on June 15, 2016, at the U.S. Senate, Washington, DC.

that cannot end gun violence in America, cannot stop terrorist activity here and abroad but that can take a step, a constructive step towards beginning to choke the flow of commonality of these incidents on American soil, and has been said time and time again, as has been said by a number of senators today, what reason was our government organized in the first place? You heard Angus King wearing the Constitution on his tie, talk to that preamble. Common defense, domestic tranquility. And so I want to frame this again, but the first frame I just have to say you and I talked about it after caucus lunch yesterday. You and I talked about it during the day. We talked about it last night. And you are not talking about it today.

You are doing it. No business as usual, and for that I'm grateful. And it is merited that we also thank the many people who are involved. When the Senate is open past midnight, hundreds of people have to be here as well, not just the people you see here on the floor. The pages who are in their first days, and that is their—one of their seminal experiences. Not the folks who are working behind the dais there, not the great Republican colleagues who have had to man that chair, but security guards and subway operators and the people who are seating folks in the gallery. And so I just want to say tonight thank you. I want to point out the fact that Chris has helped to pay for food for not only a lot of the folks here but including the Republican cloakroom. I appreciate you, Senator Murphy. But now I want to get to the framing of what this is about because there has been a lot talked about tonight, most of which I agree with. A lot discussed, a lot far afield, but you came here with a purpose around two issues that are of common sense.

One is that in the United States of America, if our investigatory authorities see people as threats, are investigating people because they are believed to be desirous of doing acts of terrorism on American soil, people who have already been banned from—in some cases from flying on airplanes, that we should take a step, we should make it the law of this land that that person who was a suspected terrorist, that person who can't get on an airplane, hey, that person also should not be able to buy an assault rifle. That is so common sense that as you said earlier today perhaps four or five hours ago, many people in America are shocked when they realize that that loophole, that terrorist loophole actually exists. What you're fighting for, Senator Murphy, is not radical. It's not out of the box. It's common sense. And what's even more important is in this day and age when partisanship does, does cripple this body from time to time on big issues, that this issue is actually not partisan. Study after study have shown, survey after survey, poll after poll says overwhelmingly Americans agree with this. In fact, overwhelmingly American gun owners, over 80% say we need to close the terrorist loophole. In fact, N.R.A. members, over 70%, say we should close a terrorist loophole.

What nation when they are at war where your enemy is actually trying to incite terrorism in your country, when your enemy is explicitly saying exploit this loophole, what country would keep that loophole wide open where it is easy for someone with terroristic aims to hurt, injure, destroy and kill? But you took it one step further, and I was happy this morning to work on an amendment with you that says you capital just close a terrorist loophole and leave open, as you called it hours ago, a back door for those terrorists to use. That means if you do background checks, they need to be universal, because if it's just the brick-and-mortar gun retailers, yeah, you go there, you're going to have to do a background check. By the way, those background checks stop people every single year, not just people that may be suspected of terrorism. Frankly they stop criminals. But we now know that we as a nation have changed where the buyers of weapons have migrated from the brick-and-mortar stores now to another market, often online or at gun shows, and unless we close those avenues for terrorists to use, they are going to use them so very much common sense again, the second thing that you are saying today is hey we need to close a terrorist loophole and we need to make sure we're doing universal background checks.

Now, those—that's the reason we're here. The grit of a Senator and the common sense of two amendments that are very critical. But I want to for a moment tell you what was perhaps the most touching time for me in this 13, 14 hours. And I went and actually checked the rules and you can't acknowledge people that are in the gallery, but I have to say tonight—they are not here now, so I'm not acknowledging anybody that's here, but your wife and child showed up. And when I heard you talk as a parent about the love of your child and how you did something that's so important for us as Americans. In fact, I think it's at the core of who we are, that this is what our country calls us to do, which is to take courageous steps of empathy and say when other people's children are dying, that that's not their problem, that it triggers empathy in me. I think about my own child, I think about my niece, I think about my nephew, I think about my family.

You see, there is a privilege in this country that is a dangerous type of privilege. It is the type of privilege that says if something is not happening to me personally, if a problem is not happening to me personally, then it's not a problem. It's not a problem if it's not happening to me personally. When that's contrary to what we say about ourselves as a country. The spirit of this country has been that we're all in this together, that we all do better when we all do better. That if there is injustice in our midst, affecting another family, another state, another neighborhood, then that's an injustice that is threatening the whole. Senator Murphy, this is one of your core values. It is expressed by great Americans. It was expressed by Martin Luther King in perhaps one of the greatest pieces of American literature, the *Letter from the Birmingham Jail*. This idea that if something is going on wrong in Connecticut, the tragedy happens there, children are murdered there, that that's not Connecticut's problem. That's all of our problems.

King said injustice anywhere is a threat to justice everywhere, that we are all caught in an inescapable network of mutuality tied in a common garment of destiny. And so that's to me a core element of our nation. It's what our founders understood when they said that we're in this together, the very Declaration of Independence ends with a nod toward that interdependence, toward that interwoven nature. It was set by our founders on the Declaration of Independence right at the end, that in order for this nation to work, we must be there for each other, we must care about each other, we must invest ourselves in each other. That if an injustice happens to our brother or my sister, it's affecting me. That Declaration of Independence ends with those words. We mutually pledge to each other our lives, our fortunes and our sacred honor. And so now we see these tragedies, and I don't want to believe that we're becoming numb to them, that we see them as some distant reality and not as a personal attack because when you attack one American, you attack us all.

And when you have an avenue where you can make a difference to preserve and protect life and you do not claim it, to me that is a sin. There is a great writer, a great thinker, great nobel laureate who once said to the effect, he said the opposite of—of—of love is not hate, it's indifference, the opposite of love is not just hate, it's action. Lack of caring, lack of compassion. And so what gets me upset about this issue is that we have commonsense tools that have been enumerated by wise colleagues of mine who have legal scholars in our caucus who understand clearly there is no absolute right when it comes to freedom of speech. That even as has been quoted many times, the majority opinion in the *Heller* case, there is no absolute right to bear arms. It has been said by multiple Senators, just closing the terrorist loophole doesn't infringe the rights of any American to bear arms, of any American sportsman, any American seeking self-defense. That this is just saying that, hey, if you're someone who is believed to be a terrorist, you should not be able to purchase a gun. You're someone on that no-fly list, you should not be able to purchase a gun. and by the way, even that, as you pointed out, there should be due process so that if you have to grieve that, there is a process for which you to grieve you being on that no-fly list.

And so for me, when I see your child come here to listen to her father, when I see parents, many of my colleagues have children, I hope that all of us, all of us when we hear about a mass shooting don't just say I'm praying for those families, begin to think that that happening to my fellow American is a threat to me, it's happening to us all, we all are lesser as a result of it, but we have to think to ourselves how would it feel if I fail to act to do what was right, to close a terrorist loophole. What if that person right now that our enemy is working to radicalize, what if that person in our country right now that our enemy is working to inspire, what about that person right now who is seeking to do harm to Americans, what happens if they exploit that loophole tomorrow, next month, next year. What happens if they exploit that loophole and this time they go to a playground, a train station, a movie theater, a church, and it happens to be your playground, your movie theater, your school, your church, your child. If you know there is something we can do to stop our enemy from getting arms and doing us harm and we have seen now from San Bernadino to Orlando, Florida, that terrorists are looking to do us harm, and we can stop our enemy with a commonsense amendment that is believed and supported by the majority of Americans, the majority of Republicans, the majority of gun owners, the majority of N.R.A. members, and yesterday this body can't do that, we are setting ourselves up for future acts of violence and terror that could have been prevented.

What if it's our child or our family or our community or our neighborhood? And there is one more step I have to mention, Senator Murphy. There is one more step that it's important to this, because if you close the terrorist loophole and make sure that those terrorists cannot exploit the back door, if you make sure those background checks are universal, again agreed to by the majority of Americans, the majority of Republicans, the majority of gun owners, the majority of N.R.A. members, you're also going to benefit by creating a background check system that stops criminals from getting guns that better undermine their ability to get their hands on weapons that they want to do to carry out violence in our neighborhoods, communities, in our cities, and that's where it gets deeply personal to me. Because like you have for your child, every American has for their kids, we have big dreams. This is a nation of dreams. We have something called the American Dream, which I say is known across the globe. It is a bold dream, it is a humble dream that this is a nation where our children can grow up, have the best of opportunity. Our children can do better than us. It is the American Dream.

But the challenge I see with American reality where we have such liberal access to weapons by people who are criminals, what that has resulted in, I have seen it myself, is so many children taken, killed, murdered time and time again, every day, every hour, time and time again, another dream destroyed, another dream devastated, another dream murdered. And that is something that's not just words to me. I have seen it across my state, in our cities, on street corners where we have set up shrines with candles and teddy bears marking the place after place, street after street where children have been murdered. I have stood on too many street corners looking down at bodies, 13-year-olds, 14-year-olds, 15-year-olds, 16-yards murdered—16-year-olds murdered in our nation with a regularity that was not seen in wars past. I've been to funerals with parents begging us to do something about the violence in our country. I've seen children that are living but yet live with trauma and stress because they hear gunshots too much in their neighborhoods. We have the power to stop this and we can't assume that these problems are not ours. Langston Hughes said it so poetically, there is a dream in this land with its back against the wall, to save the dream for one, we must save the dream for all. How many of our children's dreams must be destroyed by gun violence before we do the commonsense things that we agree on to begin to shrink those numbers? It's written in Genesis when Joseph's brothers see him approaching with murder in their eyes and said here cometh the dreamer. Let us slay him and see what becomes of his dreams. We have lost so many. So many have been slain.

But the dream of America can die. There are people who want to take it from us. They want to inject it with fear and hate. The dream of our country can die. There are rules and loopholes that allow mad men and terrorists and criminals to get their hands on assault weapons. We cannot let the dream of our country die and be dashed and be killed. We can do something about it, and it is unacceptable, when you have the power, to do nothing. And so we elected to this body, caretakers of that dream, the torch of the light of the hope of the promise of this country that still attracts so many, where hundreds of millions in our nation believe, where so many outside of our nation believe, we must make sure that we form a more perfect union, where we see unfinished business of work to be done, where we answer the call of our citizenry.

So I return to where I began. Senator Murphy, there are literally thousands of Americans taking to the streets this past week. I saw them in New Jersey, read about them in California and Florida. I see them in Washington, D.C. Here in our nation's capital. Today I'm proud that you decided that that dream was worth fighting for, that the call of our nation had to be answered, that that dream demanded something more than business as usual. Thirteen-plus hours you've stood. I don't know how long it will take, but I know this is an issue closing the terrorist loophole, closing the avenues for terrorists to go online or gun shows, just doing would is such common sense to keep us safe. I know we will win this battle. It's not a matter of if. It's a matter of when. And so as the hour grows later and later and this filibuster drags on, I just want to ask this perhaps important question. You and I both know from the incoming, you've had thousands of calls in your office, that one of the problems we have to have as we allow our inability to do everything that undermine our determination to do something, that when you have a majority of people that believe in something, that often the only thing that stops us from changing it is not that we can't. It's not a matter of can we. It's do we have the collective will. I know from scanning social media that there are thousands of people watching right now. As you speak to our colleagues and speak through the chair, perhaps my question is, can you speak to those people who tonight, many of them who were cynical about this body, found a little bit of hope in your action. Can you maybe take a moment to speak to them about how we can keep fighting this fight, what they can do to press forward, how we can make this dream of our nation stronger, mightier, more just, so that a week from now or a month from now we're not gathered together in mourning in our nation about dreams dashed by violent terrorists.

Print Citations

CMS: Booker, Cory. "A Call for Action on Gun Control Legislation." Speech at the U.S. Senate, Washington, DC, June 15, 2016. In *The Reference Shelf: Representative American Speeches, 2018–2019,* edited by Sophie Zyla, 62-67. Amenia, NY: Grey House Publishing, 2019.

MLA: Booker, Cory. "A Call for Action on Gun Control Legislation." U.S. Senate, Washington, DC, 15 June 2016, Washington, DC. Speech. *The Reference Shelf: Representative American Speeches, 2018–2019,* edited by Sophie Zyla, Grey House Publishing, 2019, pp. 62-67.

APA: Booker, C. (2016, June 15). Speech on a call for action on gun control legislation. U.S. Senate, Washington, DC. In Sophie Zyla (Ed.), *The reference shelf: Representative American speeches, 2018–2019* (pp. 62-67). Amenia, NY: Grey House Publishing.

Trump Impeachment Statement

By Nancy Pelosi

Nancy Pelosi became the first female Democratic leader of the House of Representatives in 1987 and the first female Speaker of the House in 2006, where she remained until 2010 and was reelected in 2019. She served on the Appropriations Committee and Permanent Select Committee on Intelligence. Pelosi graduated from Trinity College in Washington, D.C. Sparked by illegal attempts to conceal the whistle-blower complaint, Pelosi announced that the House of Representatives will move forward with an official impeachment inquiry against President Trump for his request for assistance from a foreign leader from Ukraine.

Good afternoon. Last Tuesday, we observed the anniversary of the adoption of the constitution on September 17th. Sadly on that day, the intelligence community Inspector General formally notified the Congress that the administration was forbidding him from turning over a whistle-blower complaint on constitution day. This is a violation of the law. Shortly thereafter, press reports began to break of a phone call by the president of the United States calling upon a foreign power to intervene in his election. This is a breach of his constitutional responsibilities.

The facts are these, the intelligence community Inspector General, who was appointed by President Trump determined that the complaint is both of urgent concern and credible. And it's disclosure, he went on to say, relates to one of the most significant, important of the Director of National Intelligence's responsibility to the American people. On Thursday, the Inspector General testified before the House Intelligence Committee stating that the acting Director of National Intelligence blocked him from disclosing the whistle-blower complaint. This is a violation of law.

The law is unequivocal. It says the DNI, D-N-I Director of National Intelligence, shall provide Congress the full whistle-blower complaint. For more than 25 years, I've served on the Intelligence Committee as a member, as the ranking member, as part of the Gang of Four even before I was in the leadership.

I was there when we created the Office of the Director of National Intelligence. That did not exist before 2004. I was there even earlier in the '90s when we wrote the whistle-blower laws and continued to write them to improve them, to ensure the security of our intelligence and the safety of our whistle-blowers. I know what their purpose was and we proceeded with balance and caution as we wrote the laws. I can say with authority, the Trump administration's actions undermine both our

---

Delivered on September 24, 2019, at the U.S. House of Representatives, Washington, DC.

national security and our intelligence and our protections of the whistle-blowers. More than both.

This Thursday, the acting DNI will appear before the house intelligence committee. At that time, he must turn over the whistle-blower's full complaint to the committee. He will have to choose whether to break the law or honor his responsibility to the constitution.

On the final day of the Constitutional Convention in 1787 when our constitution was adopted, Americans gathered on the steps of Independence Hall to await the news of the government our founders had crafted. They asked Benjamin Franklin, "What do we have a republic or monarchy?" Franklin replied, "A republic if you can keep it." Our responsibility is to keep it.

Our republic endures because of the wisdom of our constitution enshrined in three co-equal branches of government serving as checks and balances on each other. The actions taken to date by the President have seriously violated the constitution, especially when the President says, "Article two says I can do whatever I want."

For the past several months, we have been investigating in our committees and litigating in the courts so the House can gather all the relevant facts and consider whether to exercise its full article one powers, including a constitutional power of the utmost gravity approval of articles of impeachment. And this week, the President has admitted to asking the president of Ukraine to take actions which would benefit him politically. The actions of the Trump presidency revealed dishonorable fact of the President's betrayal of his oath of office, betrayal of our national security, and betrayal of the integrity of our elections.

Therefore today, I'm announcing the House of Representatives moving forward with an official impeachment inquiry. I'm directing our six committees to proceed with their investigations under that umbrella of impeachment inquiry. The President must be held accountable. No one is above the law.

Getting back to our founders, in the darkest stays at the American revolution, Thomas Payne wrote, "The times have found us." The times found them to fight for and establish our democracy. The times have found us today, not to place ourselves in the same category of greatness as our founders but to places in the urgency of protecting and defending our constitution from all enemies, foreign and domestic. In the words of Ben Franklin, to keep our republic.

I thank our chairmen, Chairman Nadler, Chairman Schiff. Chairman Nadler of Judiciary, Chairman Schiff of Intelligence, Chairman Engel of Foreign Affairs, Chairman Cummings of Oversight. And Chairman Cummings I've been in touch with constantly. He's the master of so much but including inspectors general and whistle-blowers. Congresswoman Richie Neal of the Ways and Means committee, Congresswoman Maxine Waters of the Foreign Financial Services committee. And I commend all of our our members, our colleagues for their thoughtful, thoughtful approach to all of this, for their careful statements. God bless them, and God bless America. Thank you all.

Print Citations

CMS: Pelosi, Nancy. "Trump Impeachment Statement." Speech at the U.S. House of Representatives, Washington, DC, September 24, 2019. In *The Reference Shelf: Representative American Speeches, 2018–2019,* edited by Sophie Zyla, 68-70. Amenia, NY: Grey House Publishing, 2019.

MLA: Pelosi, Nancy. "Trump Impeachment Statement." U.S. House of Representatives, 24 September 2019, Washington, DC. Speech. *The Reference Shelf: Representative American Speeches, 2018–2019,* edited by Sophie Zyla, Grey House Publishing, 2019, pp. 68-70.

APA: Pelosi, N. (2019, September 24). Speech on Trump impeachment statement. U.S. House of Representatives, Washington, DC. In Sophie Zyla (Ed.), *The reference shelf: Representative American speeches, 2018–2019* (pp. 68-70). Amenia, NY: Grey House Publishing.

Now Is the Time to Act

By John Lewis

John Lewis has served as a representative of Georgia's Fifth Congressional District since 1986. He is a senior chief deputy whip for the Democratic Party, a member of the House Ways & Means Committee, on the Subcommittee on Income Security and Family Support, and on the Subcommittee on Oversight. Lewis is dedicated to protecting human rights and in 1963 became known as "one of the Big Six leaders" of the Civil Rights Movement. He is the recipient of numerous national and international awards, including over 50 honorary degrees from colleges and universities. Lewis is a graduate of the American Baptist Theological Seminary and has a bachelor's degree in religion and philosophy from Fisk University. He shares his concerns for our democracy, our future, our ethics, and our Constitution.

Mr. Speaker, I rise to ask unanimous consent to address the House for 5 minutes.

Today I come with a heavy heart, deeply concerned about the future of our democracy. And I'm not alone. People approach me everywhere I go, whether I am traveling back and forth to Atlanta or around our country. They believe, they truly believe that our nation is descending into darkness.

They never dreamed that the United States, once seen as a beacon of hope and as an inspiration to people striving for equality and justice would be falling into such disgrace.

I share their concern for the future of our country. It keeps me up at night. We took an oath to protect this nation against all domestic enemies and foreign enemies. Sometimes I am afraid to go to sleep for fear that I will wake up and our democracy will be gone and never return.

At every turn, this administration demonstrates complete disdain and disregard for ethics, for the law and for the Constitution.

They have lied under oath. They refuse to account for their actions and appear before legislative bodies who have the constitutional right to inquire about their activities.

The people have a right to inquire. They have a right to know. The people have a right to know whether they can put their faith and trust in the outcome of our elections. They have a right to know whether the cornerstone of our democracy was undermined by people sitting in the White House today. They have a right to know whether a foreign power was asked to intervene in the 2020 election. They have a right to know whether the president is using his office to line his pockets.

Delivered on September 24, 2019, at the U.S. House of Representatives, Washington, DC.

Mr. Speaker, the people of this nation realize that if they had committed even have of these possible violations, the federal government would be swift to seek justice.

We cannot delay, we must not wait. Now is the time to act. I have been patient while we tried every other path and used every other tool.

We will never find the truth unless we use the power given to the House of Representatives, and the House alone, to begin an official investigation as dictated by the Constitution.

The future of our democracy is at stake. There comes a time when you have to be moved by the spirit of history to take action to protect and preserve the integrity of our nation.

I believe, I truly believe the time to begin impeachment proceedings against this president has come. To delay or to do otherwise would betray the foundation of our democracy. Thank you, Mr. Speaker.

Print Citations

CMS: Lewis, John. "Now Is the Time to Act." Speech at the U.S. House of Representatives, Washington, DC, September 24, 2019. In *The Reference Shelf: Representative American Speeches, 2018–2019,* edited by Sophie Zyla, 71-72. Amenia, NY: Grey House Publishing, 2019.

MLA: Lewis, John. "Now Is the Time to Act." U.S. House of Representatives, Washington, DC, 24 September 2019, Washington, DC. Speech. *The Reference Shelf: Representative American Speeches, 2018–2019,* edited by Sophie Zyla, Grey House Publishing, 2019, pp. 71-72.

APA: Lewis, J. (2019, September 24). Speech on now is the time to act. U.S. House of Representatives, Washington, DC. In Sophie Zyla (Ed.), *The reference shelf: Representative American speeches, 2018–2019* (pp. 71-72). Amenia, NY: Grey House Publishing.

Remarks by President Trump on America's Environmental Leadership: Energy & Environment

By Donald Trump

President Trump says our efforts to innovate and grow the economy will help the work to protect our environment. The United States leads the world in reducing pollution. Our legislation to reduce forest fires and red tide will make a difference. Speakers invited by the president included Bruce Hrobak, Colleen Roberts, Mary Neumayr, David Bernhardt, and Rick Perry.

THE PRESIDENT: Thank you. Thank you very much. Great to have you, and I hope you all had a truly wonderful Independence Day weekend. In spite of the heavy rain — and it was really heavy—we had a remarkable Salute to America on the National Mall. It was incredible, actually. (Applause.)

Standing on the steps of the great Lincoln Memorial and looking out at the crowds—these incredible, big, beautiful crowds, braving the weather—all the way back to the Washington Monument, we celebrated freedom in all of its magnificence while saluting our great military. It was something really special. And I will say this: It was a wonderful day for all Americans. And based on its tremendous success, we're just making the decision—and I can think we can say we've made the decision—to do it again next year, and, maybe we can say, for the foreseeable future. (Applause.)

As we celebrate our nation's founding, we're reminded once more of our profound obligation to protect America's extraordinary blessings for the next generation and many generations, frankly, to come. Among the heritage we must preserve is our country's incredible natural splendor—that is the shared obligation that brings us together today. We have some incredibly talented people that know environment and what we're doing probably better than any people on Earth.

From day one, my administration has made it a top priority to ensure that America has among the very cleanest air and cleanest water on the planet. We want the cleanest air. We want crystal-clean water, and that's what we're doing and that's what we're working on so hard.

For this afternoon's event, we are pleased to be joined by Secretary Steve Mnuchin. Steve, thank you very much. David Bernhardt—David, thank you. Secretary Wilbur Ross. Thank you, Wilbur. Secretary Alex Azar. Alex, great job. Drug

---

Delivered on July 8, 2019, at the White House, Washington, DC.

prices are coming down. I see it. (Laughter.) I'm proud of you. Secretary Elaine Chao. Elaine, thank you. Administrator Andrew Wheeler. Andrew, thank you. And Chair of the Council of Environmental Quality, Mary Neumayr. Thank you, Mary. Thank you very much.

In a few moments, we'll hear an update on some of their very important work.

Also with us are Senators Kevin Cramer, Steve Daines, John Barrasso. These are three great senators, I might add. Perhaps I'm a little prejudiced because I like them very much, but they're great senators. Thank you. Thank you, fellas. (Applause.) And Congressman Bruce Westerman. And thank you, Bruce, for being here. I appreciate it very much. Thank you all for being here. (Applause.)

As the Cabinet Secretaries will tell you, from the very beginning, I have given them clear direction to focus on addressing environmental challenges so we can provide the highest quality of life to all Americans. In addition to clean air and clean water, that means being good stewards of our public lands; prioritizing cleanup of polluted lands that threaten our most vulnerable citizens, and threaten them very dearly; and implementing pro-growth policies to unlock innovation and new technologies which will improve American life and America's environment. So important.

These are incredible goals that everyone in this country should be able to rally behind and they have rallied behind. And they've rallied behind in a very Republican and Democrat way. I really think that's something that is bipartisan.

For years, politicians told Americans that a strong economy and a vibrant energy sector were incompatible with a healthy environment. In other words, one thing doesn't go with the other. And that's wrong because we're proving the exact opposite.

A strong economy is vital to maintaining a healthy environment. When we innovate, produce, and grow, we're able to unleash technologies and processes that make the environment better while reshoring and, so importantly—you look at reshoring production all the way—taking it away from foreign polluters, and back to American soil.

The previous administration waged a relentless war on American energy. We can't do that. They sought to punish our workers, our producers, and manufacturers with ineffective global agreements that allowed the world's worst-polluting countries to continue their practices. These radical plans would not make the world cleaner; they would just make and put Americans out of work, and they put them out of work rapidly. They move production to foreign countries with lower standards—our companies were forced to do that, and they didn't want to do that—and they drive up the price of gas and electricity at home, and drive it to levels that are literally unaffordable.

And, by the way, that's happening to many other countries, but it's not happening here. Other countries—their pricing on electricity is so high, not even to be affordable. At our level, we are doing numbers that nobody has seen before. Nobody believes what we're doing and what we're producing electricity and other things for.

Punishing Americans is never the right way to produce a better environment or a better economy. We've rejected this failed approach, and we're seeing incredible results.

Since the election, we have created more than 6 million new jobs. Nobody would have believed that. I don't think anybody—(applause)—Kevin? Nobody. Nobody. (Applause.) If I would have said that during the campaign, it wouldn't have been a pretty picture the next day, as I read the headlines. (Laughter.) Six million new jobs.

Unemployment has reached the lowest rate in a half a century, and we have more people working today than have ever worked in the history of our country. We're getting very close to 160 million people, which is unthinkable. If you go back three years and you said "160 million people," they would say, "unthinkable."

We're unlocking American energy, and the United States is now a net exporter of clean, affordable, American natural gas. We're exporting all over the world. (Applause.)

And today, the United States is ranked—listen to this—number one in the world for access to clean drinking water—ranked number one in the world. (Applause.)

One of the main messages of air pollution—particulate matter—is six times lower here than the global average. So we hear so much about some countries and what everyone is doing. We're six times lower than the average. That's a tremendous number.

Since 2000, our nation's energy-related carbon emissions have declined more than any other country on Earth. Think of that. Emissions are projected to drop in 2019 and 2020. We're doing a very tough job and not everybody knows it, and that's one of the reasons we're here today to speak to you.

Every single one of the signatories to the Paris Climate Accords lags behind America in overall emissions reductions. Who would think that is possible?

For this reason, in my first year in office, I withdrew the United States from the unfair, ineffective, and very, very expensive Paris Climate Accord. (Applause.) Thank you. Thank you.

My administration is now revising the past administration's misguided regulations to better protect the environment and to protect our American workers, so importantly.

As an example, there is a very good place for solar energy. I'm a believer in solar energy. It hasn't fully developed. It's got a long way to go, but it's really got a tremendous future.

The United States does not have to sacrifice our own jobs to lead the world on the environment. My administration set the new global standard for environmental protections with unprecedented provisions in the U.S.-Mexico-Canada Agreement, commonly referred to as the "USMCA," which includes the first-ever provisions to take on the challenge of marine litter and debris.

And I'm sure you've all seen, by watching television, by maybe reading about it — it's a tremendous problem: Thousands and thousands of tons of this debris float onto our shores after it's dumped into the oceans by other countries. The tides come to us. Usually, that was a good thing, but this isn't so good. This is a tremendous problem. Thousands and thousands of tons of garbage comes to us.

While we're focused on practical solutions, more than 100 Democrats in Congress now support the so-called Green New Deal. Their plan is estimated to cost our economy nearly $100 trillion—a number unthinkable; a number not affordable even in the best of times. If you go 150 years from now and we've had great success, that's not a number that's even thought to be affordable. It'll kill millions of jobs, it'll crush the dreams of the poorest Americans, and disproportionately harm minority communities.

I will not stand for it. We will defend the environment, but we will also defend American sovereignty, American prosperity, and we will defend American jobs. (Applause.)

We've refocused the EPA back on its core mission, and, last year, the agency completed more Superfund hazardous waste clean-ups than any year of the previous administrations and set records in almost every year. We have done tremendous work on Superfunds.

To name just two examples, we've made great strides cleaning up damage near a paper plant in Kalamazoo, Michigan—something that was beyond fix-up. They thought it was never going to happen. And also, the West Lake Landfill in Missouri.

This year, we've also directed $65 million in Brownfields grants to clean up even more contaminated sites in 149 American communities. Think of that—the vast majority home to lower-income citizens. That is some project. (Applause.) That is some project.

And for the first time in nearly 30 years, we're in the process of strengthening national drinking water standards to protect vulnerable children from lead and copper exposure—something that has not been done, and we're doing it. And last month, our EPA took the first major action in nearly two decades to reduce exposure to lead-contaminated dust.

I signed America's Water Infrastructure Act, along with these great gentlemen right here. We worked very hard on that—very, very hard—and it wasn't easy, to further approve and improve drinking water infrastructure and support other critical projects.

Our administration has directed over half a billion dollars to fix Lake Okeechobee—the Herbert Hoover Dike. I was out there three months ago with your new, great governor—and senator, actually—from Florida. We had our two senators. We had Rick Scott and Marco Rubio, and our great, new governor, Ron DeSantis. We were all out and we made a certain commitment, and the commitment has already taken place, and they're fixing Lake Okeechobee. People are very happy about it in the Florida Everglades. We're restoring the ecosystems in the Everglades.

And I also signed legislation authorizing $100 million to fight red tide—a big problem that some people don't know about but, when you do know about it, that means trouble because it is bad—and other toxic algae that damages coastal areas.

It's causing tremendous havoc, and we have a way of straightening it out, and we'll get it done.

We're joined today by Bruce Hrobak, owner of Billy Bones Bait 'N Tackle in Port St. Lucie—a place I know very well—Florida. His business was devastated by toxic algae from Lake Okeechobee.

Bruce, please come up and tell us about what's happened and what we're doing for you. Where is Bruce? (Applause.) Bruce. Hi, Bruce. Please.

MR. HROBAK: I really appreciate it, sir.

THE PRESIDENT: Thank you very much.

MR. HROBAK: Hello. How are you all today? All right, we have made a big trip up here to make sure we're here. This is very important. This is my family's business, okay? I've owned the Bait 'N Tackle store since 2001 and been in Florida since 2006.

I have my son Tanner over here with me. He means the world to me. He is my best friend and my son. He's actually a brain cancer survivor. You know, he beat it and now he's 21, and—(applause)—thank you. Thank you.

I wanted to say—thank you. I wanted to say that, Mr. President, you're not only doing a tremendous job all the way around, but you jumping into this environment brings my heart to warmth, knowing that what you're doing is going—is the truth. It's going wonderfully.

My business in 2018 was so horrible, we—I own two stores—we closed several days a week because of, you know, the algae and people being frightened, if they were afraid to touch the water and everything. I have a marine mechanic—I just wanted to say really quickly—has a bad infection in his arm from the marine algae and stuff.

But basically, your completion of this Herbert Hoover Dike is going to make a tremendous difference because we can store more water in Lake Okeechobee; safely store it there so the residents that are around there are safe. We care and we're are concerned about them—us, on the coast. Believe me. And that the water does not go into the Caloosahatchee and to the St. Lucie estuary. It's full of contaminants [sic]—contaminants and fertilizers.

And, Mr. President, you mentioned about the red tide. It is a natural occurrence. This fertilizer and all these contaminants is like a super power. And we have seen devastation on the west coast like none other before, in 2018.

So, I mean, I'm just so grateful for all the work you're doing, sir, and everything. And the Everglades restoration. And also, I heard great news that the dike is going to be finished much sooner—'22 than—2022—than expected.

So I personally want to thank you because this year they're not dumping; our businesses are doing better. My wife don't yell at me as much. (Laughter.) Well, that always happens.

So, you know, she says to me, "You're going to be by the President talking." And I says, "Oh, I don't need no list or whatever. I've got a big mouth. I talk. I don't care. I'm proud." (Laughter.) I'm proud of who I am, and what I am.

I'm a licensed charter boat captain, and I've done it since 25—since I'm 25 years old. And I just want to say thank you for the opportunity to speak. Thank you for everything you are doing, sir. I speak for so many people. You are—you bring my heart to warmth for everything you're doing, and all the way around. (Applause.)

And, sir, my nephew—thank you all. My nephew Kenny Hrobak is like my son. He is in South Korea, right now, in the Army. And he's doing things. And he is so proud of you, and those boys. They all just—I've never seen people that are so proud of our President. And I just—I'm amazed.

I mean, we stayed up to watch you that day when you got elected. We were like, "He's got it! He's got it!" (Laughter.) So—I'm sorry, I'm telling the truth. (Applause.)

Listen, my dad taught me—my dad taught me, "Don't tell no lies." And when you want me to shut up, I will. But I'm telling the truth. And dad always say—he looked a little like Donald Trump; he did a little bit. But you're much handsomer. (Laughter.) Thank you. Thank you very much, sir. (Applause.)

I worked in the towers over there (inaudible). I really appreciate it. Thank you, sir. You have no idea how many people appreciate everything you've done. I mean it. Thank you so much.

THE PRESIDENT: That's really nice . I appreciate it.

MR. HROBAK: I appreciate it.

THE PRESIDENT: Thank you very much.

MR. HROBAK: And I want to say one final thing. I've got a big mouth. (Laughter.) God bless America and God bless our President! Give him a hand. (Applause.) Trump 2020.

THE PRESIDENT: Thank you, Bruce. Wow. Well, that was unexpected. We appreciate it, Bruce. (Laughter.) That's better than any speechwriter I could get, right? (Laughter.) Who am I going to get like that? I appreciate it. Thank you.

MR. HROBAK: (Inaudible.) (Off-mic.)

THE PRESIDENT: Thank you very much, Bruce.

Earlier this year, I also signed the Save Our Seas Act to protect our oceans from waste and pollution.

To improve water access worldwide, we're supporting the development of breakthrough technologies with the Department of Energy's Water Security Grand Challenge.

My administration is strongly promoting bipartisan solutions for conservation. And we're really getting along very well with the Democrats on that one. We're getting things done.

This year, I signed the largest public lands package in a decade, designating 1.3 million acres—that's a lot of land—of new wilderness and expanding recreational access.

In December, I signed a historic executive order promoting much more active forest management to prevent catastrophic wildfires like those that recently devastated California and Oregon. (Applause.)

I went to the fires in California and I said, "It's also management." It's a lot of things happening, but it's management. You can't have dirty floors. You can't have 20 years of leaves and fallen trees. After the first 17 months, they say the tree is like a piece of tinder. You have to be very careful. So you can't have that. That's why you have so many fires.

And I will say this: Spoke with the Governor of California, spoke with many people, and the process of cleaning is now really taking precedent. It—a lot of people are looking at forest management. It's a word that people didn't understand last year. Now they're getting it. And you don't have to have any forest fires. It's interesting.

I spoke to certain countries, and they said, "Sir, we're a forest nation." I never thought of a country—well-known countries: "We're a forest nation." I never heard of the term "forest nation." They live in forests and they don't have problems.

One was telling me that his trees are much more susceptible to fire than what they have in California, but they don't have fires because they manage, they clean, they do what you have to do. There's not so much to burn. And we're going to start doing that. And it's called, remember, "management." It's called "forest management." So it's a very important term.

When I went to California, they sort of scoffed at me for the first two weeks and maybe three weeks, and not so much—four weeks. (Laughter.) And after about five weeks they said, "You know, he's right. He's right."

So I think you're going to see a lot of good things. It's a lot of area. It's a lot of land. But a lot of tremendous things are happening.

We're joined today by Colleen Roberts, a County Commissioner from Jackson County, Oregon. Colleen, please come up and tell us a little bit about your approach on forest management and all of the community work you've done. It's been so successful. Please. (Applause.) Thank you very much. Thank you very much.

MS. ROBERTS: So, I want to thank our President Trump and your administration, sir, for this opportunity—this great opportunity to be here today and speak on this very important issue and in support of your executive order to reduce the hazardous fuel loads in our federal forests.

Jackson County, the county I am from—southern Oregon—has—comprises about 50 percent of federal lands to be managed by our federal agencies. And previous administrations have allowed these lands to be mismanaged, and thus are burdened with the heavy fuel loads.

Wildland fire policies also allowing management objectives to be attained through prescribed burning during our fire season is flawed. Our board has studied and successfully shared information with neighboring counties and NACo, the National Association of Counties, in an effort to achieve wildland fire policy changes.

We've suffered through years of hazardous wildfire conditions, enduring toxic smoke events for the past two years that endured not just for a day but three and four months on end. And it has adversely affected the health of our residents and our economy.

Fuels reduction, through the executive order that our President has put forth, and fire policies can work together for healthy forests and public lands that our citizens deserve.

In all of this and more, you, President Trump, have become a friend and the biggest ally to the counties in this great country. And I'm here to say "thank you" and support you. Thank you so much. (Applause.)

THE PRESIDENT: Thank you, Colleen.

And I also spoke with the governor of California about helping out with the earthquakes. And we'll be doing that. We'll—we're working very closely in California with the various representatives. And we're making a lot of progress. That was something—that was a long time—a lot of shock, lot of shake. And we are helping out. And so we're working with government.

And all across the nation, our policies are ensuring that extreme agendas do not stand in the way of responsible use of public lands. We're getting Washington bureaucrats off of their backs, and we want to make sure that they go out and help our hunters, and our fishers, and farmers, and everyone. And they want to do it. They're going to do it and they want to do it—everybody that enjoys and really loves the great outdoors.

In the proud tradition of conservation that the Republican Party inherits from Teddy Roosevelt, we will preserve this land for our magnificent people. That's what we're doing; we're preserving our land. We're making our land better and cleaner and safer.

Now I'd like to invite Administrator Andrew Wheeler up. He's at the EPA. He's doing a fantastic job. And he's keeping America clean, and we appreciate it very much. Andrew, please come up. (Applause.)

ADMINISTRATOR WHEELER: Thank you, President Trump, for your leadership and the opportunity to share our environmental progress with the American public. When you asked me to take the lead at EPA one year ago, you asked me to do three things: continue to clean up the air, continue to clean up the water, and continue to provide regulatory relief to keep the economy growing.

The President knows we can do all three at the same time. And here's the evidence: From 1970 to 2018, U.S. criteria air pollution fell 74 percent, while the economy grew by 275 percent. Under your administration, emissions of all the criteria air pollutants continue to decline. For example—(applause)—yes.

For example, the lead and sulfur dioxide have dropped by double-digit percentages over the last two years. Today, we have the cleanest air on record and we are a global leader for access to clean drinking water.

We're making tremendous environmental progress under President Trump, and the public needs to know that. Pollution is on the decline, and our focus is to accelerate its decline, particularly in the most at-risk communities.

There may be no better example than our renewed focus on Superfund—the federal program that cleans up large, hazardous sites. In the past, it wasn't unusual for a site to sit on the "Superfund: National Priorities List" for decades. We believe that a site on the National Priorities List should be just that: a national priority.

Our actions demonstrate that. In fiscal year 2018, we deleted the most sites from the National Priorities List in one year since 2005. This year, we are on track to delete even more, breaking that record.

We're also reinvigorating our Brownfields program, which transforms contaminated sites into community assets. We recently announced nearly $65 million in Brownfield grants to 149 communities nationwide. Forty percent of these communities are receiving Brownfields funding for the very first time.

And thanks to the President's historic tax reform package, we're prioritizing Opportunity Zones. Of the 149 grant recipients, 108 have identified sites designated as Opportunity Zones, including in cities such as Detroit and Green Bay.

On air quality, we're helping areas across the country reduce air pollution and meet the nation's air quality standards.

On water, we're helping communities modernize their water infrastructure. Since 2017, we've issued eight water infrastructure loans, totaling over $2 billion. These loans will help finance roughly $4 billion in water infrastructure projects, and create 6,000 jobs.

We've already invited an additional 42 projects to apply for additional funding. These projects will improve water quality for millions of Americans while creating high-paying jobs.

We're equally committed to improving the health of our oceans. The USMCA contains an historic, first-ever commitment to reduce marine litter. Sixty percent of the world's marine litter comes from six Asian countries. We have the technology and the expertise to help these nations.

The truth is, when other countries need help cleaning up their air, water, or land, they turn to us for assistance—not China, not Russia. We have the environmental laws, we develop the technologies, and we get the job done. America is and will remain the gold standard for environmental protection, and every American should know that our nation is cleaner, safer, and stronger today thanks to the leadership of President Trump. (Applause.)

THE PRESIDENT: Thank you, Andrew. Fantastic job. Who would've known that, Andrew? I'm glad you finally let people know what we're doing. (Laughter.) We're working hard. I think harder than many previous administrations. Maybe almost all of them.

I'd like to invite Mary Neumayr to the podium. And Mary has some terrific things to say, and I appreciate you being here, Mary. Thank you very much. Please. (Applause.)

MS. NEUMAYR: President Trump, thank you for your leadership in continuing to advance environmental protection.

THE PRESIDENT: Thank you.

MS. NEUMAYR: Over the past two and half years, President Trump has taken decisive action to address environmental challenges. At his direction, federal agencies are more efficiently implementing air quality standards; more actively managing our nation's forests to improve their health and reduce wildfire risks; promoting reliable water supplies and deliveries in the western United States; increasing federal coordination in the environmental review and permitting process; and efficiently managing federal operations to save energy and water, reduce waste, and cut costs.

Under the President's leadership, across the federal government, agencies have continued to improve their energy and environmental performance, and to reduce greenhouse emissions from federal operations.

One of the many important areas where President Trump has taken action is with regard to ocean policy. Our country is blessed with some of the most beautiful coastlines in the world. Our beaches are places for our families to enjoy, especially at this time of year. Our oceans provide a way of life, support diverse marine species and habitats, and offer recreational opportunities. Our oceans also support the livelihoods of millions of Americans. Coastal communities depend on clean, healthy waters.

Under President Trump's direction, agencies are improving the management of our ocean and coastal waters for present and future generations of Americans.

A little over a year ago, President Trump signed an executive order directing federal agencies to improve coordination on ocean-related matters; work with state-led and regional ocean partnerships; expand federal—access to federal ocean-related data; and maximize the effectiveness of agency investments in ocean research.

Federal agencies are working with state, regional, and other stakeholders to address coastal and ocean management challenges. The agencies are also prioritizing research to better understand and protect our coastal environment, to improve our knowledge of our vast oceans, and to develop next-generation ocean technologies.

This fall, the administration will convene a summit to promote partnerships in ocean science and technology. And the summit will showcase American leadership and engage the research community and the private sector to explore the unknown ocean, advance marine science, and promote new technologies.

In addition to implementing the Save Our Seas Act, signed by President Trump, our federal agencies have also prioritized addressing the harmful effects of marine debris. This administration has engaged with members of Congress, conservation organizations, the private sector, and other nations.

It is critical that we effectively take action on this issue and improve the health of our oceans.

The administration is committed to ensuring that we are good stewards of our environment, while supporting American prosperity. We look forward to continuing to address our nation's environmental challenges and to improving quality of life for all Americans. (Applause.)

THE PRESIDENT: Thank you very much. What a great job you're doing. Thank you very much. Appreciate it.

So a man who was very responsible for our tremendous success, Salute to America—Department of Interiors. They kept you very busy. Right, David?

SECRETARY BERNHARDT: Yes, sir.

THE PRESIDENT: David Bernhardt. Come on up. Thank you. (Applause.)

SECRETARY BERNHARDT: Good afternoon. It is an honor to serve a President who has been focused on conservation stewardship since day one. The President mentioned that he signed into law the largest public lands legislation in over a decade. Thank you all on your side.

We are aggressively implementing this act, which, among other things, designated 1.3 million acres of public land as wilderness, as you said. To put that into perspective, 1.3 million acres exceeds the entire size of the state of Rhode Island.

Today, the geographic area of our nation's wilderness system is actually larger than every state in the union except for Texas and Alaska. We are ensuring that future generations receive the benefit of an enduring wilderness system.

Mr. President, throughout your term, Interior has also been focused on strengthening the North American Wildlife Conservation Model, which is the best in the world. The model was originally conceived by American hunters and anglers, who were the first to crusade for wildlife protection, and retain some of today's most important conservation leadership.

The success of this model depends on a strong federal-state partnership and the continued commitment and participation of the hunters and anglers. These important relationships were frayed under the prior administration. In contrast, your administration has fostered stewardship collaboration by working with the states, not unilaterally, on our shared mission to conserve fish and wildlife and preserve their habitats for future generations.

For example, since 2017, at Interior we have released 292 million sportfish, which provide recreational angling opportunities while contributing to species restoration and recovery goals. We have removed 325 barriers opening over 8,000 river miles for native fish through our National Fish Passage Program.

Public access and outdoor recreation opportunities are critical for wildlife conservation. Since January of 2017, across the refuge system, we have devoted more than $52 million to restore, retain, and enhance access to outdoor recreation sites and support habitat infrastructure. During that time, we've also opened or expanded hunting and fishing access to 385,000 of acres on refuged lands.

And last month, we announced our plan to open or expand an additional 1.4 million acres in several national wildlife refuges and fish hatcheries for new hunting, fishing, and recreational activities. America leads—(applause)—it's a big number.

The reality is that America leads the world in wilderness and wildlife conservation efforts. And under President Trump's commonsense leadership, every day at Interior we are increasing access to our public lands, increasing recreational opportunities on those public lands, and enhancing our conservation efforts.

So, thank you. (Applause.)

THE PRESIDENT: Well, thank you very much, David.

I got to know this one, David. You, I didn't know, but I got to know this one. He's a tough competitor on the campaign trail. He wanted this position. And we fought and we fought, and I said, "You know, I want him someday. If I win, I'm going to get him in some capacity." (Laughter.) And who's better to get than a man who successfully ran Texas for 12 years? Is that what it is? Twelve years, right? A long time. Great state. And you did a great job.

So I said, "I want Rick Perry working for us." And he knows more about energy than anybody. Come on up, Rick. (Applause.)

SECRETARY PERRY: Thank you. Mr. President, I want to tell you that last Thursday was a big day for me. In the morning, I got to welcome my first grandson into the world. (Applause.)

And that afternoon, I got to watch the President of the United States give one of the greatest history lessons that I have ever seen before and to celebrate the American military like I'd never seen it celebrated before. I am proud to be standing with you, proud to be working in this Cabinet with these men and women. This is a great moment for America. It's a great moment for America for a lot of reasons. (Applause.)

And today, I'm really proud to get to stand up here in front of America—and of the world, for that matter—as they watch this, and to recognize how important today is because the chance to tell a story that often doesn't get told in a proper way, and a story about what this administration is doing to clean up the environment; what this administration is doing on policies that are having an effect on our environment.

At the Department of Energy, we have championed both the historic development of our nation's resources and the technological breakthroughs that are just literally cascading across this country in ways to use energy more cleanly, more efficiently, than anyone ever thought possible before.

We know that by investing in innovative solutions—like carbon capture, utilization, sequestration, zero emission works like our nuclear power, exporting those technologies to other countries and—we're being able to share our technologies around the world of cleaner energy without singling—I mean, without surrendering one single fuel, one iota of growth, one iota of opportunity. That's what this President is all about. That's your record, Mr. President.

We're seeing, on your watch, America become the number-one producer of oil and gas in the world. (Applause.) We're seeing emissions being reduced around the world. I was with some of our friends from the European Union, and reminding them about what you're being able to do in this country with the innovation. We're being able to deliver liquefied natural gas to them so they can move away from these dirty or burning old, inefficient plants, and bring a cleaner environment to those countries.

You know, it's our national labs at the Department of Energy. Elaine, we've talked about this, and you've seen this through your years where this technology—this technological revolution that is occurring. And we're not only increasing our energy supply, but we're making it cleaner. We're doing it in a way that the world is enjoying with us.

So—and at your direction, Mr. President, DOE launched, as you mentioned earlier, the Water Security Grand Challenge. Using the power of competition, the Water Security Grand Challenge will spur innovation and advances in transformational technology that are going to meet the global need for safe, affordable, beautiful crystal-clear water. (Applause.)

And, Mr. President, it's been your policies, it's been your focus, that greater energy security for America while at the same time enhancing our environmental stewardship. I think the world needs to look at your leadership. Look at what you've done.

You know, for too long, there's been this conventional wisdom that you've got to choose between economic growth and environmental protection. That's a false choice, and it's one that you've talked about, Mr. President. It's always been this country, and this country that leads—just like you reminded people last Thursday—the greatness of America, the innovation of America. And the future of this world will rely greatly upon America and this administration.

Thank you, Mr. President, for the opportunity. (Applause.)

THE PRESIDENT: Thank you.

SECRETARY PERRY: Yes, sir.

THE PRESIDENT: And what Rick has done with our nuclear supply—nuclear energy, and all forms nuclear—has been absolutely incredible in very a short period of time. I want to thank you. That's fantastic. So important the job you're doing. Thank you very much, Rick.

When I ran for President, I pledged a strong, growing economy and a healthy environment because I believe that we can pursue both at the same time.

We have only one America. We have only one planet. That's why, every day of my presidency, we will fight for a cleaner environment and a better quality of life for every one of our great citizens. Above all, we will remain loyal to the American people and be faithful stewards of God's glorious creation, from sea to shining sea.

Thank you all very much for being here. God bless you. And God bless America. Thank you. (Applause.) Thank you.

Print Citations

CMS: Trump, Donald. "Remarks by President Trump on America's Environmental Leadership: Energy & Environment." Speech at the White House, Washington, DC, July 8, 2019. In *The Reference Shelf: Representative American Speeches, 2018–2019*, edited by Sophie Zyla, 73-85. Amenia, NY: Grey House Publishing, 2019.

MLA: Trump, Donald. "Remarks by President Trump on America's Environmental Leadership: Energy & Environment." The White House, 8 July 2019, Washington, DC. Speech. *The Reference Shelf: Representative American Speeches, 2018–2019*, edited by Sophie Zyla, Grey House Publishing, 2019, pp. 73-85.

APA: Trump, D. (2019, July 8). Remarks by President Trump on America's environmental leadership: Energy & environment. The White House, Washington, DC. In Sophie Zyla (Ed.), *The reference shelf: Representative American speeches, 2018–2019* (pp. 73-85). Amenia, NY: Grey House Publishing.

3
Responses in Controversial Political Times

By Gage Skidmore, via Wikimedia.

Senator and presidential candidate Cory Booker was "profoundly disturbed" by racial and ethnic comments made by President Trump, and also by former Homeland Security secretary Kirstjen Nielsen's apparent inability to recall them.

Opening Statement to the Senate Judiciary Committee

By Christine Blasey Ford

Christine Blasey Ford received a bachelor's degree from the University of North Carolina, a master's degree in psychology from Pepperdine University, a PhD in educational psychology from University of Southern California, and a master's in education from Stanford. She is a professor of psychology at Palo Alto University and a research psychologist at Stanford University.

Chairman Grassley, Ranking Member Feinstein, Members of the Committee. My name is Christine Blasey Ford. I am a Professor of Psychology at Palo Alto University and a Research Psychologist at the Stanford University School of Medicine.

I was an undergraduate at the University of North Carolina and earned my degree in Experimental Psychology in 1988. I received a Master's degree in 1991 in Clinical Psychology from Pepperdine University. In 1996, I received a PhD in Educational Psychology from the University of Southern California. I earned a Master's degree in Epidemiology from the Stanford University School of Medicine in 2009.

I have been married to Russell Ford since 2002 and we have two children.

I am here today not because I want to be. I am terrified. I am here because I believe it is my civic duty to tell you what happened to me while Brett Kavanaugh and I were in high school. I have described the events publicly before. I summarized them in my letter to Ranking Member Feinstein, and again in my letter to Chairman Grassley. I understand and appreciate the importance of your hearing from me directly about what happened to me and the impact it has had on my life and on my family.

I grew up in the suburbs of Washington, D.C. I attended the Holton-Arms School in Bethesda, Maryland, from 1980 to 1984. Holton-Arms is an all-girls school that opened in 1901. During my time at the school, girls at Holton-Arms frequently met and became friendly with boys from all-boys schools in the area, including Landon School, Georgetown Prep, Gonzaga High School, country clubs, and other places where kids and their families socialized. This is how I met Brett Kavanaugh, the boy who sexually assaulted me.

In my freshman and sophomore school years, when I was 14 and 15 years old, my group of friends intersected with Brett and his friends for a short period of time. I had been friendly with a classmate of Brett's for a short time during my freshman

---

Delivered on September 26, 2018, to the U.S. Senate Judiciary Committee, Washington, DC.

year, and it was through that connection that I attended a number of parties that Brett also attended. We did not know each other well, but I knew him and he knew me. In the summer of 1982, like most summers, I spent almost every day at the Columbia Country Club in Chevy Chase, Maryland swimming and practicing diving.

One evening that summer, after a day of swimming at the club, I attended a small gathering at a house in the Chevy Chase/Bethesda area. There were four boys I remember being there: Brett Kavanaugh, Mark Judge, P.J. Smyth, and one other boy whose name I cannot recall. I remember my friend Leland Ingham attending. I do not remember all of the details of how that gathering came together, but like many that summer, it was almost surely a spur of the moment gathering. I truly wish I could provide detailed answers to all of the questions that have been and will be asked about how I got to the party, where it took place, and so forth. I don't have all the answers, and I don't remember as much as I would like to. But the details about that night that bring me here today are ones I will never forget. They have been seared into my memory and have haunted me episodically as an adult.

When I got to the small gathering, people were drinking beer in a small living room on the first floor of the house. I drank one beer that evening. Brett and Mark were visibly drunk. Early in the evening, I went up a narrow set of stairs leading from the living room to a second floor to use the bathroom. When I got to the top of the stairs, I was pushed from behind into a bedroom. I couldn't see who pushed me. Brett and Mark came into the bedroom and locked the door behind them. There was music already playing in the bedroom. It was turned up louder by either Brett or Mark once we were in the room. I was pushed onto the bed and Brett got on top of me. He began running his hands over my body and grinding his hips into me. I yelled, hoping someone downstairs might hear me, and tried to get away from him, but his weight was heavy. Brett groped me and tried to take off my clothes. He had a hard time because he was so drunk, and because I was wearing a one-piece bathing suit under my clothes. I believed he was going to rape me. I tried to yell for help. When I did, Brett put his hand over my mouth to stop me from screaming. This was what terrified me the most, and has had the most lasting impact on my life. It was hard for me to breathe, and I thought that Brett was accidentally going to kill me. Both Brett and Mark were drunkenly laughing during the attack. They both seemed to be having a good time. Mark was urging Brett on, although at times he told Brett to stop. A couple of times I made eye contact with Mark and thought he might try to help me, but he did not.

During this assault, Mark came over and jumped on the bed twice while Brett was on top of me. The last time he did this, we toppled over and Brett was no longer on top of me. I was able to get up and run out of the room. Directly across from the bedroom was a small bathroom. I ran inside the bathroom and locked the door. I heard Brett and Mark leave the bedroom laughing and loudly walk down the narrow stairs, pin-balling off the walls on the way down. I waited and when I did not hear them come back up the stairs, I left the bathroom, ran down the stairs, through the living room, and left the house. I remember being on the street and feeling an enormous sense of relief that I had escaped from the house and that Brett and Mark were not coming after me.

Brett's assault on me drastically altered my life. For a very long time, I was too afraid and ashamed to tell anyone the details. I did not want to tell my parents that I, at age 15, was in a house without any parents present, drinking beer with boys. I tried to convince myself that because Brett did not rape me, I should be able to move on and just pretend that it had never happened. Over the years, I told very few friends that I had this traumatic experience. I told my husband before we were married that I had experienced a sexual assault. I had never told the details to anyone until May 2012, during a couples counseling session. The reason this came up in counseling is that my husband and I had completed an extensive remodel of our home, and I insisted on a second front door, an idea that he and others disagreed with and could not understand. In explaining why I wanted to have a second front door, I described the assault in detail. I recall saying that the boy who assaulted me could someday be on the U.S. Supreme Court and spoke a bit about his background. My husband recalls that I named my attacker as Brett Kavanaugh.

After that May 2012 therapy session, I did my best to suppress memories of the assault because recounting the details caused me to relive the experience, and caused panic attacks and anxiety. Occasionally I would discuss the assault in individual therapy, but talking about it caused me to relive the trauma, so I tried not to think about it or discuss it. But over the years, I went through periods where I thought about Brett's attack. I confided in some close friends that I had an experience with sexual assault. Occasionally I stated that my assailant was a prominent lawyer or judge but I did not use his name. I do not recall each person I spoke to about Brett's assault, and some friends have reminded me of these conversations since the publication of the *Washington Post* story on September 16, 2018. But until July 2018, I had never named Mr. Kavanaugh as my attacker outside of therapy.

This all changed in early July 2018. I saw press reports stating that Brett Kavanaugh was on the "short list" of potential Supreme Court nominees. I thought it was my civic duty to relay the information I had about Mr. Kavanaugh's conduct so that those considering his potential nomination would know about the assault.

On July 6, 2018, I had a sense of urgency to relay the information to the Senate and the President as soon as possible before a nominee was selected. I called my congressional representative and let her receptionist know that someone on the President's shortlist had attacked me. I also sent a message to the *Washington Post's* confidential tip line. I did not use my name, but I provided the names of Brett Kavanaugh and Mark Judge. I stated that Mr. Kavanaugh had assaulted me in the 1980s in Maryland. This was an extremely hard thing for me to do, but I felt I couldn't NOT do it. Over the next two days, I told a couple of close friends on the beach in California that Mr. Kavanaugh had sexually assaulted me. I was conflicted about whether to speak out.

On July 9, 2018, I received a call from the office of Congresswoman Anna Eshoo after Mr. Kavanaugh had become the nominee. I met with her staff on July 11 and with her on July 13, describing the assault and discussing my fear about coming forward. Later, we discussed the possibility of sending a letter to Ranking Member Feinstein, who is one of my state's Senators, describing what occurred. My understanding is that Representative Eshoo's office delivered a copy of my letter to Senator Feinstein's office on July 30, 2018. The letter included my name, but requested that the letter be kept confidential.

My hope was that providing the information confidentially would be sufficient to allow the Senate to consider Mr. Kavanaugh's serious misconduct without having to make myself, my family, or anyone's family vulnerable to the personal attacks and invasions of privacy we have faced since my name became public. In a letter on August 31, 2018, Senator Feinstein wrote that she would not share the letter without my consent. I greatly appreciated this commitment. All sexual assault victims should be able to decide for themselves whether their private experience is made public.

As the hearing date got closer, I struggled with a terrible choice: Do I share the facts with the Senate and put myself and my family in the public spotlight? Or do I preserve our privacy and allow the Senate to make its decision on Mr. Kavanaugh's nomination without knowing the full truth about his past behavior?

I agonized daily with this decision throughout August and early September 2018. The sense of duty that motivated me to reach out confidentially to the *Washington Post*, Representative Eshoo's office, and Senator Feinstein's office was always there, but my fears of the consequences of speaking out started to increase.

During August 2018, the press reported that Mr. Kavanaugh's confirmation was virtually certain. His allies painted him as a champion of women's rights and empowerment. I believed that if I came forward, my voice would be drowned out by a chorus of powerful supporters. By the time of the confirmation hearings, I had resigned myself to remaining quiet and letting the Committee and the Senate make their decision without knowing what Mr. Kavanaugh had done to me.

Once the press started reporting on the existence of the letter I had sent to Senator Feinstein, I faced mounting pressure. Reporters appeared at my home and at my job demanding information about this letter, including in the presence of my graduate students. They called my boss and coworkers and left me many messages, making it clear that my name would inevitably be released to the media. I decided to speak out publicly to a journalist who had responded to the tip I had sent to the *Washington Post* and who had gained my trust. It was important to me to describe the details of the assault in my own words.

Since September 16, the date of the *Washington Post* story, I have experienced an outpouring of support from people in every state of this country. Thousands of people who have had their lives dramatically altered by sexual violence have reached out to share their own experiences with me and have thanked me for coming forward. We have received tremendous support from friends and our community.

At the same time, my greatest fears have been realized—and the reality has been far worse than what I expected. My family and I have been the target of constant harassment and death threats. I have been called the most vile and hateful names imaginable. These messages, while far fewer than the expressions of support, have been terrifying to receive and have rocked me to my core. People have posted my personal information on the internet. This has resulted in additional emails, calls, and threats. My family and I were forced to move out of our home. Since September 16, my family and I have been living in various secure locales, with guards. This past Tuesday evening, my work email account was hacked and messages were sent out supposedly recanting my description of the sexual assault.

Apart from the assault itself, these last couple of weeks have been the hardest of my life. I have had to relive my trauma in front of the entire world, and have seen my life picked apart by people on television, in the media, and in this body who have never met me or spoken with me. I have been accused of acting out of partisan political motives. Those who say that do not know me. I am a fiercely independent person and I am no one's pawn. My motivation in coming forward was to provide the facts about how Mr. Kavanaugh's actions have damaged my life, so that you can take that into serious consideration as you make your decision about how to proceed. It is not my responsibility to determine whether Mr. Kavanaugh deserves to sit on the Supreme Court. My responsibility is to tell the truth.

I understand that the Majority has hired a professional prosecutor to ask me some questions, and I am committed to doing my very best to answer them. At the same time, because the Committee Members will be judging my credibility, I hope to be able to engage directly with each of you.

At this point, I will do my best to answer your questions.

Print Citations

CMS: "Christine Blasey Ford's Opening Statement to the Senate Judiciary Committee." Presentation to the U.S. Senate, Washington, DC, September 26, 2018. In *The Reference Shelf: Representative American Speeches, 2018–2019,* edited by Sophie Zyla, 89-93. Amenia, NY: Grey House Publishing, 2019.

MLA: "Christine Blasey Ford's Opening Statement to the Senate Judiciary Committee." U.S. Senate, 26 September 2018, Washington, DC. Presentation. *The Reference Shelf: Representative American Speeches, 2018–2019,* edited by Sophie Zyla, Grey House Publishing, 2019, pp. 89-93.

APA: Politico Staff. (2018, September 26). Presentation of Christine Blasey Ford's opening statement to the Senate Judiciary Committee. U.S. Senate, Washington, DC. In Sophie Zyla (Ed.), *The reference shelf: Representative American speeches, 2018–2019* (pp. 89-93). Amenia, NY: Grey House Publishing.

Vote to Confirm Brett Kavanaugh

By Susan Collins

Susan M. Collins is a senator from Maine. Collins worked for Senator William Cohen from 1981–1987, and in 1996 she was elected to the U.S. Senate. Collins was reelected in 2002, 2008, and 2014. She serves as chair for the Committee on Governmental Affairs, Committee on Homeland Security and Governmental Affairs, and Committee on Aging. She has a degree from St. Lawrence University in Canton, New York. The controversy sparked by the Brett Kavanaugh nomination and the Christine Blasey Ford hearing prompted her to provide insight on her determination process in a complicated case.

President, the five previous times that I've come to the floor to explain my vote on the nomination of a justice to the United States Supreme Court, I have begun my floor remarks explaining my decision with a recognition of the solemn nature and the importance of the occasion. But today we have come to the conclusion of a confirmation process that has become so dysfunctional, it looks more like a caricature of a gutter-level political campaign than a solemn occasion.

The president nominated Brett Kavanaugh on July 9. Within moments of that announcement, special interest groups raced to be the first to oppose him, including one organization that didn't even bother to fill in the judge's name on its pre-written press release. They simply wrote that they opposed Donald Trump's nomination of "XX" to the Supreme Court of the United States. A number of senators joined the race to announce their opposition, but they were beaten to the punch by one of our colleagues who actually announced opposition before the nominee's identity was even known.

Since that time, we have seen special interest groups whip their followers into a frenzy by spreading misrepresentations and outright falsehoods about Judge Kavanaugh's judicial record. Over-the-top rhetoric and distortions of his record and testimony at his first hearing produced short-lived headlines, which although debunked hours later, continued to live on and be spread through social media. Interest groups have also spent an unprecedented amount of dark money opposing this nomination. Our Supreme Court confirmation process has been in steady decline for more than 30 years.

One can only hope that the Kavanaugh nomination is where the process has finally hit rock bottom. Against this backdrop, it is up to each individual senator to decide what the Constitution's advice and consent duty means. Informed by

---

Delivered on October 5, 2018, at the U.S. Senate, Washington, DC.

Alexander Hamilton's *Federalist 76*, I have interpreted this to mean that the president has broad discretion to consider a nominee's philosophy, whereas my duty as a senator is to focus on the nominee's qualifications as long as that nominee's philosophy is within the mainstream of judicial thought.

I have always opposed litmus tests for judicial nominees with respect to their personal views or politics, but I fully expect them to be able to put aside any and all personal preferences in deciding the cases that come before them. I've never considered the president's identity or party when evaluating Supreme Court nominations. As a result, I voted in favor of Justices Roberts and Alito, who were nominated by President Bush. Justices Sotomayor and Kagan, who were nominated by President Obama. And Justice Gorsuch, who was nominated by President Trump.

So I began my evaluation of Judge Kavanaugh's nomination by reviewing his 12-year record on the DC Circuit Court of Appeals, including his more than 300 opinions and his many speeches and law review articles. Nineteen attorneys, including lawyers from the nonpartisan congressional research service, briefed me many times each week and assisted me in evaluating the Judge's extensive record. I met with Judge Kavanaugh for more than two hours in my office. I listened carefully to the testimony at the committee hearings. I spoke with people who knew him personally, such as Condoleezza Rice and many others. And I talked with Judge Kavanaugh a second time by phone for another hour to ask him very specific additional questions. I also have met with thousands of my constituents, both advocates and many opponents, regarding Judge Kavanaugh.

One concern that I frequently heard was that the judge would be likely to eliminate the Affordable Care Act's vital protections for people with preexisting conditions. I disagree with this. In a dissent in *Seven-Sky v. Holder*, Judge Kavanaugh rejected a challenge to the ACA on narrow procedural grounds, preserving the law in full. Many experts have said that his dissent informed Justice Roberts's opinion upholding the ACA at the Supreme Court.

Furthermore, Judge Kavanaugh's approach toward the doctrine of sever-ability is narrow. When a part of a statute is challenged on constitutional grounds, he has argued for severing the invalid clause as surgically as possible while allowing the overall law to remain intact. This was his approach in a case that involved a challenge to the structure of the consumer financial protection bureau. In his dissent, Judge Kavanaugh argued for "severing any problematic portions while leaving the remainder intact." Given the current challenges to the ACA proponents, including myself, of protections for people with preexisting conditions should want a justice who would take just this kind of approach.

Another assertion that I have heard often that Judge Kavanaugh cannot be trusted if a case involving alleged wrongdoing by the president were to come before the court. The basis for this argument seems to be two-fold.

First, Judge Kavanaugh has written that he believes that Congress should enact legislation to protect presidents from criminal prosecution or civil liability while in office. Mr. President, I believe opponents missed the mark on this issue. The fact that Judge Kavanaugh offered this legislative proposal suggests that he believes that the president does not have such protection currently.

Second, there are some who argue that given the current special counsel investigation, President Trump should not even be allowed to nominate a justice. That argument ignores our recent history. President Clinton in 1993 nominated Justice Ginsburg after the Whitewater investigation was already underway, and she was confirmed 96 to 3. The next year, just three months after independent counsel Robert Fisk was named to lead the Whitewater investigation, President Clinton nominated Justice Breyer. He was confirmed 87 to 9.

Supreme Court justices have not hesitated to rule against the presidents who have nominated them. Perhaps most notably in the *United States v. Nixon*, three Nixon appointees who heard the case joined the unanimous opinion against him. Judge Kavanaugh has been unequivocal in his belief that no president is above the law. He has stated that *Marbury v. Madison*, *Youngstown Steel v. Sawyer* and the *United States v. Nixon* are three of the greatest Supreme Court cases in history. What do they have in common? Each of them is a case where Congress served as a check on presidential power.

And I would note that the fourth case that Judge Kavanaugh has pointed to as the greatest in history was *Brown v. the Board of Education*. One Kavanaugh decision illustrates the point about the check on presidential power directly. He wrote the opinion in *Hamdan v. the United States*, a case that challenges the Bush administration's military commission prosecution of an associate of Osama bin Laden. This conviction was very important to the Bush administration, but Judge Kavanaugh, who had been appointed to the DC Circuit by President Bush and had worked in President Bush's White House, ruled that the conviction was unlawful. As he explained during the hearing, "we don't make decisions based on who people are or their policy preferences or the moment. We base decisions on the law."

Others I've met with have expressed concerns that Justice Kennedy's retirement threatens the right of same-sex couples to marry. Yet, Judge Kavanaugh described the Obergefell decision, which legalized same-gender marriages, as an important landmark precedent. He also cited Justice Kennedy's recent masterpiece cake shop opinion for the court's majority stating that "the days of treating gay and lesbian Americans, or gay and lesbian couples as second-class citizens who are inferior in dignity and worth are over in the Supreme Court."

Others have suggested that the judge holds extreme views on birth control. In one case Judge Kavanaugh incurred the disfavor of both sides of the political spectrum for seeking to ensure the availability of contraceptive services for women while minimizing the involvement of employers with religious objections. Although his critics frequently overlook this point, Judge Kavanaugh's dissent rejected arguments that the government did not have a compelling interest in facilitating access to contraception. In fact, he wrote that the Supreme Court precedent strongly suggested that there was a compelling interest in facilitating access to birth control.

There has also been considerable focus on the future of abortion rights based on the concern that Judge Kavanaugh would seek to overturn *Roe v. Wade*. Protecting this right is important to me. To my knowledge, Judge Kavanaugh is the first Supreme Court nominee to express the view that precedent is not merely a practice and tradition, but rooted in Article 3 of our Constitution itself. He believes that precedent is not just a judicial policy, it is constitutionally dictated to pay attention and pay heed to rules of precedent. In other words, precedent isn't a goal or an aspiration. It is a constitutional tenet that has to be followed except in the most extraordinary circumstances.

The judge further explained that precedent provides stability, predictability, reliance and fairness. There are, of course, rare and extraordinary times where the Supreme Court would rightly overturn a precedent. The most famous example was when the Supreme Court in *Brown v. the Board of Education* overruled *Plessy v. Ferguson*, correcting a "grievously wrong decision" to use the judge's term, allowing racial inequality. But someone who believes that the importance of precedent has been rooted in the Constitution would follow long-established precedent except in those rare circumstances where a decision is grievously wrong or deeply inconsistent with the law. Those are Judge Kavanaugh's phrases.

As the judge asserted to me, a long-established precedent is not something to be trimmed, narrowed, discarded, or overlooked. Its roots in the Constitution give the concept of stare decisis greater weight simply because a judge might want to on a whim. In short, his views on honoring precedent would preclude attempts to do by stealth that which one has committed not to do overtly.

Noting that *Roe v. Wade* was decided 45 years ago and reaffirmed 19 years later in *Planned Parenthood v. Casey*, I asked Judge Kavanaugh whether the passage of time is relevant to following precedent. He said decisions become part of our legal framework with the passage of time and that honoring precedent is essential to maintaining public confidence. Our discussion then turned to the right of privacy on which the Supreme Court relied in *Griswold v. Connecticut*, a case that struck down a law banning the use and sale of contraceptions. Griswold established the legal foundation that led to *Roe* eight years later. In describing Griswold as settled law, Judge Kavanaugh observed that it was the correct application of two famous cases from the 1920's, Meyer and Pierce that are not seriously challenged by anyone today.

Finally, in his testimony, he noted repeatedly that *Roe* had been upheld by *Planned Parenthood v. Casey*, describing it as a precedent. When I asked him would it be sufficient to overturn a long-established precedent if five current justices believed that it was wrongly decided, he emphatically said "no."

Opponents frequently cite then-candidate Donald Trump's campaign pledge to nominate only judges who would overturn *Roe*. The Republican platform for all presidential campaigns has included this pledge since at least 1980. During this time Republican presidents have appointed Justices O'Connor, Souter and Kennedy to the Supreme Court. These are the very three Republican president appointed justices who authored the Casey decision which reaffirmed *Roe*.

Furthermore, pro-choice groups vigorously oppose each of these justice's nominations. Incredibly, they even circulated buttons with the slogan "Stop Souter or women will die." Just two years later Justice Souter coauthored the Casey opinion reaffirming a woman's right to choose. Suffice it to say, prominent advocacy organizations have been wrong.

These same interest groups have speculated that Judge Kavanaugh was selected to do the bidding of conservative ideologues despite his record of judicial Independence. I asked the judge point-blank whether he had made any commitments or pledges to anyone at the White House, to the Federalist Society, to any outside group on how he would decide cases. He unequivocally assured me that he had not.

Judge Kavanaugh has received rave reviews for his 12-year track record as a judge, including for his judicial temperament. The American Bar Association gave him its highest possible rating. Its standing committee on the federal judiciary conducted an extraordinarily thorough assessment, soliciting input from almost 500 people, including his judicial colleagues. The ABA concluded that his integrity, judicial temperament and professional competence met the highest standards.

Lisa Blatt, who has argued more cases before the Supreme Court than any other woman in history, testified, "By any objective measure, Judge Kavanaugh is clearly qualified to serve on the Supreme Court. His opinions are invariably thoughtful and fair." Ms. Blatt, who clerked for and is an ardent admirer of Justice Ginsburg and who is, in her own words, an unapologetic defender of a woman's right to choose, says that Judge Kavanaugh fits within the mainstream of legal thought. She also observed that Judge Kavanaugh is remarkably committed to promoting women in the legal profession.

That Judge Kavanaugh is more of a centrist than some of his critics maintain is reflected in the fact that he and Chief Judge Merrick Garland voted the same way in 93 percent of the cases that they heard together. Indeed, Chief Judge Garland joined in more than 96 percent of the majority opinions authored by Judge Kavanaugh, dissenting only once.

Despite all this, after weeks of reviewing Judge Kavanaugh's record and listening record and listening to 32 hours of his testimony, the Senate's advice and consent was thrown into a tailspin following the allegations of sexual assault by Professor Christine Blasey Ford. The confirmation process now involved evaluating whether or not Judge Kavanaugh committed sexual assault and lied about it to the Judiciary Committee.

Some argue that because this is a lifetime appointment to our highest court, the public interest requires that it be resolved against the nominee. Others see the public interest as embodied in our long-established tradition of affording to those accused of misconduct a presumption of innocence or in cases in which the facts are unclear, they would argue that the question should be resolved in favor of the nominee.

Mr. President, I understand both viewpoints. And this debate is complicated further by the fact that the Senate confirmation process is not a trial. But certain fundamentally legal principles about due process, the presumption of innocence, and fairness do bear on my thinking, and I cannot abandon them. In evaluating any given claim of misconduct we will be ill served in the long republic if we abandon the presumption of innocence and fairness tempting though it may be.

We must always remember that it is when passions are most inflamed that fairness is most in jeopardy. The presumption of innocence is relevant to the advice and consent function when an accusation departs from a nominees otherwise exemplary record. I worry that departing from this presumption could a lead to a lack of public faith in the judiciary and would be hugely damaging to the confirmation process moving forward.

Some of the allegations levied against Judge Kavanaugh illustrate why the presumption of innocence is so important. I am thinking in particular not at the allegations raised by professor Ford, but of the allegations that when he was a teenager Judge Kavanaugh drugged multiple girls and used their weakened state to facility gang rape.

This outlandish allegation was put forth without any credible supporting evidence and simply parroted public statements of others. That's such an allegation can find its way into the Supreme Court confirmation process is a stark reminder about why the presumption of innocence is so ingrained in our a American consciousness.

Mr. President, I listened carefully to Christine Blasey Ford's testimony before the Judiciary Committee. I found her testimony to be sincere, painful, and compelling. I believe that she is a survivor of a sexual assault and that this trauma has upended her life.

Nevertheless, the four witnesses she named could not corroborate any of the events of that evening gathering where she says the assault occurred. None of the individuals Prof. Ford says were at the party has any recollection at all of that night. Judge Kavanaugh forcefully denied the allegations under penalty of perjury. Mark Judge denied under penalty of felony that he had witnessed an assault. P.J. Smith, another person allegedly at the party, denied that he was there under penalty of felony. Professor Ford's lifelong friend, Leland Kaiser, indicated that under penalty of felony she does not remember that party. And Ms. Kaiser went further. She indicated that not only does she not remember a night like that, but also that she does not even know Brett Kavanaugh.

In addition to the lack of corroborating evidence we also learn facts that have raised more questions. For instance, since these allegations have become public, Prof. Ford testified that not a single person has contacted her to say I was at the party that night.

Furthermore the professor testified that although she does not remember how she got home that evening, she knew that because of the distance she would have needed a ride. Yet, not a single person has come forward to say that they were the ones who drove her home or were in the car with her that night.

And Prof. Ford also indicated that even though she left that small gathering of six or so people abruptly, and without saying goodbye, and distraught, none of them called her the next day or ever to ask why she left. "Is she okay?" Not even her closest friend, Ms. Kaiser.

Mr. President, the Constitution does not provide guidance on how we are supposed to evaluate these competing claims. It leaves that decision up to each senator. This is not a criminal trial, and I do not believe that claims such as these need to be proved beyond a reasonable doubt, nevertheless fairness of this terrible problem.

I have been alarmed and disturbed, however, by some who have suggested that unless Judge Kavanaugh's nomination is rejected, the Senate is somehow condoning sexual assault. Nothing could be further from the truth. Every person, man or woman, who makes a charge of sexual assault deserves to be heard and treated with respect. The #MeToo movement is real. It matters. It is needed. And it is long overdue.

We know that rape and sexual assault are less likely to be reported to the police than other forms of assault. On average, an estimated 211,000 rapes and sexual assaults go unreported every year. We must listen to survivors, and every day we must seek to stop the criminal behavior that has hurt so many. We owe this to ourselves, our children, and generations to come.

Since the hearing, I have listened to many survivors of sexual assault. Many were total strangers who told me their heart-wrenching stories for the first time in their lives. Some were friends that I had known for decades. Yet with the exception of one woman who had confided in me years ago, I had no idea that they had been the victims of sexual attacks. I am grateful for their courage and their willingness to come forward and I hope that in heightening public awareness they have also lightened burden that they have been quietly bearing for so many years.

To them I pledge to do all that I can to ensure that their daughters and granddaughters never share their experiences. Over the past few weeks, I have been emphatic that the Senate has an obligation to investigate and evaluate the serious allegations of sexual assault. I called for and supported the additional hearing to hear from both Prof. Ford and Judge Kavanaugh. I also pushed for and supported the FBI's supplemental background check investigation. This was the right thing to do.

Christine Ford never sought the spotlight. She indicated that she was terrified to appear before the Senate Judiciary Committee, and she has shunned attention since then. She seemed completely unaware of Chairman Grassley's offer to allow her to testify confidentially in California. Watching her, Mr. President, I could not help but feel that some people who wanted to engineer the defeat of this nomination cared little, if at all, for her well-being.

Prof. Ford testified that a very limited of number people had access to her letter, yet that letter found its way into the public domain. She testified that she never gave permission for that very private letter to be released, and yet here we are. We are in the middle of a fight that she never sought, arguing about claims that she wanted to raise confidentially.

Now, one theory I've heard espoused repeatedly is that our colleague Sen. Feinstein leaked Prof. Ford's letter at the 11th hour to derail this process. I want to state this very clearly. I know Senator Dianne Feinstein extremely well, and I believe that she would never do that. I knew that to be the case before she even stated it at the hearing. She is a person of integrity and I stand by her.

I have also heard some argue that the chairman of the committee somehow treated Prof. Ford unfairly. Nothing could be further from the truth. Chairman Grassley along with his excellent staff treated Prof. Ford with compassion and respect throughout the entire process. And that is the way the senator from Iowa has conducted himself throughout a lifetime dedicated to public service.

But the fact remains, Mr. President, someone leaked this letter against professor Ford's expressed wishes. I suspect regrettably that we will never know for certain who did it. To that leaker who I hope is listening now, let me say that what you did was unconscionable. You have taken a survivor who was not only entitled to your respect but who also trusted you to protect her, and you have sacrificed her well-being in a misguided attempt to win whatever political crusade you think you are fighting.

My only hope is that your callous act has turned this process into such a dysfunctional circus that it will cause the Senate and indeed all Americans to reconsider how we evaluate Supreme Court if that happens, then the appalling lack of compassion you afforded Prof. Ford will at least have some unintended positive consequences.

Mr. President, the politically charged atmosphere surrounding this nomination has reached a fever pitch even before these allegations were known, and it has been challenging even then to separate fact from fiction. We live in a time of such great disunity as the bitter fight over this nomination both in the Senate and among the public clearly demonstrates. It is not merely a case of differing groups having different opinions. It is a case of people bearing extreme ill will toward those who disagree with them. In our intense focus on our differences, we have forgotten the common values that bind us together as Americans.

When some of our best minds are seeking to develop even more sophisticated algorithms designed to link us to websites that only reinforce and cater to our views, we can only expect our differences to intensify. This would have alarmed the drafters of our constitution who were acutely aware that different values and interests could prevent Americans from becoming and remaining a single people.

Indeed, of the six objectives they invoked in the Preamble to the Constitution, the one that they put first was the formation of a more perfect union. Their vision of a more perfect union does not exist today if anything, we appear to be moving farther away from it. It is particularly worrisome that the Supreme Court, the institution that most Americans see as the principle guardian of our shared constitutional heritage is viewed as part of the problem through a political lens.

Mr. President, we've heard a lot of charges and countercharges about Judge Kavanaugh, but as those who have known him best have attested, he has been an exemplary public servant, judge, teacher, coach, husband, and father. Despite the turbulent, bitter fight surrounding his nomination, my fervent hope is that Brett Kavanaugh will work to lessen the divisions in the Supreme Court so that we have far fewer 5 to 4 decisions and so that public confidence in our judiciary and our highest court is restored.

Mr. President, I will vote to confirm Judge Kavanaugh. Thank you, Mr. President.

Print Citations

CMS: Collins, Susan. "I Will Vote to Confirm Brett Kavanaugh." Speech at the U.S. Senate, Washington, DC, October 5, 2018. In *The Reference Shelf: Representative American Speeches, 2018–2019,* edited by Sophie Zyla, 94-102. Amenia, NY: Grey House Publishing, 2019.

MLA: Collins, Susan. "I Will Vote to Confirm Brett Kavanaugh." U.S. Senate, 5 October 2018, Washington, DC. Speech. *The Reference Shelf: Representative American Speeches, 2018–2019,* edited by Sophie Zyla, Grey House Publishing, 2019, pp. 94-102.

APA: Collins, S. (2018, October 5). Speech on I will vote to confirm Brett Kavanaugh. U.S. Senate, Washington, DC. In Sophie Zyla (Ed.), *The reference shelf: Representative American speeches, 2018–2019* (pp. 94-102). Amenia, NY: Grey House Publishing.

I'll Be the Bad Guy

By Alexandria Ocasio-Cortez

Alexandria Ocasio-Cortez, popularly referred to as AOC, is an American politician and activist who serves as the U.S. Representative for New York's 14th congressional district. The district includes the eastern part of the Bronx and portions of north-central Queens in New York City. She is the youngest congresswoman ever elected.

AOC: Thank you, chair. Let's play a game.

Let's play a lightning round game. I'm gonna be the bad guy, which I'm sure half the room would agree anyway, and I want to get away with as much bad things as possible, ideally to enrich myself and advance my interests, even if that means putting my interests ahead of the American people.

So, Mrs. Hobert Flynn. And by the way, I have enlisted all of you as my co-conspirators. So you're gonna help me legally get away with all of this.

So, Mrs. Hobert Flynn. I want to run. If I want to run a campaign that is entirely funded by corporate political action committees is there anything that legally prevents me from doing that?

Karen Hobert Flynn: No.

AOC: Okay. So there's nothing stopping me from being entirely funded by corporate PACs say from the fossil fuel industry, the healthcare industry, Big Pharma. I'm entirely, 100 percent lobbyist PAC funded.

Okay, so, let's say, I'm a really, really bad guy.

And let's say I have some skeletons in my closet that I need to cover up so that I can get elected. Mr. Smith, is it true that you wrote this article, this opinion piece for the *Washington Post* entitled "These payments to women were unseemly that doesn't mean they were illegal."

Mr. Smith: Well, I can't see the piece, but I wrote a piece under that headline in the *Post*, so I assume that's right.

AOC: Okay, great, so, green light for hush money. I can do all sorts of terrible things. It's totally legal right now for me to pay people off and that is considered speech. That money is considered speech.

So I used my special interests dark money funded campaign to pay off folks that I needed to pay off and get elected. So, now, I'm elected and now I'm in, I've got the power to draft, lobby, and shape the laws that govern the United States of America.

Fabulous.

Delivered on February 28, 2019, at the U.S. House of Representatives, Washington, DC.

Now, is there any hard limit that I have, perhaps, . . . Mrs. Hobert Flynn? Is there any hard limit that I have in terms of what legislation I'm allowed to touch? Are there any limits on the laws I can write or influence, especially if I'm—based on the special interest funds that accepted to finance my campaign that get me elected in the first place?

Karen Hobert Flynn: There's no limit.

AOC: So, there's none. So I can totally be funded by oil and gas. I can totally be funded by Big Pharma. I can come in, write Big Pharma laws and there's no limits to that whatsoever.

Karen Hobert Flynn: That's right.

AOC: Okay, so. Awesome. Now, Mr. Mehrbani, the last thing I want to do is get rich with as little work as possible. That's really what I'm trying to do with as a bad guy, right? So, is there anything preventing me from holding stocks say in an oil or gas company and then writing laws to deregulate that industry and cause—could potentially cause the stock value to soar and accrue a lot of money in that time.

Rudy Mehrbani: You can do that.

AOC: So I could do that? I could do that now with the way our current laws are set up? Yes?

Rudy Mehrbani: Yes.

AOC: Okay, great. So, my last question is, or one of my last questions I guess I'd say. Is it possible that any elements of this story apply to our current public servants right now?

Rudy Mehrbani: Yes.

AOC: Yes. So we have a system that is fundamentally broken. We have these influences existing in this body, which means that these influences are here in this committee shaping the questions that are being asked of you all right now. Would you say that's correct? Mr. Mehrbani? Or Mr. Shaub?

Mr. Mehrbani: Yes.

AOC: Alright. So. One last thing, Mr. Shaub. In regulation to congressional oversight that we have, the limits that are placed on me as a congresswoman compared to the executive branch and compared to say the President of the United States. Would you say that Congress has the same sort of standard of accountability?

Are there—is there more teeth in that regulation in Congress on the president or would you say it's about even? Or more so on the federal?

Walter Shaub: In terms of laws that apply to the president, yeah, there's almost no laws at all that apply to the president.

AOC: So I'm being held and every person in this body is being held to a higher ethical standard than the President of the United States?

Walter Shaub: That's right because there are some committee, ethics committee rules that apply to you.

AOC: And it's already super legal as we've seen for me to be a pretty bad guy. So, it's even easier for the President of the United States to be one, I would assume.

Walter Shaub: That's right.

AOC: Thank you very much.

Print Citations

- **CMS:** Ocasio-Cortez, Alexandria. "I'll Be the Bad Guy." Speech at the U.S. House of Representatives, Washington, DC, February 28, 2019. In *The Reference Shelf: Representative American Speeches, 2018–2019,* edited by Sophie Zyla, 103-105. Amenia, NY: Grey House Publishing, 2019.

- **MLA:** Ocasio-Cortez, Alexandria. "I'll Be the Bad Guy." U.S. House of Representatives, 28 February 2019, Washington, DC. Speech. *The Reference Shelf: Representative American Speeches, 2018–2019,* edited by Sophie Zyla, Grey House Publishing, 2019, pp. 103-105.

- **APA:** Ocasio-Cortez, A. (2019, February 28). Speech on I'll be the bad guy. U.S. House of Representatives, Washington, DC. In Sophie Zyla (Ed.), *The reference shelf: Representative American speeches, 2018–2019* (pp. 103-105). Amenia, NY: Grey House Publishing.

Harris Kicks Off Her Presidential Campaign

By Kamala Harris

Kamala Harris was sworn in as U.S. senator for California in 2017. She was the second African American woman and first South Asian American senator in history. Harris' passion is fighting injustice and advocating for those who can not defend themselves. She has an undergraduate degree from Howard University and a law degree from the University of California. She served two terms as the district attorney of San Francisco before serving as California's attorney general. Harris' goals include working on a flawed criminal justice system, fighting for middle-class families, and stopping the trafficking of drugs, guns, and people.

Thank you, thank you, thank you, thank you. . . . Oh, my heart is full right now, thank you.

Let me start, I want to thank Libby Schaaf, the great mayor of the City of Oakland here, for giving that incredible introduction, and our longstanding friendship, you know, our mothers were friends together also here in Oakland and I can't thank you Olivia enough for your leadership and your friendship. So here we are. Let me tell you, I am so proud to be a daughter of Oakland, California. And as most of you know, I was born just up the road at Kaiser Hospital. And it was just a few miles away my parents first met as graduate students at UC Berkeley where they were active in the civil rights movement.

And they were born half a world apart from each other. My father, Donald, came from Jamaica to study economics. My mother, Shyamala, came from India to study the science of fighting disease.

And they came here in pursuit of more than just knowledge. Like so many others, they came in pursuit of a dream. And that dream was a dream for themselves, for me and for my sister Maya.

As children growing up here in the East Bay, we were raised by a community with a deep belief in the promise of our country—and, a deep understanding of the parts of that promise that still remain unfulfilled.

We were raised in a community where we were taught to see a world, beyond just ourselves. To be conscious and compassionate about the struggles of all people.

We were raised to believe public service is a noble cause and the fight for justice is everyone's responsibility.

Delivered on January 27, 2019, at the Frank Ogawa Plaza, Oakland, CA.

In fact, my mother used to say "Don't sit around and complain about things, do something." And basically I think she was saying, "You've got to get up and stand up and don't give up the fight!"

And it is this deep-rooted belief that inspired me to become a lawyer and a prosecutor.

It was just a couple of blocks from this very spot that nearly 30 years ago as a young district attorney I walked into the courtroom for the first time and said the five words that would guide my life's work:

"Kamala Harris, for the people."

Now, I knew our criminal justice system was deeply flawed.

But I also knew the profound impact law enforcement has on people's lives, and it's responsibility to give them safety and dignity.

I knew I wanted to protect people.

And I knew that the people in our society who are most often targeted by predators are also most often the voiceless and vulnerable.

I believe, and on that point I believed then as I do now, no one should be left to fight alone.

Because you see, in our system of justice, we believe that a harm against any one of us is a har against all of us. That is why when a case is filed it doesn't read the name of the victim. It reads, "The People."

And this is a point I have often explained to console and counsel survivors of crime, people who faced great harm, often at the hands of someone they trust—be it a relative or a bank or a big corporation.

I would remind them, you are not invisible. We all stand together, because that's the power of the people.

And my whole life, I've only had one client: the people.

Fighting for the people meant fighting on behalf of survivors of sexual assault—a fight not just against predators but a fight against silence and stigma.

For the people meant fighting for a more fair criminal justice system.

At a time when prevention and redemption were not in the vocabulary or mindset of most district attorneys, we created an initiative to get skills and job training instead of jail time for young people arrested for drugs.

For the people meant fighting for middle class families who had been defrauded by banks and were losing their homes by the millions in the Great Recession.

And I'll tell you, sitting across the table from the big banks, I witnessed the arrogance of power. Wealthy bankers accusing innocent homeowners of fault, as if Wall Street's mess was of the people's making.

So we went after the five biggest banks in the United States. We won 20 billion dollars and together we passed the strongest anti-foreclosure law in the United States of America.

For the people meant fighting transnational gangs who traffic in drugs and guns and human beings. And I saw their sophistication, their persistence and their ruthlessness.

And folks, on the subject of transnational gangs, let's be perfectly clear: the president's medieval vanity project is not going to stop them.

And in the fight for the people to hold this administration accountable, I have seen the amazing spirit of the American people.

During the health care fight, I saw parents and children with grave illnesses walk the halls of the United States Congress, families who had travelled across the country at incredible sacrifice.

They came to our nation's capital believing that if their stories were heard, and if they were seen, their leaders would do the right thing.

I saw the same thing with our Dreamers. They came by the thousands. By plane, train and automobile. I'm sure they were sleeping ten-deep on someone's living room floor.

And they came because they believe in our democracy and the only country they've ever known as home.

I met survivors who shared their deepest, most painful personal experiences—who told stories they had never before revealed, even to their closest loved ones—because they believed that if they were seen, that their leaders would do the right thing and protect the highest court in our land.

Together we took on these battles.

And to be sure we won and we've lost, but we have never stopped fighting.

And that's why we are here today.

We are here knowing we are at an inflection point in the history of our world.

We are at an inflection point in the history of our nation.

We are here because the American Dream and our American democracy are under attack and on the line like never before.

We are here at this moment in time because we must answer a fundamental question.

Who are we? Who are we as Americans?

So, let's answer that question, to the world, and each other, right here and right now.

America, we are better than this.

When we have leaders who will bully and attack a free press and undermine our democratic institutions that's not our America.

When white supremacists march and murder in Charlottesville or massacre innocent worshipers in a Pittsburgh synagogue that's not our America.

When we have children in cages crying for their mothers and fathers, don't you dare call that border security, that's a human rights abuse.

When we have leaders who attack public schools and vilify public school teachers that is not our America.

When bankers who crashed our economy get bonuses but the workers who brought our kids' country back can't even get a raise that's not our America.

And when American families are barely living paycheck to paycheck, what is this administration's response?

Their response is to try to take health care away from millions of families.

Their response is to give away a trillion dollars to the biggest corporations in this country.

And their response is to blame immigrants as the source of all our problems.

And guys lets understand what is happening here: People in power are trying to convince us that the villain in our American story is each other.

But that is not our story. That is not who we are. That's not our America.

You see, our United States of America is not about us versus them. It's about We the people.

And in this moment, we must all speak truth about what's happening.

We must seek truth, speak truth and fight for the truth.

So let's speak some truth.

Let's speak truth about our economy. Our economy today is not working for working people.

The cost of living is going up, but paychecks aren't keeping up.

For so many Americans, a decent retirement feels out of reach and the American Dream feels out of touch.

The truth, is our people are drowning in debt.

Record student loan debt, car loan debt, credit card debt. Resorting to payday lenders because you can't keep up with the bills.

People are drowning in America.

We have a whole generation of Americans living with the sinking fear that they won't do as well as their parents.

And let's speak another truth about our economy. Women are paid on average 80 cents on the dollar, black women, 63 cents, Latinas, 53 cents.

And here's the thing. When we lift up the women of our country, we lift up the children of our country. We lift up the families of our country. And society benefits.

Let's speak another truth. Big pharmaceutical companies have unleashed an opioid crisis from the California coast to the mountains of West Virginia. And people once and for all we have got to call drug addiction what it is: a national public health emergency. And what we don't need is another War on Drugs.

Let's speak truth. Climate change is real and it is happening. From wildfires in the west to hurricanes in the east, to floods and droughts in the heartland. But we're not gonna buy the lie. We're gonna act, based on science fact, not science fiction.

And let's speak an uncomfortable but honest truth with one another: racism, sexism, anti-Semitism, homophobia, transphobia are real in this country. And they are age-old forms of hate with new fuel. And we need to speak that truth so we can deal with it.

Let's also speak the truth that too many unarmed black men and women are killed in America. Too many black and brown Americans are being locked up. From mass incarceration to cash bail to policing, our criminal justice system needs drastic repair. Let's speak that truth.

And let's speak truth. Under this administration, America's position in the world has never been weaker. When democratic values are under attack around the globe. When authoritarianism is on the march. When nuclear proliferation is on the rise.

When we have foreign powers infecting the White House like malware. Let's speak truth about what are clear and present dangers.

And let's speak the biggest truth, the biggest truth of all: In the face of powerful forces trying to sow hate and division among us, the truth is that as Americans we have much more in common than what separates us. Let's speak that truth.

And, let's not buy that stuff that some folks are are trying to peddle. Let's never forget, that on the fundamental issues, we all have so much more in common than what separates us.

And you know, some will say that we need to search to find that common ground. Here's what I say, I think we need to recognize we are already standing on common ground.

I say we rise together or we fall together as one nation, indivisible.

And I want to be perfectly clear: I'm not talking about unity for the sake of unity. So hear me out. I'm not talking about unity for the sake of unity.

I'm not talking about some façade of unity.

And I believe we must acknowledge that the word unity has often been used to shut people up or to preserve the status quo.

After all let's remember: when women fought for suffrage, those in power said they were dividing the sexes and disturbing the peace.

Let's remember, when abolitionists spoke out and civil rights workers marched, their oppressors said they were dividing the races and violating the word of God.

But Fredrick Douglass said it best and Harriet Tubman and Dr. King knew.

To love the religion of Jesus is to hate the religion of the slave master.

When we have true unity, no one will be subjugated for others. It's about fighting for a country with equal treatment, collective purpose and freedom for all.

That's who we are.

And so, I stand before you today, clear-eyed about the fight ahead and what has to be done—with faith in God, with fidelity to country, and with the fighting spirit I got from my mother. I stand before you today to announce my candidacy for President of the United States.

And I will tell you I'm running for president because I love my country. I love my country.

I'm running to be president, of the people, by the people, and for all people.

I'm running to fight for an America where the economy works for working people, for an America where you only have to work one job to pay the bills, and where hard work is rewarded and where any worker can join a union.

I am running to declare, once and for all, that health care is a fundamental right, and we will deliver that right with Medicare for All!

I am running to declare education is a fundamental right, and we will guarantee that right with universal pre-k and debt free college!

I am running to guarantee working and middle class families an overdue pay increase. We will deliver the largest working and middle-class tax cut in a generation. Up to $500 a month to help America's families make ends meet.

And we'll pay for it by reversing this administration's giveaways to the top.

I'm running to fight for an America where our democracy and its institutions are protected against all enemies, foreign and domestic.

Which is why I will defend this nation against all threats to our cybersecurity.

We will secure our elections and our critical infrastructure to protect our democracy.

And we will honor our service members and veterans—so no one who has served this country has to wait in line for weeks and months to get what they are owed when they return home on first day.

I'm running to fight for an America where no mother or father has to teach their young son that people may stop him, arrest him, chase him, or kill him, because of his race.

An America where every parent can send their children to school without being haunted by the horror of yet another killing spree.

Where we treat attacks on voting rights and civil rights and women's rights and immigrant rights as attacks on our country itself.

An America where we welcome refugees and bring people out of the shadows, and provide a pathway to citizenship.

An America where our daughters and our sisters and our mothers and our grandmothers are respected where they live and where they work.

Where reproductive rights are not just protected by the Constitution of the United States but guaranteed in every state.

I'll fight for an America where we keep our word and where we honor our promises.

Because that's our America.

And that's the America I believe in.

That's the America I know we believe in. And as we embark on this campaign, I will tell you this: I am not perfect. Lord knows, I am not perfect. But I will always speak with decency and moral clarity and treat all people with dignity and respect. I will lead with integrity. And I will speak the truth.

And of course, we know this is not going to be easy guys. It's not gonna be easy.

We know what the doubters will say.

It's the same thing they've always said.

They'll say it's not your time. They'll say wait your turn. They'll say the odds are long. They'll say it can't be done.

But America's story has always been written by people who can see what can be unburdened by what has been. That is our story. That is our story.

As Robert Kennedy many years ago said, "Only those who dare to fail greatly can ever achieve greatly."

He also said, "I do not lightly dismiss the dangers and the difficulties of challenging an incumbent President, but these are not ordinary times and this is not an ordinary election." He said, "At stake is not simply the leadership of our party and even our country. It is our right to moral leadership of this planet."

So today I say to you my friends, these are not ordinary times. And this will not be an ordinary election. But this is our America.

And so here's the thing. It's up to us.
It's up to us. Each and every one of us.
So let's remember in this fight we have the power of the people.
We can achieve the dreams of our parents and grandparents.
We can heal our nation.
We can give our children the future they deserve.
We can reclaim the American Dream for every single person in our country.
And we can restore America's moral leadership on this planet.
So let's do this.
And let's do it together.
And let's start now.
Thank you. God bless you. And God bless the United States of America.

Print Citations

CMS: Harris, Kamala. "Harris Kicks Off Her Presidential Campaign." Frank Ogawa Plaza, Oakland, CA, January 27, 2019. In *The Reference Shelf: Representative American Speeches, 2018–2019,* edited by Sophie Zyla, 106-112. Amenia, NY: Grey House Publishing, 2019.

MLA: Harris, Kamala. "Harris Kicks Off Her Presidential Campaign." Frank Ogawa Plaza, 27 January 2019, Oakland, CA. Speech. *The Reference Shelf: Representative American Speeches, 2018–2019,* edited by Sophie Zyla, Grey House Publishing, 2019, pp. 106-112.

APA: Harris, K. (2019, January 27). Speech on Harris kicks off her presidential campaign. Frank Ogawa Plaza, Oakland, CA. In Sophie Zyla (Ed.), *The reference shelf: Representative American speeches, 2018–2019* (pp. 106-112). Amenia, NY: Grey House Publishing.

New York City Campaign Rally

By Elizabeth Warren

Elizabeth Warren was the first women elected to the Senate in Massachusetts; she was reelected for a second term to the U.S. Senate. Warren graduated from the University of Houston and Rutgers School of Law. She has been a law professor for over 30 years and has written over a hundred articles and published eleven books, including four best-sellers. She is a leading progressive voice and an advocate for middle-class families. In her speech at a New York City Rally, Warren talks about the giant corporations' role in our government, climate change, gun safety, and healthcare.

Audience: Warren! Warren! Warren!

Senator Warren: Thank you, Maurice. And can we hear it for State Senator Biaggi and Assemblywoman Niou, fabulous. Hello, New York. Now, some of you know this. I never thought I'd get into politics, not in a million years, but when I got into this fight, I quickly found out nobody makes it on their own. If you're going to make any kind of progress in this country, you need allies who know how to fight. And more importantly, you need allies who know how to win. The Working Families Party has been on the front lines of fighting for racial and economic justice and building a grassroots movement to elect the next generation and I am honored to have their support. And tonight with all of you as witnesses, I'm going to make a promise and that is when I'm in the White House, working families will have a champion.

Senator Warren: Thank you Maurice and thank you to the Working Families Party. Now when so many good people show up, I usually do a town hall followed by selfies. Tonight, it's a little something different. I want to tell you a story that I haven't had a chance to tell before. It's an important story about our past and about our future. But I'll stay afterwards for as long as anyone wants to take selfies. Some things we just don't mess with. So I am especially glad to be here in Washington Square Park. I wanted to give this speech right here and not because of the arch behind me or the president that this square is named for, nope. We are not here today because of famous arches or famous men. In fact, we're not here because of men at all.

Senator Warren: We're here because of some hardworking women. Women, who more than a 100 years ago worked long hours in a brown, 10 story building, just a block that way. Women who worked at the Triangle Shirtwaist Factory. So here's what I want you to hear. It was March 25th, 1911, it was a Saturday. And at about 4:45 in the afternoon, people walking through this very park looked up and saw

---

Delivered on September 16, 2019, Washington Square Park, New York, NY.

black smoke billowing into the sky. A fire had started in that building and inside that building on the top three floors, deadly flames leaped from a bin to the oily floors and from the floors to the walls sweeping across workrooms and trapping the workers fighting for their lives. Women, girls really, some as young as 14 raced to escape, but the exit doors were locked. Others ran to the windows, waving their arms and screaming for help. No help was coming. The fire department's ladders could only reach to the sixth floor. The flames leaped higher and women started crawling out onto the ledges. And as people on the ground stood in shocked silence, a woman jumped and then another and then another. They hit the ground with a sickening thud. They died on impact so many so fast that the women's bodies piled up on the sidewalk. Their blood ran into the gutters. Dozens more were tracked inside, trapped because the door to the staircase was locked, locked by bosses afraid that the workers might steal scraps of cloth. Firefighters would later find a pile of burned bodies next to that locked door. It took 18 minutes for 146 people to die. Mostly women, mostly immigrants, Jewish and Italian, mostly people who made as little as five dollars a week to get their shot at the American dream. It was one of the worst industrial disasters in American history, one of the worst, but it should not have been a surprise.

Senator Warren: For years across the city, women factory workers and their allies had been sounding the alarm about dangerous and squalid conditions. Fighting for shorter hours and higher pay. They protested, they went on strike, they got coverage in the press. Everyone knew about these problems, but the fat profits were making New York's factory owners rich and they had no plans to give that up. Instead of changing conditions at the factories, the owners worked their political connections. They made campaign contributions and talked with their friends in the legislature. They had greased the state government so thoroughly that nothing changed. Business owners got richer, politicians got more powerful and working people paid the price. Does any of this sound familiar?

Audience: Yes!

Senator Warren: Take any big problem we have in America today and you don't have to dig very deep to see the same system at work. Climate change, gun safety, healthcare. On the face of it these three are totally different issues, but despite our being the strongest and wealthiest country in the history of the world, our democracy is paralyzed. And why? Because giant corporations have bought off our government. Americans are killed by floods and fires in a rapidly warming planet. Why? Because huge fossil fuel corporations have bought off our government.

Audience: Boo!

Senator Warren: Americans are killed with unthinkable speed and efficiency in our streets and our stores and our schools. Why? Because the gun industry has bought off our government.

Audience: Boo!

Senator Warren: Americans are dying because they can't afford to fill prescriptions or pay for treatment. Why? Because health insurance companies and drug companies have bought off our government.

Audience: Boo!

Senator Warren: Now, Americans disagree on many things, but we don't want each other's homes burned down by wildfires. We don't want each other's children murdered at school and we don't want each other's families bankrupted by medical bills. What we want is for our government to do something. And yet, our federal government is unable to act, unable to take even the most basic steps to protect the American people. Now when you see a government that works great for those with money and connections and doesn't work for much of anyone else, that's corruption plain and simple and we need to call it out for what it is! Corruption has put our planet at risk. Corruption has broken our economy, and corruption is breaking our democracy. I know what's broken, I've got a plan to fix it and hat's why I'm running for President of the United States. There it is. [Inaudible 00:29:09].

Audience: Warren! Warren! Warren! Warren! Warren! Warren!

Senator Warren: Okay, so let's start with the obvious. Donald Trump is corruption in the flesh. He's sworn to serve the people of the United States, but he only serves himself and his partners in corruption. He tries to divide us, white against black, Christians against Muslim, straight against queer and trans and everyone against immigrants.

Senator Warren: Queer and trans and everyone against immigrants. Because if we're all busy fighting each other, no one will notice that he and his buddies are stealing more and more of our country's wealth, and destroying the future for everyone else.

Senator Warren: Now, as bad as things are, we have to recognize our problems didn't start with Donald Trump. He made them worse, but we need to take a deep breath and recognize that a country that elects Donald Trump is already in serious trouble. Republican politicians sold out a long time ago, filling the courts with judges who expand the rights of corporations while they destroy the rights of citizens, passing tax cuts for wealthy donors while doing nothing to help working families, and sucking up corporate donations while lying about climate change, lying about guns and lying about health care. And too many politicians in both parties have convinced themselves that playing the money for influence game is the only way to get something done.

Senator Warren: So, what has this corrupt business as usual gotten us the extinction of one species after another as the earth heats up, children slaughtered by assault weapons, the highest levels of inequality in a century, wages that barely budge, crippling student loan debt, shrinking opportunity for the next generation, and the one after that, and the one after that. The American people get it and they are sick of it. Corruption has taken over our government and we're running out of time. We must rooted out and return our democracy to the people. And yes, I got a plan for that. Okay, so, I got a lot of plans, but they all come back to one simple idea: put economic and political power in the hands of the people. Yeah. And we start by rooting out corruption in government. No more business as usual. Let's attack corruption head on. You ready?

Senator Warren: So, I've got the biggest anti-corruption plan since Watergate. It's a plan to shut down the ability of the rich and powerful to use their money to tilt every decision in Washington. So, I just want to give you a sample of what we can do. End lobbying as we know it. We can do this. No high ranking public official should be thinking about their next job while they're collecting a paycheck to represent the American people. So I have a lifetime ban on senators, congressmen, and cabinet secretaries from ever being lobbyists. And no more hiring corporate lobbyists to staff up the federal government. Look, the right of every person in this country to petition their government does not protect a multibillion dollar influence industry, whose sole purpose is to undermine democracy and tilt every decision in favor of those who can pay. So, let's shut this industry down and return our government to the people. Oh, and there's more. No more secret meetings. Every single meeting between a lobbyist and a public official should be a matter of public record. No more lobbying on behalf of foreign governments, and no more campaign contributions or bundling by lobbyists. Contributing to a campaign at the same time that you're paid to influence those same elected officials is the very definition of bribery, and we're going to put a stop to it.

Senator Warren: And here's another. Anyone, anyone, who wants to run for federal office will have to put their tax returns online. And there's more. Presidents, cabinet members, members of Congress will be barred from owning businesses on the side, barred from trading in individual stocks. You know, look, take care of the people's business or take care of your own business, but you can't do both at the same time.

Senator Warren: Corruption and influence peddling has seeped into every corner of our government, so it's time for some new plans for our regulators. Far too many agencies act like wholly owned subsidiaries of the companies they are supposed to regulate. When these agencies are captured, the results are pollution and financial advisers who cheat people, all while regulators look the other way. Enough is enough. We're going to take down the for sale signs hanging outside of every federal building in Washington.

Senator Warren: Oh, and here's another one. It's also time to call out corruption in the federal judiciary. Increasingly, bigshot corporate lawyers are getting appointed as federal judges, and they turn out one decision after another in favor of corporations and against the interests of American consumers, against unions and against vulnerable people who must count on the courts to protect their rights. Shadowy right wing groups have spent millions of dollars to ram through aggressively unqualified nominees who are likely to advance their causes. No one should be surprised that public confidence in our federal courts is at an all time low, but we can fix it.

Senator Warren: We will rewrite the basic code of ethics for federal judges, and we will appoint a whole new generation of judges with diverse backgrounds and a wide range of legal experiences. Judges who actually believe in fundamental principles like rule of law, civil rights, and equal justice.

Senator Warren: And finally, we will end the corruption of our campaign finance system, overturn Citizens United. Democracy is not for sale. Get rid of super PACs and secret spending by the billionaires, and break the big donors' stranglehold by creating a system of public funding for our elections. Look, I get it. I know that some people will always have more money, so they can own more shoes or more clothes than other people, but no one should own more of our democracy.

Senator Warren: Corruption comes in other forms, too, and I have plans for those. A planned end, the corrupt practice of selling fancy ambassadorships to wealthy donors, because American diplomacy should not be for sale. A plan to abolish private prisons. No one should make a profit locking people up, and no one should have a financial incentive to lobby Congress to lock up even more people. A plan to stop selling access to federal lands and national parks to giant polluters. And to break the stranglehold of the coal industry and the oil industry in energy production and transportation.

Senator Warren: And yeah, when we're talking corruption, we need to call it out in the Oval Office. I read all 448 pages of the Mueller report. No one is above the law, not even the United States president. Impeachment is our constitutional duty. So, there it is.

Audience: Warren! Warren! Warren! Warren! Warren! Warren! Warren! Warren! Warren! Warren! Warren! Warren!

Senator Warren: So, there it is. Step one: tackle corruption head on. Step two: transform our economy so that every person, no matter where they live, no matter who their parents are, no matter how much money they have, every person has real opportunity. The chance to work hard, to play by the same set of rules, and to take care of themselves and the people they love. Corruption in Washington has allowed the rich and the powerful to tilt the rules and grow richer and more powerful. But this small slice at the top hasn't just scooped up a huge chunk of the wealth that all of us have worked so hard to produce. They have gobbled up opportunity itself.

Senator Warren: For the rich and the powerful in this country. There are first, second, third, and fourth chances to get ahead. But for a lot of Americans, especially for people of color, there is barely one, or for some, no chance at all. We have the power to fix that. We are the wealthiest nation in the history of the world.

Audience: Warren! Warren! Warren! Warren! Warren! Warren! Warren! Warren! Warren! Warren! Warren! Warren! Warren!

Senator Warren: We can afford Medicare for all to save our people and a Green New Deal to save our planet. We just need real investments in working people. So, let's start with more power in the hands of workers. Make it easier to join a union and give unions more power when they negotiate. And yes, it's time for a wealth tax.

Audience: Two cents! Two cents! Two cents! Two cents! Two cents! Two cents! Two cents! Two cents! Two cents! Two cents! Two cents! Two cents!

Senator Warren: Yes! Yes, that is a 2 cent tax on fortunes over $50 million. Your first 50 million, don't worry, you're in the clear. But for your 50 millionth and 1st dollar, you got to pitch in 2 cents, and 2 cents for every dollar after that, just two cents.

Audience: Two cents! Two cents! Two cents! Two cents! Two cents! Two cents! Two cents! Two cents! Two cents! Two cents! Two cents!

Senator Warren: So, I look at it this way. You built a great fortune here in this country, worked hard, stayed up late, unlike anyone else. Yeah, you worked hard, you built a great fortune, or you inherited one. Good for you. But I guarantee that any great fortune in America was built, at least in part, using workers all of us helped pay to educate. Built at least in part getting your goods to market on roads and bridges all of us helped pay to build. Built, at least in part, protected by police and firefighters. All of us help pay their salaries.

Senator Warren: And we're happy to do it. This is America. We're happy to invest in opportunities for everyone. But we're saying that if you make it big, really big, really, really big, the top one 10th of 1%, bigger than $50 million, then pitch in two cents so everyone else gets a chance to make it. Yeah.

Audience: Two cents! Two cents! Two cents! Two cents! Two cents! Two cents! Two cents! Two cents! Two cents! Two cents!

Senator Warren: And what can we do with two cents? Oh, universal child care for every baby in this country age zero to five, universal pre-K for every three year old and four year olds in America, and raise the wages of every childcare worker and preschool teacher in this country. All that for two cents and more.

Senator Warren: We can make technical school, community college and four year college tuition free for everyone who wants to get an education. And we can truly level the playing field, and put $50 billion directly into our historically black colleges and universities, and other minority serving institutions. All of that, and we can cancel student loan debt for 95% of the folks who've got it.

Senator Warren: So, think of what that means. Real opportunity, not just opportunity for people born into privilege, opportunity for everyone. And opportunity, real opportunity, requires honesty. Working families all across this country have been denied the opportunities they deserve. But the path for Black and Brown and Native families has been even steeper. And that is why my plans tackle historical injustice head on. And here are a few examples.

Senator Warren: My student debt cancellation plan will help close the wealth gap between black and white families. My criminal justice plan well end the practice of mass incarceration that has destroyed the lives of so many Black and Brown men. My housing plan will help families living in formerly redlined areas buy a home and start building the kind of wealth that government-sponsored discrimination denied their parents and grandparents. My climate plan includes justice for the Black and Brown communities that have struggled with the impact of pollution. And my plan respects the rights of Native Americans to protect their lands and be good stewards of this Earth. And on day one of my administration, I love the thought of what a president can do all by herself.

Senator Warren: On day one of my administration, I will use my executive authority to start closing the pay gap between women of color and everyone else because it's about time we valued the work of women of color. We must recognize the systemic discrimination that infects our economy, and we must work actively and deliberately to root it out and set this country on a better path. The time for holding back is over. We need big, structural change.

Senator Warren: Now, I know what some of you are thinking. I do. Whoa, too much. Too big. Too hard.

Audience: No!

Senator Warren: Okay, nobody here, but we know there's some people over there, way, way out. Okay. But, you know, I know this change is possible, and I know it because America has made big, structural change before.

Senator Warren: Let me take you back to the day of that fire. A woman was visiting friends who lived in a townhouse right behind me. When the fire broke out, she hurried into the street. She joined the crowds as they ran across the park and headed to the Triangle Factory. And when she got there, she stood and she watched. She watched as women on the ledge, begged for help. She watched as they held each other. She watched as they jumped to their deaths.

Senator Warren: The woman watching was Francis Perkins. She was 30 years old and already a worker's rights activist, but that day set change in motion. A week later, the women's trade unions organized a funeral March and a half a million people showed up to march on Fifth Avenue right behind me. Half a million people in 1911. And it wasn't their first march, but this time it was different.

Senator Warren: While the women of the trade unions kept pushing from the outside, Francis pushed from the inside. She understood that those women died because of the greed of their bosses and the corruption of elected officials. So, she went up to Albany ready to fight. She worked to create a commission investigating factory conditions, and then she served as its lead investigator. Now, everybody just remember, this was years before women could even vote, let alone hold major roles in government. But Francis had a plan.

Senator Warren: She and her fellow activists fought for fire safety and they got it. So, the next time you do a fire drill at school or at work, you see a plainly marked fire exit, think of Francis and the Triangle Women, because they are the reason the laws changed. But they didn't stop with fire safety. With Francis working the system from the inside, and the women workers organizing and applying pressure from the outside, they rewrote New York state's labor laws from top to bottom, to protect workers. Now, over time, Francis Perkins became the state's leading expert on working conditions, and later, when Franklin Roosevelt was elected governor, he appointed her to head his labor department in Albany. And four years after that, in the depths of the Great Depression, when Roosevelt became president, he asked Francis to come to Washington to address the crisis as Secretary of Labor for the entire nation.

Senator Warren: Francis Perkins became the first woman in history to serve in the cabinet. Yeah. And what did she push for when she got there? Big structural change. She used the same model that she and her friends had used after the Triangle fire. She worked the political system relentlessly from the inside, while a sustained movement applied pressure from the outside. As Francis Perkins put it, the Triangle fire was the day the New Deal was born.

Senator Warren: So, here's what I want you to think about. What did one woman, one very persistent woman, one woman backed up by millions of people across this country get done? Social security, unemployment insurance, abolition of child labor, minimum wage, the right to join a union, and even the very existence of the weekend! That's big, structural change! One woman and millions of people to back her up.

Senator Warren: The tragic story of the Triangle Factory fire is a story about power, a story of what happens when the rich and the powerful take control of government and use it to increase their own profits while they stick it to working people. But what happened in the aftermath of the fire is a different story about power. A story about our power, a story about what's possible when we fight together as one.

Senator Warren: Over and over throughout our history, Americans have been told that big, structural change just wasn't possible, and that they should just give up. The abolitionists were told, "It's just too hard. Give up now." The suffragettes were told, "Too hard. Give up now." The early union organizers were told, "It's just too hard. Give up now." Foot soldiers in the Civil Rights Movement were told, "Too hard. Give up now." LGBTQ activists were told, "It's just too hard. Give up now." But they didn't give up!

Senator Warren: No. They didn't give up. They organized, they built a grassroots movement. They persisted, and they changed the course of American history.

Audience: Warren! Warren! Warren! Warren! Warren! Warren! Warren! Warren! Warren! Warren! Warren! Warren! Warren! Warren!

Senator Warren: 2020 is about the direction our America goes, not just for four years, but for generations to come. And yeah, there's a lot at stake in this election, and I know people are scared, but we can't choose a candidate we don't believe in just because we're too scared to do anything else. And Democrats can't win if we're scared and looking backward. We win when we meet the moment. We win when we stand up for what is right. We win when we get out there and fight.

Audience: Warren! Warren! Warren!

Senator Warren: I am not afraid. And you can't be afraid either. So, if you're ready to fight, then join me. Go to elizabethwarren.com, help us organize, volunteer, donate five bucks, text FIGHT to 24477. We need everyone.

Print Citations

CMS: Warren, Elizabeth. "New York City Campaign Rally." Speech at Washington Square Park, New York, NY, September 16, 2019. In *The Reference Shelf: Representative American Speeches, 2018–2019,* edited by Sophie Zyla, 113-121. Amenia, NY: Grey House Publishing, 2019.

MLA: Warren, Elizabeth. "New York City Campaign Rally." Washington Square Park, 16 September 2019, New York, NY. Speech. *The Reference Shelf: Representative American Speeches, 2018–2019,* edited by Sophie Zyla, Grey House Publishing, 2019, pp. 113-121.

APA: Warren, E. (2019, September 16). Speech at New York City campaign rally. Washington Square Park, New York, NY. In Sophie Zyla (Ed.), *The reference shelf: Representative American speeches, 2018–2019* (pp. 113-121). Amenia, NY: Grey House Publishing.

Exploring a 2020 Run Against Donald Trump

By Bill Weld

Bill Weld is a Republican presidential candidate for 2020. Weld was the governor of Massachusetts from 1991–1997, assistant attorney general for the U.S. Criminal Division from 1986-1988, and U.S. attorney for Massachusetts from 1981–1986. He received a bachelor's degree from Harvard College, a diploma in international economics from Oxford University, and a JD from Harvard Law School. Weld believes that it is possible to cut federal spending, to restructure the tax system, and ensure freedom for consumers to choose health care providers and where they will purchase pharmaceutical drugs. Weld believes that addiction is a national health emergency.

Thank you, Jim Brett, my longtime friend and colleague. May I say what a pleasure it always is to be back in New Hampshire. Since I was a boy, I've had a happy relationship with the waters and woods of New Hampshire, enjoying visits to Henniker, Center Sandwich and Gilsum. I have my share of vivid political memories in New Hampshire as well. I was present in Nashua for the famous Reagan-Bush debate in 1980, I campaigned with Bush 41 in 1992, manning the microphone on primary night, and I enjoyed traveling the state with Governor Judd Gregg when he campaigned successfully for the Senate. But it is not my fond memories of New Hampshire that bring me here today.

I'm here because I think our country is in grave peril, and I cannot sit quietly on the sidelines any longer. We have a President who openly praises and encourages despotic and authoritarian leaders abroad, while going out of his way to insult and even humiliate our democratic allies. Why? We have a President who has set out to unravel, rather than promote, arms control agreements with other nuclear powers. Why? He has lightly tossed around threats of the United States itself using nuclear weapons. Why? He has railed against the very idea of the rule of law, the cornerstone of our individual freedoms. Why? He has virtually spat upon the idea that we should have freedom of the press. Why? He has failed to call out and denounce appalling instances of racism. Why? He ridicules and dismisses the looming threats from climate change. Why? He has demonstrated a repeated pattern of vindictiveness. (He calls it "counterpunching," but it's actually vindictiveness.) He acts like a schoolyard bully, except of course when he is around other bullies, like Mr. Putin, and then he turns ingratiating, all smiles, kicks the American press out of the Oval

---

Delivered on February 15, 2019, at the Bedford Village Inn, Bedford, NH.

Office, and has his summit meeting with no news media present except Tass—the Russian state organ! For what possible reason?

The answer to all these questions, and I say this with a heavy heart, is that we have a President whose priorities are skewed toward promotion of himself rather than toward the good of the country. He may have great energy and considerable raw talent, but he does not use them in ways that promote democracy, truth, justice and equal opportunity for all. To compound matters, our President is simply too unstable to carry out the duties of the highest executive office—which include the specific duty to take care that the laws be faithfully executed—in a competent and professional manner. He is simply in the wrong place.

They say the President has captured the Republican party in Washington. Sad. But even sadder is that many Republicans exhibit all the symptoms of Stockholm Syndrome, identifying with their captor.

The truth is that we have wasted an enormous amount of time by humoring this President, indulging him in his narcissism and his compulsive, irrational behaviors. Recently there have been occasions when our national government seemed almost a charade: the lights are on in the White House, but no one's home. Many people around the President are consumed in passively admiring the emperor's new clothes—as he insists.

The situation is not yet hopeless, but we do need a mid-course correction. We don't need six more years of the antics we have seen. We need to make a change, and install leaders who know that character counts.

Many aspects of our current morass in Washington cry out for bold action—before it is too late. First of all, the amount of extra debt being run up in Washington is completely crazy. The Administration is spending a trillion dollars a year more than it takes in. And they call themselves conservatives! That's a trillion dollars of debt for our children and grandchildren to pay off. That's not fair, to put it mildly, to members of the X-generation or to millennials.

None of the States do this. Most States require by their Constitution that the Governor's budget be balanced. Unfortunately, especially in the left wing of the Democratic party, socialism seems to have replaced any notion of spending restraint.

We need the opposite of socialism. In the federal budget, the two most important tasks are to cut spending and to cut taxes—and spending comes first. We need to "zero base" the federal budget, basing each appropriation on outcomes actually achieved, not on last year's appropriation plus 5 per cent, which is what too many folks in Washington use as a starting point.

It is actually possible to cut spending year over year. I did that when I got into office, and I was rated the most fiscally conservative Governor in the country by the *Wall Street Journal* and the Cato Institute. This President should be able to do the same. Don't worry, Mr. President, it doesn't hurt the economy: our unemployment rate in Massachusetts went from the highest rate to the lowest rate among all the industrialized states, in my first three years in office.

There's also a huge opportunity to cut federal spending by contracting out the provision of social services to the private sector, particularly the vast network of non-profit organizations. Based on our experience in Massachusetts, this will save a great deal of taxpayers' money and improve the quality of the services and the degree of compassion and dignity afforded to the people receiving the services. The reason is that monopoly services are always less efficient than competitively priced services. So the key distinction is not public versus private: it's monopoly versus competition.

The best way to deal with government spending is to deal with it as Smokey the Bear recommends dealing with fire: keep it small, keep it in a confined area, and keep it under observation.

Right after cutting spending comes cutting taxes. Federal taxes need serious adjustment downward. I favor repealing the federal death tax, for example, and cutting the capital gains tax rate to 10%. These taxes are not major revenue raisers, and they both have the perverse effect of penalizing people for a lifetime of hard work. Eliminating them will increase our aggregate national wealth, which should always be a key priority of the United States government.

But we also need to restructure our entire tax system. We don't need to choose between Robin Hood-style confiscatory taxation and deficit-creating tax cuts for the super-rich. We should instead take a good long look at some other models, such as a 19% flat tax on income, and the famous "post card" tax return. I have read extensively on the subject, and I believe the savings from the dramatic simplification of the Internal Revenue Code and the whole process of taxation would be enormous.

As to health care, instead of arguing endlessly and fruitlessly about whether the Affordable Care Act should be repealed—because let's face it, we do not have a consensus in Congress—there are various commonsense health care issues that could be addressed immediately, across party lines. Consumers should be permitted to establish personal health care savings accounts, and to choose their health care provider. They should be free to purchase pharmaceutical drugs across state lines and also in other countries. Their choice, not the government's.

Veterans should be permitted to receive health care from hospitals and health care providers outside the exclusive network of V.A. hospitals. They should be permitted to use cannabis for the relief of post-traumatic stress disorder without losing their veteran's benefits, as is the case under current V.A. law.

The elderly must be permitted to have full access to non-addictive drugs which are useful for the relief of pain, including cannabis and CBD.

Addiction of all types should be treated as the national public health emergency that it is, rather than as a crime of status and a top priority for the US criminal justice system. We should also move on to bail reform, funding for reentry programs, and other criminal justice reforms not reached by the recent First Step legislation.

In fairness to millennials, who may never receive the benefits of social security, the government should permit the establishment of individual retirement accounts. In fairness to young adults in the military, they should not be asked to risk their lives in order to engineer regime changes in foreign countries at the whim of the US government, in the absence of any substantial threat to the United States.

With respect to the environment and climate change, the approach of the current Administration is antithetical to every principle of conservation and conservatism, and every tenet of Theodore Roosevelt's Grand Old Party.

Whether as protection of a fragile ecosystem or as stewardship of God's creation, there is a pressing need to act on climate change. The United States must rejoin the Paris climate accords, and adopt targets consonant with those of other industrialized nations.

We must protect our economy, yes, but we must also recognize that increased natural disasters and unfamiliar weather patterns threaten to strip the snow from our White Mountains, and to melt all the mountain glaciers worldwide upon which hundreds of millions of people depend for their only source of water. Europe has its cathedrals and monuments; we have our mountains, canyons, valleys, rivers and streams—and we had damn well better take care of them. Our borders are safe in New Hampshire, but it is not a stretch to say that if climate change is not addressed, our coastlines and those of all other countries will over time be obliterated by storm surge and the melting of the polar ice cap. Yet climate skeptics claim that they are conservative!

On the international front, the United States should return to a regime of free trade rather than having constant recourse to tariffs. Mr. Smoot and Mr. Hawley tried tariffs in June, 1930, and fanned the flames of the Great Depression.

When it comes to immigration, we should adopt a robust guest worker program, to assist our agricultural and construction industries, particularly in the western states. We don't need a path to citizenship for eleven million people, but we do need more and longer work visas. Under the current regime, we're simply educating our competition in our graduate schools, and then sending them home to China and other economic competitors of the U.S. We may not need a long impenetrable wall, but we do need short-term bridges.

Domestically, our most immediate priority must be jobs and wages. What are we going to do about the fact that 25% of all the jobs in the United States today won't exist in 15 years? This is not caused by the unseen hands of globalization or the internet, but rather by the soon to be all-too-visible hands of robotics, drones, machine learning, artificial intelligence, and autonomous vehicles. The old jobs will be replaced by new and different jobs, but the problem is that today's workers don't yet possess the skill sets that the replacement jobs will require. This truly is a national emergency, and it's going to require a nationwide response.

The skills required by the new jobs correspond roughly to the skills now taught in the first two years of post-secondary education, or the community college level. But a displaced worker can't take two years off and pay two years' tuition to acquire those skills. Accordingly, we should adjust our budget priorities to cover the cost of in-state tuition for those displaced workers, as we did for our returning veterans under the G.I. Bill following World War II. In addition, to cut down on room and board expense, we should encourage and embrace on-line education. It has now been proved that distance learning is as effective as learning in a bricks and mortar classroom, so we should take advantage of that.

What I am suggesting will be a tiny budget adjustment—the equivalent of a small round hole in the snow, particularly if shared with the federal government—but it will solve an enormous problem. It will make all the difference in the world to those workers. If we do this educational component right, we should be able to ensure that the new jobs—the replacement jobs—have higher wages than the old jobs. That would truly be a happy ending. But if we don't do this, the door to the middle class may be closed to the working poor. That would be an end game that we as a society cannot afford.

A system for delivering new skill sets is not the only area of education that cries out for action in the future. Parents need more options regarding the education of their children. We need to support school choice. We need to support home schooling. We need to support charter schools. And we need to consider abolishing the U.S. Department of Education, transferring decision-making authority to the States and the parents of school-age and college-age children.

Oh, and the current federal provision which prevents the renegotiation of student debt? We need to repeal it immediately.

Finally, it should go without saying, but as was deeply impressed on me during my seven years in the U.S. Justice Department, our country must always stand tall for integrity and the rule of law, without fear or favor; we must insist on the rule of law!

As you can tell from my remarks, I care a great deal about the kind of government we have in Washington, and I hope to see the Republican Party assume once again the mantle of being the party of Lincoln. It upsets me that our energies as a society are being sapped by the President's culture of divisiveness in Washington. The United States was founded in the spirit of national unity. America is stronger, and can afford to be more generous, when it is united rather than divided. There is a place and time for opposition and dissent, there is always room for healthy debate. But there should be no hatred, no intimidation, no name- 8 calling between the various arms of the federal government, or between groups of citizens. Like President Reagan, like President Eisenhower, our leaders in government should seek to unite us and make us all proud to be Americans—and never, ever seek to divide us.

Because of the many concerns I have talked of today, I am establishing an Exploratory Committee to pursue the possibility of my running for the Presidency of the United States as a Republican in the 2020 election. I encourage those of you who are watching the current administration nervously but saying nothing to stand up and speak out when lines are crossed in dangerous ways. We cannot sit passively as our precious democracy slips quietly into darkness. Congress must do its duty, and as citizens we must do ours.

As we move toward the 2020 election year, each of us must also strive to remember and uphold the difference between the open heart, open mind and open handedness of patriotism versus the hard heart, closed mind and clenched fist of nativism and nationalism.

In every country there comes a time when patriotic men and women must stand up and speak out to protect their own individual rights and the overall health of the nation. In our country, this is such a time. It is time for all people of good will—and our country is filled with people of good will—to take a stand and plant a flag.

Abraham Lincoln might have called it the flag of the Union. Today we call it the flag of the United—yes, United! —States of America.

Thank you all very much.

Print Citations

CMS: DeCosta-Klipa, Nik. "Bill Weld's Speech on Exploring a 2020 Run against Donald Trump." Speech at the Bedford Village Inn, Bedford, NH, February 15, 2019. In *The Reference Shelf: Representative American Speeches, 2018–2019,* edited by Sophie Zyla, 122-127. Amenia, NY: Grey House Publishing, 2019.

MLA: DeCosta-Klipa, Nik. "Bill Weld's Speech on Exploring a 2020 Run against Donald Trump." Bedford Village Inn, 15 February 2019, Bedford, NH. Speech. *The Reference Shelf: Representative American Speeches, 2018–2019,* edited by Sophie Zyla, Grey House Publishing, 2019, pp. 122-127.

APA: DeCosta-Klipa, N. (2019, February 15). Bill Weld's speech on exploring a 2020 run against Donald Trump. Bedford Inn, Bedford, NH. In Sophie Zyla (Ed.), *The reference shelf: Representative American speeches, 2018–2019* (pp. 122-127). Amenia, NY: Grey House Publishing.

Hearing of Former Attorney to President Donald Trump

By Michael Cohen

Michael Cohen began his career as a private injury lawyer and opened his own practice before expanding into the taxicab business in New York and Chicago. He also dealt in New York City real estate, a casino cruise ship business, and medical clinics and billing companies. Cohen began working for Donald Trump in 2007 as a legal and real estate advisor, and he eventually became special counsel and executive vice president of the Trump Organization. Cohen continued to defend Trump in the early period of his presidency as his personal attorney. Cohen has a degree from American University and a law degree from Thomas M. Cooley Law School.

Chairman Cummings, Ranking Member Jordan, and members of the committee, thank you for inviting me here today. I have asked this committee to ensure that my family be protected from Presidential threats, and that the committee be sensitive to the questions pertaining to ongoing investigations. I thank you for your help and for your understanding.

I am here under oath to correct the record, to answer the committee's questions truthfully, and to offer the American people what I know about President Trump. I recognize that some of you may doubt and attack me on my credibility. It is for this reason that I have incorporated into this opening statement documents that are irrefutable, and demonstrate that the information you will hear is accurate and truthful.

Never in a million years did I imagine when I accepted a job in 2007 to work for Donald Trump that he would one day run for the presidency, to launch a campaign on a platform of hate and intolerance, and actively win. I regret the day I said yes to Mr. Trump. I regret all the help and support I gave him along the way. I am ashamed of my own failings and publicly accepted responsibility for them by pleading guilty in the Southern District of New York. I am ashamed of my weakness and my misplaced loyalty of the things I did for Mr. Trump in an effort to protect and promote him.

I am ashamed that I chose to take part in concealing Mr. Trump's illicit acts rather than listening to my own conscience. I am ashamed, because I know what Mr. Trump is. He is a racist, he is a con man, and he is a cheat.

Delivered on February 27, 2019, at the U.S. House of Representatives, Washington, DC.

He was a Presidential candidate who knew that Roger Stone was talking with Julian Assange about a WikiLeaks drop on Democratic National Committee emails. And I will explain each in a few moments.

I am providing the committee today with several documents, and these include a copy of a check Mr. Trump wrote from his personal bank account, after he became President, to reimburse me for the hush money payments I made to cover up his affair with an adult film star, and to prevent damage to his campaign. Copies of financial statements from 2011, 2012, and 2013 that he gave to such institutions such as Deutsche Bank, a copy of an article with Mr. Trump's handwriting on it that reported on the auction of a portrait of himself that he arranged for the bidder ahead of time and then reimbursed the bidder from the account of his nonprofit charitable foundation, with the picture now hanging in one of his country clubs, and copies of letters I wrote at Mr. Trump's direction that threatened his high school, colleges, and the College Board not to release his grades or SAT scores.

I hope my appearance here today, my guilty plea, and my work with law enforcement agencies are steps along a path of redemption that will restore faith in me and help this country understand our President better.

Before going further, I want to apologize to each member, to you as Congress, as a whole. The last time I appeared before Congress, I came to protect Mr. Trump. Today, I am here to tell the truth about Mr. Trump. I lied to Congress when Mr. Trump stopped negotiating the Moscow tower project in Russia. I stated that we stopped negotiating in January 2016. That was false. Our negotiations continued for months later during the campaign.

Mr. Trump did not directly tell me to lie to Congress. That's not how he operates. In conversations we had during the campaign, at the same time, I was actively negotiating in Russia for him, he would look me in the eye and tell me, there's no Russian business, and then go on to lie to the American people by saying the same thing. In his way, he was telling me to lie.

There are at least a half a dozen times between the Iowa caucus in January 2016 and the end of June when he would ask me how's it going in Russia, referring to the Moscow tower project.

You need to know that Mr. Trump's personal lawyers reviewed and edited my statement to Congress about the timing of the Moscow tower negotiations before I gave it. So to be clear, Mr. Trump knew of and directed the Trump-Moscow negotiations throughout the campaign and lied about it. He lied about it because he never expected to win. He also lied about it because he stood to make hundreds of millions of dollars on the Moscow real estate project.

So I lied about it too, because Mr. Trump had made clear to me, through his personal statements to me that we both knew to be false and through his lies to the country, that he wanted me to lie. And he made it clear to me, because his personal attorneys reviewed my statement before I gave it to Congress.

Over the past two years, I have been smeared as a rat by the President of the United States. The truth is much different. And let me take a brief moment to introduce myself.

My name is Michael Dean Cohen, and I am a blessed husband of 24 years and a father to an incredible daughter and son.

When I married my wife, I promised her that I would love her, I would cherish her, and I would protect her. As my father said countless times throughout my childhood, you, my wife, and you, my children, are the air that I breathe.

So to my Laura and to my Sami, and to my Jake, there is nothing I wouldn't do to protect you.

I have always tried to live a life of loyalty, friendship, generosity, and compassion. It is qualities my parents engrained in my siblings and me since childhood. My father survived the Holocaust. Thanks to the compassion and selfless acts of others, he was helped by many who put themselves in harm's way to do what they knew was right. And that is why my first instinct has always been to help those in need. And Mom and Dad, I am sorry I let you down.

As the many people that know me best would say, I am the person that they call at 3 a.m. if they needed help. And I proudly remember being the emergency contact for many of my children's friends when they were growing up, because their parents knew that I would drop everything and care for them as if they were my own.

Yet last fall, I pled guilty in Federal court to felonies for the benefit of, at the direction of, and in coordination with individual No. 1. And for the record, individual No. 1 is President Donald J. Trump.

It is painful to admit that I was motivated by ambition at times. It is even more painful to admit that many times I ignored my conscience and acted loyal to a man when I should not have. Sitting here today, it seems unbelievable that I was so mesmerized by Donald Trump that I was willing to do things for him that I knew were absolutely wrong. For that reason, I have come here to apologize to my family, to my government, and to the American people.

Accordingly, let me now tell you about Mr. Trump.

I got to know him very well working very closely with him for more than 10 years as his executive vice president and special counsel, and then as personal attorney when he became President.

When I first met Mr. Trump, he was a successful entrepreneur, a real estate giant, and an icon. Being around Mr. Trump was intoxicating. When you were in his presence, you felt like you were involved in something greater than yourself, that you were somehow changing the world. I wound up touting the Trump narrative for over a decade. That was my job. Always stay on message. Always defend. It monopolized my life.

At first, I worked mostly on real estate developments and other business transactions. Shortly thereafter, Mr. Trump brought me into his personal life and private dealings. Over time, I saw his true character revealed.

Mr. Trump is an enigma. He is complicated, as am I. He is both good and bad, as are we all. But the bad far outweighs the good. And since taking office, he has become the worst version of himself.

He is capable of behaving kindly, but he is not kind. He is capable of committing acts of generosity, but he is not generous. He is capable of being loyal, but he is fundamentally disloyal.

Donald Trump is a man who ran for office to make his brand great, not to make our country great. He had no desire or intention to lead this Nation, only to market himself and to build his wealth and power.

Mr. Trump would often say this campaign was going to be the greatest infomercial in political history. He never expected to win the primary. He never expected to win the general election. The campaign for him was always a marketing opportunity.

I knew early on in my work for Mr. Trump that he would direct me to lie to further his business interests. And I am ashamed to say that when it was for a real estate mogul in the private sector, I considered it trivial. As the President, I consider it significant and dangerous.

In the mix, lying for Mr. Trump was normalized, and no one around him questioned it. In fairness, no one around him today questions it either. A lot of people have asked me about whether Mr. Trump knew about the release of the hacked documents, the Democratic National Committee emails ahead of time. And the answer is yes.

As I earlier stated, Mr. Trump knew from Roger Stone in advance about the WikiLeaks drop of emails. In July 2016, days before the Democratic Convention, I was in Mr. Trump's office when his secretary announced that Roger Stone was on the phone. Mr. Trump put Mr. Stone on the speaker phone. Mr. Stone told Mr. Trump that he had just gotten off the phone with Julian Assange, and that Mr. Assange told Mr. Stone that within a couple of days, there would be a massive dump of emails that would damage Hillary Clinton's campaign.

Mr. Trump responded by stating to the effect, Wouldn't that be great.

Mr. Trump is a racist. The country has seen Mr. Trump court white supremacists and bigots. You have heard him call poorer countries shitholes. His private—in private he is even worse.

He once asked me if I can name a country run by a black person that wasn't a shithole. This was when Barack Obama was President of the United States. And while we were once driving through a struggling neighborhood in Chicago, he commented that only black people could live that way. And he told me that black people would never vote for him because they were too stupid. And yet, I continued to work for him.

Mr. Trump is a cheat. As previously stated, I am giving to the committee today three years of Mr. Trump's personal financial statements from 2011, 2012, and 2013, which he gave to Deutsche Bank to inquire about a loan to buy the Buffalo Bills and to Forbes. These are exhibits 1A, 1B, and 1C to my testimony.

It was my experience that Mr. Trump inflated his total assets when it served his purposes, such as trying to be listed amongst the wealthiest people in *Forbes* and deflated his assets to reduce his real estate taxes.

I'm sharing with you two newspaper articles side-by-side that are examples of Mr. Trump inflating and deflating his assets, as I said, to suit his financial interests. These are exhibit 2 to my testimony.

As I noted, I'm giving the committee today an article he wrote on and sent to me that reported on an auction of a portrait of Mr. Trump. This is exhibit 3A to my testimony. Mr. Trump directed me to find a straw bidder to purchase a portrait of him that was being auctioned off at an art Hampton's event. The objective was to ensure that this portrait, which was going to be auctioned last, would go for the highest price of any portrait that afternoon. The portrait was purchased by the fake bidder for $60,000.

Mr. Trump directed the Trump Foundation, which is supposed to be a charitable organization, to repay the fake bidder, despite keeping the art for himself. And please see exhibit 3B to my testimony.

It should come as no surprise that one of my more common responsibilities was that Mr. Trump directed me to call business owners, many of whom are small businesses, that were owed money for their services and told them that no payment or a reduced payment would be coming. When I asked Mr. Trump—or when I told Mr. Trump of my success, he actually reveled in it. And yet, I continued to work for him.

Mr. Trump is a con man. He asked me to pay off an adult film star with whom he had an affair, and to lie about it to his wife, which I did. And lying to the First Lady is one of my biggest regrets, because she is a kind, good person, and I respect her greatly. And she did not deserve that.

I am giving the committee today a copy of the $130,000 wire transfer from me to Ms. Clifford's attorney during the closing days of the Presidential campaign that was demanded by Ms. Clifford to maintain her silence about her affair with Mr. Trump. And this is exhibit 4 to my testimony.

Mr. Trump directed me to use my own personal funds from a home equity line of credit to avoid any money being traced back to him that could negatively impact his campaign. And I did that too, without bothering to consider whether that was improper much less whether it was the right thing to do, or how it would impact me, my family, or the public. And I am going to jail, in part, because of my decision to help Mr. Trump hide that payment from the American people before they voted a few days later.

As exhibit 5A to my testimony shows, I am providing a copy of a $35,000 check that President Trump personally signed from his personal bank account on August 1 of 2017, when he was President of the United States, pursuant to the cover-up which was the basis of my guilty plea to reimburse me, the word used by Mr. Trump's TV lawyer for the illegal hush money I paid on his behalf.

This $35,000 check was one of 11 check installments that was paid throughout the year while he was President. Other checks to reimburse me for the hush money payments were signed by Donald Trump, Jr., and Allen Weisselberg. And see that example, 5B.

The President of the United States thus wrote a personal check for the payment of hush money as part of a criminal scheme to violate campaign finance laws. And you can find the details of that scheme directed by Mr. Trump in the pleadings in the U.S. District Court for the Southern District of New York.

So picture this scene. In February 2017, one month into his presidency, I'm visiting President Trump in the oval office for the first time, and it's truthfully awe-inspiring. He's showing me all around and pointing to different paintings. And he says to me something to the effect of, Don't worry, Michael. Your January and February reimbursement checks are coming. They were FedEx'd from New York. And it takes a while for that to get through the White House system.

As he promised, I received the first check for the reimbursement of $70,000 not long thereafter.

When I say con man, I'm talking about a man who declares himself brilliant, but directed me to threaten his high school, his colleges, and the College Board to never release his grades or SAT scores. As I mentioned, I'm giving the committee today copies of a letter I sent at Mr. Trump's direction, threatening these schools with civil and criminal actions if Mr. Trump's grades or SAT scores were ever disclosed without his permission. And these are under exhibit 6.

The irony wasn't lost on me at the time that Mr. Trump, in 2011, had strongly criticized President Obama for not releasing his grades. As you can see in exhibit 7, Mr. Trump declared, Let him show his records, after calling President Obama a terrible student.

The sad fact is that I never heard Mr. Trump say anything in private that led me to believe he loved our Nation or wanted to make it better. In fact, he did the opposite. When telling me in 2008 or 2009 that he was cutting employees' salaries in half, including mine. He showed me what he claimed was a $10 million IRS tax refund. And he said that he could not believe how stupid the government was for giving someone like him that much money back.

During the campaign, Mr. Trump said that he did not consider Vietnam veteran and prisoner of war, Senator John McCain, to be a hero because he likes people who weren't captured. At the same time, Mr. Trump tasked me to handle the negative press surrounding his medical deferment from the Vietnam draft.

Mr. Trump claimed it was because of a bone spur. But when I asked for medical records, he gave me none and said that there was no surgery. He told me not to answer the specific questions by reporters, but rather, offer simply the fact that he received a medical deferment. He finished the conversation with the following comment. "You think I'm stupid? I'm not going to Vietnam." And I find it ironic, Mr. President, that you are in Vietnam right now. And yet, I continued to work for him.

The questions have been raised about whether I know of direct evidence that Mr. Trump or his campaign colluded with Russia. I do not. And I want to be clear. But I have my suspicions.

Sometime in the summer of 2017, I read all over the media that there had been a meeting in Trump Tower in June 2016 involving Don Jr. and others from the campaign with Russians, including a representative of the Russian Government, and an email setting up the meeting with the subject line, Dirt on Hillary Clinton.

Something clicked in my mind. I remembered being in a room with Mr. Trump, probably in early June 2016, when something peculiar happened. Don Trump, Jr. came into the room and walked behind his father's desk, which in and of itself was unusual. People didn't just walk behind Mr. Trump's desk to talk to him.

I recalled Don Jr. leaning over to his father and speaking in a low voice, which I could clearly hear, and saying, "The meeting is all set." And I remember Mr. Trump saying, "OK. Good. Let me know."

What struck me as I look back and thought about the exchange between Don Jr. and his father was, first, that Mr. Trump had frequently told me and others that his son Don Jr. had the worst judgment of anyone in the world. And also that Don Jr. would never set up any meeting of significance alone, and certainly not without checking with his father.

I also knew that nothing went on in Trump world, especially the campaign, without Mr. Trump's knowledge and approval. So I concluded that Don Jr. was referring to that June 2016 Trump Tower meeting about dirt on Hillary with the Russian representatives when he walked behind his dad's desk that day, and that Mr. Trump knew that was the meeting Don Jr. was talking about when he said, That's good. Let me know.

Over the past year or so, I have done some real soul searching. And I see now that my ambition and the intoxication of Trump power had much to do with the bad decisions in part that I made. And to you, Chairman Cummings and Ranking Member Jordan, the other members of this committee, the members of the House and Senate, I am sorry for my lies and for lying to Congress. And to our Nation, I am sorry for actively working to hide from you the truth about Mr. Trump when you needed it most.

For those who question my motives for being here today, I understand. I have lied. But I am not a liar. And I have done bad things, but I am not a bad man. I have fixed things, but I am no longer your fixer, Mr. Trump. And I am going to prison and have shattered the safety and security that I tried so hard to provide for my family.

My testimony certainly does not diminish the pain that I have caused my family and my friends. Nothing can do that. And I have never asked for, nor would I accept a pardon from President Trump.

By coming today, I have caused my family to be the target of personal, scurrilous attacks by the President and his lawyer trying to intimidate me from appearing before this panel.

Mr. Trump called me a rat for choosing to tell the truth, much like a mobster would do when one of his men decides to cooperate with the government. And as exhibit 8 shows, I have provided the committee with copies of tweets that Mr. Trump posted attacking me and my family. Only someone burying his head in the sand would not recognize them for what they are. It's encouragement to someone to do harm to me and my family.

I never imagined that he would engage in vicious, false attacks on my family, and unleash his TV lawyer to do the same. And I hope this committee, and all Members of Congress on both sides of the aisle, make it clear that, as a Nation, we should not tolerate attempts to intimidate witnesses before Congress, and attacks on family are out of bounds and not acceptable.

I wish to especially thank Speaker Pelosi for her statements, it's exhibit 9, to protect this institution and me, and the chairman of the House Permanent Select Committee on Intelligence, Adam Schiff, and you, Chairman Cummings, for likewise defending the institution and my family against the attacks by Mr. Trump, and also the many Republicans who have admonished the President as well.

I am not a perfect man. I have done things I am not proud of. And I will live with the consequences of my actions for the rest of my life. But today, I get to decide the example that I set for my children, and how I attempt to change how history will remember me. I may not be able to change the past, but I can do right by the American people here today.

I thank you for your attention, and I'm happy to answer the committee's questions.

Print Citations

CMS: Cohen, Michael. "Hearing of Former Attorney to President Donald Trump." Presentation to the U.S. House of Representatives, Washington, DC, February 27, 2019. In *The Reference Shelf: Representative American Speeches, 2018–2019,* edited by Sophie Zyla, 128-135. Amenia, NY: Grey House Publishing, 2019.

MLA: Cohen, Michael. "Hearing of Former Attorney to President Donald Trump." U.S. House of Representatives, 27 February 2019, Washington, DC. Presentation. *The Reference Shelf: Representative American Speeches, 2018–2019,* edited by Sophie Zyla, Grey House Publishing, 2019, pp. 128-135.

APA: Cohen, M. (2019, February 27). Presentation at hearing of former attorney to president Donald Trump. U.S. House of Representatives, Washington, DC. In Sophie Zyla (Ed.), *The reference shelf: Representative American speeches, 2018–2019* (pp. 128-135). Amenia, NY: Grey House Publishing.

Analyzing Trump's Comments on the Whistle-Blower in a Private Meeting

By Gregory Korte, Jennifer Jacobs, and Nick Wadhams

The president spoke to a limited group of diplomats and guests, making reference to the whistle-blower as being a spy, with no actual knowledge of events. The rest of his remarks touched on the Bidens, coal mining, the press, his crowds at events, and how well his diplomatic appointees do. Analysis is enclosed in parentheses.

Meeting behind closed doors with U.S. diplomats and invited guests in New York on Thursday, President Donald Trump gave a free-wheeling, rally-like performance in which he mocked Democratic rival Joe Biden, accused a whistle-blower of treason and falsely claimed that Australia had eradicated black lung disease. The speech Thursday came less than two hours after the release of a whistle-blower report alleging that Trump pressured Ukrainian President Volodymyr Zelenskiy to investigate a political rival, Democratic presidential candidate Joe Biden. Here's an annotated copy of that speech explaining key elements.

Kelly is going to be a star.

(Trump was introduced by Kelly Craft, the new U.S. Ambassador to the United Nations. Before being sworn in at the White House Sept. 12, she was the ambassador to Canada, and she and her husband are prominent Republican donors.)

And the only way you're a star, no matter how you look or feel or talk, is when you make good deals. [Inaudible] You've got to make good deals, otherwise it's over. And, uh, she's going to make great deals. I was with her now for three days and she's developed incredible relationships in a very short period of time. And, um, we appreciate it. You'll be out there, you'll be in the firing line today, for instance.

I just heard, you know while I'm coming up here, you know they have a whistle-blower. And he turned out to be a fake. He's a fake. Highly partisan whistle-blower. The lawyers contributed to Biden,

(Andrew Bakaj, the whistle-blower's lead lawyer, contributed $100 to Biden through the fundrasising portal ActBlue. Another lawyer, Mark Zaid, has not contributed.)

they contributed—the whole thing is—but more importantly, you know what the whistle-blower was? The same letter that we announced yesterday. Which was perfect. It was—I couldn't have written it better if I wrote it myself. I could not have

---

Delivered on September 27, 2019, at a private meeting in New York, NY. Used with permission of Bloomberg L.P. Copyright © 2017. All rights reserved.

said it or had a better conversation, and we had a really nice gentleman in, president of Ukraine. And, uh, he was, he was—they said, 'Was he pressuring you?'

(Trump met with Zelenskiy at the United Nations Wednesday, when reporters asked if Trump pressured him to investigate the Bidens. "It was normal. We spoke about many things. And I—so I think, and you read it, that nobody pushed—pushed me, Zelenskiy said)

You know, these animals in the press.

They're animals [inaudible]. Some of the worst human beings you'll ever meet.

[Audience member, male: "Thank you!"]

[Applause.]

They're scum. Many of them are scum. Then you have some good reporters but not many, I'll be honest with you. And that's one of the things we battle. You'll find out. [To Craft] But they'll probably like you better than they like me, right? But I had to get us here, right?

[Audience member, male. "Right!"]

But they're total just terrible dishonest people. And, uh—They couldn't figure out, what do we say bad about this conversation. Then it turns that they have out senators, Democrat senators, that went over there and strong-armed the guy. "You better damn well do this or you're not going to get any money from the Congress."

(In May 2018, three Democratic senators wrote to the Ukrainian prosecutor general to "express great concern" that he was failing to cooperate with the U.S. investigation into Russian interference in the 2016 election. Those senators—Robert Menendez of New Jersey, Dick Durbin of Illinois and Patrick Leahy of Vermont—made no mention of U.S. funding to Ukraine.)

Oh I see, that's OK?

And then you have sleepy Joe Biden who's dumb as a rock.

[Audience laughs.]

This guy's dumb on his best day. And he's not having his best day right now. He's dumb as a rock.

So you have sleepy Joe, and he goes up and—and his kid, who's got a lot of problems. He got thrown out of the Navy.

(Hunter Biden is Joe Biden's second son. He was commissioned as a Navy ensign in 2013 at the age of 43. He was discharged the next year after testing positive for cocaine.)

Little problems. I mean look, I'm not going to—it's a problem. That's a problem. So we won't get into why and all that. But he got thrown out of the Navy and now this kid goes into Ukraine, walks away with millions of dollars, and becomes a consultant for 50,000 a month.

(Hunter Biden worked as a lawyer, a lobbyist and a venture capitalist before taking a board seat on the Ukrainian energy company Burisma Holdings in 2014.)

And he doesn't know anything compared to anybody in this room. OK? He's a stiff. He knows nothing. He's walking away with 50,000—or as you would say in the old days, fifty-K a month.

Not bad. Would anybody else in this room like to represent Ukraine for 50,000 a month?

[Audience laughs.]

That's on top—[inaudible]—that's on top of, that's on top of hundreds of thousands of millions of dollars. But that's not the best one. The best one is China. Just came up. So now he goes to China. And I was with the head of Blackstone,

(New York-based private equity firm)

which is a big deal. Steve Schwarzman

(Schwarzman is a prominent Trump adviser who led the president's economic advisory council before it was disbanded. He has also cultivated ties to China. He ranks 60th on the Bloomberg list of the world's richest people, with a net worth of $17.5 billion.)

And I said, "Steve is that possible?" "No. Why? Why, who got that? Who got that?" And I said, "Biden's son." "Ooh." Well then you know, he says, "Maybe I shouldn't get involved. You know if it was very political."

But I say, I say, "Steve, what happens when you come off a vice presidential plane—it's called Air Force Two

(Hunter Biden accompanied his father on the vice presidential plane during an official visit to China in 2013.)

—your father's with you, you walk into a room in China, and they give you a fund of 1.5 billion!" Billion dollars.

(Hunter Biden is a 10% owner of BHR Partners, which advises Chinese firms wanting to invest outside of China. The company says its net worth is about $4.2 million, making Biden's share worth $420,000. Biden has said he has not received any profits from the company. Trump's timeline is off: BHR had already negotiated a deal with Chinese officials by the time of the December 2013 visit.)

You make hundreds of thousands of dollars, and millions of dollars off that. And that's probably not all they gave him, they gave him plenty more, I'm sure. We might never find out.

And then they talk about me and I didn't do anything. I don't know if I'm the most innocent person in the world.

[Audience: chuckling.]

But you know you look at that—most presidential, they always said

(Trump is quoting himself. "I say, with the exception of the late great Abraham Lincoln, I can be more presidential than any president that has ever held this office, I can tell you," he said at a 2017 campaign rally.)

I'm the most presidential except for possibly Abe Lincoln when he wore the hat. That was tough to beat.

[Audience: laughter.]

Honest Abe, when he wore that hat, that was tough to beat. But I can't do that, that hat wouldn't work for me.

[Audience member, male: "Go ahead."]

Yeah, I have better hair than him.

But Honest Abe was tough to beat. Remember we used to do that during the campaign? They used to say, when I speak, the crowd would be crazy, I'd go crazy—we'd all go crazy. We had a lot of fun together.

We had 25,000—we've never had an empty seat.

(Trump uses rally attendance as a measurement of political support, and has often exaggerated the size of the crowds.)

From the day I came down the escalator, with a potential, unbelievable woman, who became our first lady.

[Audience: applause and cheers.]

We've never had—they do, the crowds love her, the people love her.

But we've never had an empty seat, not one. I really—I really believe that. There was one case where we had a tremendous snow storm, it was—and it was just about frozen. Massive. It was like a monster storm. I don't even know how we got there. I said, "How's the crowd?" "It's just about full, sir." I said, "What does that mean?" Like there's about two seats on top. Thousands and thousands of people couldn't get in there.

So they show pictures of the empty seats. They don't say there's—there's the worst storm they've had in years. They show pictures of like nine empty seats. Could have been people just went to the bathroom together.

[Audience: laughter.]

But we've never—and I always say, just get the biggest arena. Good location if you can, but get the biggest arena. We did it the other night, Tuesday night. We had, uh, two congressmen. One was possibly going to win, he was up by two. He won by about 27,

(Republican Greg Murphy defeated Democrat Allen Thomas in a special election for North Carolina's 3rd congressional district on Sept. 10, 62% to 38%.)

I think, or something like that. A lot. The other one was down by 17.

(Republican Dan Bishop defeated Democrat Dan McCready, 50.2% to 48.6%, to win a special election to North Carolina's 9th congressional district Sept. 10. There are no public polls showing he was ever down by 17 points. The district has voted reliably Republican since 1963.)

And they said, "Sir, don't campaign for him, please." "Why?" "Because if he loses, they're going to kill you, the press." I said, "They're going to kill me whether I campaign or not."

It'll make it a little bit worse. You know they'll say, "He worked, and he failed. Trump failed."

The guy was down 17 points and he ended up winning by a lot.

(Bishop won by 2 percentage points. Trump won the district by 12 points in 2016.)

You know, he ended up winning by a lot.

In fact, the whole night, CNN, who had built the most beautiful, $2 million maybe they spent—no wonder they're losing their ass. They have no ratings and they're building studios all over the place but they had a studio, the studio was going to stay up for weeks and toward the end of the night they were taking it down. Their so-called stars were leaving. They had stars. There's not many stars, I'll tell you, less than 10.

But they were taking—the stars were leaving. And, uh, they didn't want to report it.

But the candidate, Dan Bishop, won—by a lot. He was down by 17, and they had lines a mile long. I mean the lines going into those voting booths were unbelievable. And without the rally speech, and a couple of tweets, the Twitter stuff is good—we have like way over 100 million people on six or seven different platforms. It's actually much higher than that even. Higher than just about everybody.

And it helps. It helps. They have signs oftentimes when I speak. It said, "Please keep"—this woman the other night, beautiful woman, she's got a sign"Please keep tweeting sir, it matters."

And it does matter. Because we get our voice out. You know, if we don't do that, we don't get the voice—I can't say what a great job Kelly's doing, and uh, I can't say what a wonderful husband she has.

(Joe Craft is Kelly Craft's third husband. He's CEO of Alliance Resource Partners, the third largest coal producer in the United States.)

Look at how devoted he is. He'a a rich man, too. He's loaded.

(Forbes estimated Joe Craft's net worth at $1.4 billion in 2011.)

What are you doing here? Why aren't you working? He's so proud of his wife he can't leave his office. That's really great though, huh? It's great.

Are you all proud of her?

He said very much. And he's really a fantastic guy, he's been a friend of mine for a long time. Before I met Kelly, I met Joe. And Joe, uh, impressed me because of his knowledge of energy. Now he could be paying—OK, you're going to pay a guy, 50—now he wouldn't take it. For him that's not, uh, that's not quite good enough. Although he might. He might. It's easy money, Joe, you have to say. But he would be an expert on energy, he'd be a real expert, and he would be, uh, somebody that you [inaudible] a lot of money too, but not Biden's son.

So the whistle-blower came out and said, nothing. He said, "a couple of people told me, he had a conversation with Ukraine—we're in a war. These people are sick. They're sick. And nobody's called it out like I do. I don't understand. People are afraid to call it out, they're afraid to say that the press is crooked. We have a crooked press. We have a dishonest media.

So now they're devastated. But they'll always find something. I'm sure there'll be something they'll find in this report that will suit [inaudible]. But basically that person never saw the report, never saw the call. They never saw the call. Heard something. And decided that he or she, whoever the hell it is—almost a spy.

I want to know, who's the person that gave the whistle-blower—who's the person that gave the whistle-blower the information because that's close to a spy. You know what we used to do in the old days when were smart, right, with spies and treason? We used to handle it a little differently than we do now.

(Trump is accusing the whistle-blower and those who cooperated with him of treason, a crime that carries a punishment of at least five years in prison or the death penalty. [Only one person has ever been executed by the United States for treason, during the Civil War.])

[Audience: light laughter.]

Now you have guys like, uh, little Adam Schiff

(Adam Schiff is chairman of the House Intelligence Committee. He is a Democrat from California.)

defending you.

[Audience member, male: "Pencil-neck"]

(One of Trump's nicknames for Schiff. "Little pencil neck Adam Schiff," he said at a March rally in Grand Rapids, Michigan. "He's got the smallest, thinnest neck I've ever seen. He is not a long ball hitter.")

He says "pencil-neck"—that name stuck.

[Audience: light laughter. Audience member, male: mostly inaudible but repeats "Pencil-neck."]

He's got a neck about this big. [Holds right hand up in an "OK" sign.] He's got shirts that are too big because you can't buy shirts that are that small. He was never a coal miner, Joe, let's put it that way. I don't think he worked in the mines, you think? I don't think so. These miners come out—we love our miners—they come out, they have hands, arms, they shake, "aw I love you sir, I love you sir." But we gave them back their jobs.

(Coal mining jobs have increased from 50,8000 when Trump was inaugurated to 53,000 in July, according to the Bureau of Labor Stastics.)

They were dead. And you know, Hillary came in just before West Virginia and says, "No, we want the miners we want to re-train them, and they'll be doing—can you imagine a miner with, you know, massive arms, shoulders, they love what they're doing, in a line, with little tiny widgets? They're putting little tiny computer parts together. These big strong—and they don't want to be doing that. And I said to them—it's the only time they ever got angry at me, I said to them—'Now listen, suppose, is there any truth, suppose we would take you out of that business and we do retrain you, and you go into, uh, technology, OK?' They almost threw up all over the place."

[Audience: light laughter.]

And it's a funny thing. You know, I call it dangerous, rough stuff. But it's become much safer. In Australia now they have no black lung disease.

(As of February there were 102 confirmed and 250 suspected black lung cases in the coal mining Australian state of Queensland, according to the Mine Dust Diseases Victims Group.)

They really got all of that dust out of there. And they've done a fantastic job, we're copying that system, we give credit where credit it is due. But, uh, it's incredible.

But, you know, they were talking about retraining these guys. By the way, I was thinking about doing, walking in, I look at these big rough guys and I say, "Nah, they don't want to do that. " And I said to them, "Would you want that, would you want any re-training, " uh, and the one guy looks at me, he says, "Sir, my great-grandfather was a miner, my grandfather, my father, and I'm a miner, and we love our life. We want to dig coal. That's what we want to do, sir, we don't want anything else. We want to just dig coal. It's true. You couldn't—if I said, "I'm going to give you an apartment on Fifth Avenue, you come with me, you're going to have a great time in New York, they would say, 'No thank you. That's just the way it is, you know. That's their life, that's what they want. They love it. They don't want a—they don't want to do anything different. And I understand that. I'm the only fool that decided to do something—I had a great life."

[Audience: laughter.]

And then I said, "Let's run for president, let's help this country out." And we've been hit harder than anybody in history.

[Audience member, male: "Great job!" Audience: applause, cheers.]

Thank you. I'll tell you one thing I tell people, though—no rich guy's ever going to run for politics, I can tell you, if anybody did this, I don't think they're going to run. But I love doing it. I guess I love it because we've made so much progress. And you're a really big part of it. And you know our deputy permanent representative ambassador, Jonathan Cohen

(Cohen is the acting deputy representative to the United Nations. He was recently confirmed as ambassador to Egypt.)

may be here, where's Jonathan, is he here? [To Craft] Doing a great job, right? [Craft: "Excellent."]

Is everybody saying what a, what a good job he's doing. So Jonathan, thank you, good luck, do well. You've got plenty to work on, Jonathan. [chuckles] We have plenty of, I call them points of confliction, right? Points of confliction. But you don't realize how important you are. What you do, you make it all possible. And I've always said about the United Nations, it has more potential than any institution that I've ever dealt with. It really does. It hasn't lived up to its potential. It's starting to more. I think one of the reasons is because I feel that way. I will use the United Nations to our benefit as a country. And because I'm doing it, others are doing it and we're sort of getting together and doing things differently.

And Nikki did great job.

(Nikki Haley was U.S. ambassador to the United Nations until leaving at the end of last year.)

And Kelly's going to do a great job. And it's very important—this position is so important. So important. Um, it's uh—another thing that I think was underrated [turns to Craft]—the importance of your position. I think it was very underrated. But, a—you have the right person in that position. But the United Nations is going to finally live up to its potential. It's, uh, it's really got something. And I like your secretary-general.

(U.N. Secretary-General António Guterres of Portugal.)

He's really working hard. He's always on the ball. He's always there for me. I really like him. So I think he has—you know, I think he has the stuff. The right stuff, as they say. Right? You know as they say in a couple of very good movies.

But I just came over this morning, I wanted to thank you, I wanted to congratulate everyone, I wanted to congratulate Jonathan and Kelly—I didn't know Joe was going to be here, but I'm happy to see you Joe. And, uh, you folks are fantastic, and just keep it going. We've got it really rocking. We're looking good. We're looking good for another four years [inaudable].

[Audience: Applause, cheers]

[inaudible] I have a certain group of reporters, I say we're looking good for another four years, and then if we want to another four, and maybe another four.

(The 22nd Amendment to the Constitution limits presidents to two four-year terms. Trump has repeatedly joked about serving for 20 or more years.)

[Audience: laughter, applause.]

And they go crazy. The whack job Bill Maher.

(Host of HBO's "Real Time with Bill Maher.")

He goes to somebody over there, he goes, "You know he's going to win, don't you? " It's just some idiot, that he's on TV, and he goes, "You know he's going to win. " "No, no, I think we can… " "You know he's going to win. And you know he's not leaving don't you? " And the guy's like "What do you mean? "He's not leaving. He's not leaving. " And I thought he was kidding—he's being serious [laughs]. So uh, did anybody ever see the *Time* magazine cover where we have it 2020, 2024, 2028, 2032

(A *Time* magazine cover story last year had the headline "How Trumpism Outlasts Trump," with an illustration of Trump yard signs up through "Trump 2044.")—in other words—we do that to drive them fricking crazy.

[Audience: laughter, applause.]

So I just want to thank you, congratulations to Kelly, Jonathan, and everyone in this room, you make it work and it's so important. It's called world peace. And we've got to have it. We'll have it. We'll have it. We have a lot of good things going. Tremendous things. Problems with India and Pakistan. Big. Problems with … North Korea? We're doing all right, we have a pretty good relationship going, I'll tell you, we have a good relationship going. But we have a lot of great things going and you make it possible. Thank you very much everybody."

Print Citations

CMS: Korte, Gregory, Jennifer Jacobs, and Nick Wadhams. "Analyzing Trump's Comments on the Whistle-Blower in a Private Meeting." Remarks on private meeting, New York NY, September 27, 2019. In *The Reference Shelf: Representative American Speeches, 2018–2019,* edited by Sophie Zyla, 136-143. Amenia, NY: Grey House Publishing, 2019.

MLA: Korte, Gregory, Jennifer Jacobs, and Nick Wadhams. "Analyzing Trump's Comments on the Whistle-Blower in a Private Meeting." Private Meeting, 27 September 2019, New York, NY. Remarks. *The Reference Shelf: Representative American Speeches, 2018–2019,* edited by Sophie Zyla, Grey House Publishing, 2019, pp. 136-143.

APA: Korte, G., Jacobs, J., & Wadhams, N. (2019, September 27). Remarks on analyzing Trump's comments on the whistle-blower in a private meeting. Private meeting, New York, NY. In Sophie Zyla (Ed.), *The reference shelf: Representative American speeches, 2018–2019* (pp. 136-143). Amenia, NY: Grey House Publishing.

4
Scientists and Activists

Photo by NASA/Liaison/Getty Images.

Dr. Ellen Ochoa, the first Latina director of the Johnson Space Center and the first chosen to go into space, spoke of transcending borders at a SACNAS National Diversity in STEM conference.

SACNAS: National Diversity in STEM Conference Keynote Address

By Ellen Ochoa

Dr. Ellen Ochoa was the 11th director of the Johnson Space Center, the first Hispanic director, second female director, and prior deputy center director and director of flight crew operations. Ochoa, a research engineer at National Aeronautics and Space Administration (NASA) Ames Research Center, was selected as the first Hispanic women to go into space on the shuttle Discovery *and has flown into space four times with the Johnson Space Center. She is the recipient of NASA's Distinguished Service Medal and the Presidential Rank Award, she has six schools named after her, and she is a Fellow of the American Association for the Advancement of Science (AAAS) and the American Institute of Aeronautics and Astronautics (AIAA). Ochoa has a bachelor's degree in physics from San Diego State University, and a master's degree and doctorate in electrical engineering from Stanford University. Ochoa talks of the space frontier as a place where boundaries are pushed, much like her work with NASA and her time spent in space.*

[Applause]

Thank you so much, and the first thing I want to do is thank Agnes for having me here today.

I spoke at a couple of SACNAS events early in my career, you know, probably 25 years ago, but it's been a while and I'm just so thrilled to see how SACNAS has grown over the years and to see all of you here today. Congratulations on your 45th anniversary and I always think anniversaries, are a great time to reflect on the success that you've had over the last 45 years but of course also a good time for all of us to think about how we can continue to help encourage diversity in STEM. So one of the things I was going to mention very first of all today was, we had a crew that was launching to the International Space Station very early this morning here and so I was going to talk about them—they should have docked by now—and a little bit about what's currently going on. But if you've seen the news you probably saw that they had an anomaly during the launch and the crew needed to do an abort. However they landed safely and both, they're both fine. We had a NASA astronaut and a cosmonaut on board, so I think it serves as a reminder that space flight's still hard and it really requires the best of engineers and scientists to really make it happen

---

Delivered on October 11, 2018, at 2018 SACNAS—The National Diversity in STEM Conference hosted by SACNAS—Advancing Chicanos/Hispanics & Native Americans in Science.

and that we always have to be prepared. And that's something that we really specialized at NASA.

The other thing I wanted to mention is, because I hope you all know but you may not, that the second Latina to go into space is in space right now living and working on the International Space Station, Serena Auñón-Chancellor. And so I hope you're following along with her mission. You can follow her on Twitter at @AstroSerena. By the way feel free to tag me at Astro underscore Ellen and you can follow along with her. And if you go outside tonight at 8:52 p.m. and there's not too many clouds, you can see the Space Station fly over, and there's an even better pass tomorrow at 8 p.m. So just go to your computer and put in "Spot the Station," put in "San Antonio," and they'll tell you exactly when and where to look. And I hope you all will feel part of the space program by watching the Space Station fly over and of course cheering on Serena.

So a few years ago one of our astronauts returned from the International Space Station, and he talked about living and working on the frontier. And that was a phrase that really kind of spoke to me about the excitement and the challenge of working in human space exploration. And a frontier is a place, it's often an actual place, where explorers come and pioneers settle. But sometimes it's more of a metaphor, and I think it's something that we all can relate to because a frontier is a place where boundaries are pushed. And certainly I've had the opportunity in my career to live and work on the frontier. But many, many of you in this room are also very familiar with frontiers and pushing boundaries.

I've had an amazing career with NASA, being able to live and work on the frontier, being able to do research and development in space, helping to assemble the International Space Station and learn how to operate it and how to train for it, and of course being the first Latina in space and the first Hispanic director of the Johnson Space Center. So I wanted to tell you a little bit more about that. My career was really possible for a variety of reasons. Certainly the development of the Space Shuttle and some of the changes going on in our country during the 1970s, but also through my family's focus on education. So my dad's parents were Mexican and they moved first to Arizona and then to California, and that's where my dad, who was the youngest of 12 kids, was born. And

education was important in their family. He was a good student and he was able to get a tuition-free college education by getting an appointment to the Naval Academy. My mom wasn't able to go to college when she was young. In fact she didn't even finish high school for health reasons until she was in her 30s. But she always loved learning and she really passed that on to me and to my four brothers and sisters. And during the whole time that she was raising us we lived in San Diego, a suburb of San Diego, and our local university was San Diego State University. And she would take like a class a semester for a long time just because she loved to learn about all different kinds of things. And she eventually did get her college degree a year after I graduated from San Diego State University. But her example really had a big impression on me and my brothers and sisters and we all went to college.

Now when I went off to college I had actually no idea what I was going to do, certainly never thought about the astronaut program at that time and I wasn't even in science and engineering. I thought maybe I'd major in business or music but wasn't really sure what exactly that meant for my future career. I did take a lot of math in high school and I liked it. I was good at it and so at San Diego State I ended up taking more math classes and when I talked to the people, the other students, in those classes—you know I was finishing up the calculus series—I was asking them, you know, what they were taking. And you know most of them were in engineering, also physics, and they asked me what I was in there for, and I said, well just for fun. I like calculus, so, but they're like, you know, maybe you should go find out, you know, what subjects actually used calculus. And so I went to talk to a couple different professors at San Diego State University. One was in the electrical engineering department and, you know, this professor, to be honest, was pretty discouraging. He was like, wow, we had a woman come through the program once and you know it's a pretty difficult program and, you know, he was picking up different components on his desk—like capacitors and things—saying you know you'll have to work with these. I, you know, I really don't know that that's something you'd be interested in.

But then I went to talk to a physics professor and so one of the first things he asked about was my math background. And when I told him what I had already studied he just got really excited. He said, that's terrific. He said, you've already learned the language of physics and so, you know, if you come to our major and take our classes you'll be able to focus on the concepts, whereas the other students will be doing that simultaneously. And he said, I think you'd do really well. And then the other important thing he told me was some careers that you can do when you major in physics. And that was really important to me because to be honest I wasn't completely sure what physics was. And I really, you know, I didn't know any scientists. I didn't know any engineers. I'm sure I share that with many of you in this room. So I couldn't really picture what a career was or what somebody did with the major in physics. So it's really important that he helped to paint that picture. And, you know, after those two conversations it's probably not too surprising that I actually chose physics as my major.

At that point I also had the opportunity to attend a conference at San Diego State that was put on by women in science and engineering. And there were a number of women who came and talked about what their job was really like, and that was also really important to me. So I know there are so many people here, there are professors, there are professionals. I just hope you understand how important the words that you say to the students coming up are. You can see how it affected my career. And even for the students here, the graduate students' undergraduate career, you have that opportunity to talk to and affect high school students and middle school students. And what you say can really be very important for their future. I had the opportunity while I was at San Diego State to spend a couple different summers working in a research lab, and at one of them I was actually mentored by one of the women's staff members. They are one of the very, very few women staff members there, and she was really the first one that talked to me about graduate school. She asked me if I liked doing research and I said, yeah, yeah, I'm just getting a first taste of it but I enjoy it, something I might want to do. And she said, well then graduate school is really important. She actually mentioned the name of a professor at Stanford that had recently come to their lab to speak, and what it turned out is about a year later I was actually at Stanford as a graduate student working for that specific professor, who became my PhD advisor. And in fact I'm still in contact with him today, and he's really been a supporter of mine over the years.

So it was while I was at Stanford, actually in the first year there, when I was getting my Master's, that the Space Shuttle flew for the first time. And that was a big deal, because it was a very different kind of spacecraft than we had ever flown in the United States before. And it had so many more capabilities than you have in a capsule design, and a lot of what it was designed to do with science and engineering research in space. And because of that, a few years before when NASA was selecting the first group of astronauts that would actually fly on the Space Shuttle, they realized they needed scientists, they needed engineers, they needed medical doctors—all these people who could perform the research in space. And it really expanded the view of who they would look at for astronauts. And that, along with the equal rights movement and the civil rights movement in the country, opened up the Astronaut Corps. for the very first time for women and minorities. And the first class that included them, of course, was the 1978 class. So again in '81 is when it flew for the first time.

Two years later Sally Ride flew in space, another huge march forward, first American woman in space. And when I looked at Sally from afar, you know, I could see that we had to connect. Some connections, not only that we were both women, of course, but she had majored in physics as I had, she had gone to Stanford, which is where I was at the moment. And those connections really helped me dream much bigger than I would have otherwise and start to think about, you know, the astronaut program, and is that something that I could really possibly be a part of. I can say I basically almost talked myself out of it just thinking, you know, there's so many thousands of other people who apply and they're probably way more, you know, qualified than I am. So one of the things we always have to watch out for is not to talk ourselves out of these potential opportunities and these dreams that we have but instead just try to work toward them and find those people who will help encourage you. I certainly had the encouragement of my thesis advisors when I went off to my, I applied for the program as soon as I got my PhD. But I never actually expected to hear back from NASA, so I went off to, first of all, Sandia National Labs. I worked in Livermore California, and I was able to do research there. And between my work at Stanford—Sandia was a co-inventor on three patents during that time—as well as a number of journal articles as well, but while I was at Sandia, I did get called by NASA to come for the interview at Johnson Space Center.

And I didn't know it till I got there, but that meant that out of a few thousand applications I was down to one of about a hundred and twenty people that they actually invited to come interview. It was my first chance to be at a NASA center, and of course Johnson Space Center, as a home in human spaceflight, got to meet and talk with other astronauts for the first time, find out a little bit more about what the job was like, got to tour around and see the training facilities, got lots and lots and lots of medical testing and had the chance to interview. And I wasn't selected that year, but I was even more excited about going for it in the future. And I realized, you know, some holes in my background, one of them being I'd mainly had an academic and research background. And of course as an astronaut you work in an operational environment, and they want to make sure that you can operate in an environment where things are happening quickly, where you have to prioritize information, make decisions. So one of the things I did after that was get a private pilot's license to help give me some of that experience. I also decided I wanted to work for NASA, you know, even if I never was selected as an astronaut. Because I was interested in space exploration and really of being part of something bigger than myself, working as part of a team.

So I went off to NASA Ames Research Center in Northern California, and after just six months was actually offered a position as a supervisor of a group of about 35 people. So three years after that initial interview I was called—the next selection was happening for astronauts, and I was called to interview again. And that was the year that I was selected, in 1990, and went off to Johnson Space Center, where I spent the next 28 years. And just as I hoped when I first thought about the astronaut program, my first two flights were part of doing science research in space. And those missions were specifically focused on atmospheric research and the problem of ozone depletion and the ozone hole. And we had a whole suite of instruments in the payload bay and we were trying to understand, you know, what was really causing the ozone hole and ozone depletion and how much of it was due to human activities and how much of it was due to the natural solar cycle of the sun. So and some of the instruments that we were using were optical instruments, so I was pretty familiar with how they operated, and of course part of my job was to actually explain to the public what it is that we were doing on that mission and how these instruments were helping us collect the data that would help us understand more about our atmosphere.

So after those first two missions I then had the opportunity to start to support the International Space Station program. And at this time—this was the mid 1990s—it was not too long after we had joined forces with the Russian Space Agency and of course we were already working with the European, Japanese, and Canadian Space Agencies on this project, and so we were sort of in the midst of a redesign and just starting to develop hardware and get into more of the details of the design but also trying to figure out how we were actually going to operate the Space Station. So one of my jobs became, you know, going to Russia, negotiating with members of the Russian Space Agency and some of their contractors, and really trying to figure out, you know, how is a joint crew going to operate on the station, how are we going to select those crews, what language are we going to speak during training, what language are we going to speak on the International Space Station—just all of those things we had to put together, that whole operational concept.

So it was an incredible time to be involved in that, and a few years later one of the other jobs that I got to do was to lead the group of astronauts that work in Mission Control. They're called Capcom's because they're the ones that communicate with the astronauts on board, and we had to transform our Mission Control Center from one that operated, you know, usually ten days at a time or so during a shuttle mission to one that was going to operate 24/7 well into the future and understand how that was going to work and how we were best going to support a mission that was now going to be day-in-and-day-out. And I hope you know that we've now had astronauts and cosmonauts in orbit, next month it will be 18 years straight. So for anybody who is a senior in high school this year, every minute that they've been alive we've had our astronauts in space. And we've been able to keep them safe and productive and doing research in a whole variety of areas. And that's one of the things that I have loved being involved with. And the second, the third, and fourth missions that I had on the Space Station, thank you, the third and fourth missions that I was able to fly in the astronaut office were part of assembling the International Space Station.

One of them was the very first shuttle to dock with the station. This was back in 1999, it was only two modules, one that had been launched from Russia one that had been launched from the US. There were no people living on board yet because we didn't have a habitation module, so our job was to go up and transfer supplies both inside and outside in order to prepare it for the first crew. And then I got to go back three years later when the station of course was much larger. We had a crew of three living on board, we were still in the middle of assembly, and our crew brought up the very first piece of the truss structure, about 40 feet long, and we added it to the station. And that truss structure of course now is about 350 feet long, and the four large solar arrays hang off it and those are what power the entire station, including the US laboratory and laboratories that have been put up by the European Space Agency and the Japanese Space Agency. So getting a chance to be a part of that assembly—that was, you know, an absolute highlight in my career.

After my fourth mission is when I really had the opportunity to go into management and leadership positions at Johnson Space Center, first as deputy and then as director of the organization that managed the astronaut office and our aircraft ops division, and then as deputy center director, and finally for the last five and a half years up until May when I retired as the director of Johnson Space Center. And I do want to say every person I've ever worked for in my career has been a man, and yet they have all been so very supportive of my career and they provided me lots of opportunities. So I want to make sure, like, we're all in this together, right? We need to provide that support and encouragement to those who are coming up behind us and to provide the opportunities so that each of us can reach our potential. I also learned how important it was to kind of find my own voice, to speak up, to understand where I could add value in the meetings that I supported and in leading people. It's been a hugely exciting time. Over that time we of course finished the assembly of the International Space Station, during the time that I was in management. And we've had a real focus on moving forward.

At Johnson Space Center as Center Director I had an initiative called JSC 2.0, and it was about advancing human spaceflight by being lean, agile, and adaptive to change. And I think that's something that all organizations have, that same challenge of how do we move forward, how do we innovate, especially if we've been successful in how we're operating today. But we know that the world changes and of course there's all kinds of changes going on in human spaceflight. We have a lot more companies involved now, a lot of them have just started up in the last 10 years or so. NASA works with all of those companies, and we've had to figure out a new way of working with them where they actually own the spacecraft and the rockets that they use and we buy services from them and they operate them. And we work together in a way that was different than the way we worked in our history. One of the things that we focused on in order to help innovate is the idea of tying innovation and inclusion together, because it's really voices coming from all different kinds of backgrounds that helped bring us new ideas. And it's also really imperative that we use and value every single person that we have at Johnson Space Center. And that to me was so important for inclusion. It's the right thing to do.

But it's also an imperative for us to be successful and for us to be safe. If there are people at our Center that had a concern about a safety issue, something that could actually affect the lives of our astronauts, if they're not feeling valued or respected they may hesitate to speak up. We may not hear that voice, and it could lead directly to a tragedy for us. So it's absolutely critical that all of our folks feel valued, feel respected, and know they can speak up. And one of the mechanisms we used was employee resource groups, and of course we have a very thriving Hispanic employee resource group who has added so much to our Center, and in fact was recognized by the White House two or three years ago as part of their Hispanic education initiative because of the great work that we do. And we tried to develop all kinds of processes that would make sure that we were trying to include all of the people who worked at Johnson Space Center.

So I wanted to say just in the final minute or two that I'm up here a little bit about what I'm doing now since I retired from NASA in May. One of the main activities that I do is I'm the vice chair of the National Science Board, and the NSB has two roles. It governs the National Science Foundation, so I'm very thrilled that this conference is partially funded by the National Science Foundation, which is important to me and to our country. And their other role is to provide science and engineering advice to the nation, and so I'm still very, very involved in STEM. And one of the things I mentioned, which I think speaks to a lot of the messages that some of our previous speakers today have talked about, is I hope that you have noticed that just in the last few months a lot of these government and professional organizations—like NASA, like NSF, like the American Association for the Advancement of Science—have all recently updated and given a lot of attention to policies related to harassment. And they are really working hard to ensure that we improve the culture that we have for everybody that works in our organizations, whether it's STEM-related or not. But I'm very happy to see that these STEM-related organizations are working on that, and it is important to these organizations. I can tell you, being a part of them, that it is important. And when I look out and I see the thousands of you here, and the great work that you are doing, I'm very, very optimistic for the future. And I want to thank you again for having me today as your speaker.

[Applause]

Print Citations

CMS: Ochoa, Ellen. "SACNAS: National Diversity in STEM Conference." Keynote Address at SACNAS, STEM Conference, San Antonio, TX, October 11, 2018. In *The Reference Shelf: Representative American Speeches, 2018–2019*, edited by Sophie Zyla, 147-154. Amenia, NY: Grey House Publishing, 2019.

MLA: Ochoa, Ellen. "SACNAS: National Diversity in STEM Conference." SACNAS, STEM Conference, 11 October 2018, San Antonio, TX. Keynote Address. *The Reference Shelf: Representative American Speeches, 2018–2019*, edited by Sophie Zyla, Grey House Publishing, 2019, pp. 147-154.

APA: Ochoa, E. (2018, October 11). Keynote Address on SACNAS: National diversity in STEM conference. SACNAS, STEM Conference, San Antonio, TX. In Sophie Zyla (Ed.), *The reference shelf: Representative American speeches, 2018–2019* (pp. 147-154). Amenia, NY: Grey House Publishing.

Scientific Integrity in Federal Agencies (Excerpt)

By Michael Halpern

Michael Halpern is deputy director of the Center for Science and Democracy at the Union of Concerned Scientists. He works to promote solutions that ensure government decisions are fully informed by scientific information, and also oversees efforts to enable scientists to more effectively engage the public. Halpern speaks regularly on the use and misuse of science in decision making. He blogs regularly in the Guardian *and has appeared in national and international media outlets, including the* Associated Press, *the* Boston Globe, CNN, National Public Radio, NBC, *the* New York Times, *and the* Washington Post. *Michael holds a B.A. in sociology and communication studies from Macalester College.*

Thank you, Chairwoman Stevens and Chairwoman Sherrill, and also Ranking Member Baird and Ranking Member Norman, for holding this important hearing, and thank you for the opportunity to testify. My name is Michael Halpern, and I am the Deputy Director of the Center for Science and Democracy at the Union of Concerned Scientists. I have been working to protect science in decision making and scientific integrity since 2004 at a national and international level, and have authored numerous articles and reports about the problem of political interference in science and solutions to it.

The Environmental Protection Agency (EPA), Centers for Disease Control and Prevention (CDC), Department of Interior (DOI), and Food and Drug Administration (FDA) are supposed to use independent science to protect and improve public health and the environment. Much of the time, they do. But sometimes presidential administrations want to sideline, manipulate, misrepresent, or suppress information that comes out of federal agencies—especially if it doesn't support the policies they want to put forward. When that happens, valuable information is kept from the public, and it becomes easier for politicians to justify ill-advised public health and environmental protection decisions. This makes people sicker and degrades the environment.

A lack of protection for science makes it easier for the White House to try to get away with actions like censoring a study on chemical contamination of drinking water,[1] or why employees can be reprimanded for tweeting about climate change.[2] Absent these protections, employees feel the need to self-censor, and avoid talking

---

Delivered on July 17, 2019, at the U.S. House of Representatives, Washington, DC.

publicly about their research results. Such a climate of censorship harms the public trust in science-based policymaking, erodes the public understanding of the scientific record, and threatens to fundamentally alter the strength of our democracy.

Since 2004, the Union of Concerned Scientists has regularly monitored agencies for actions that compromise the use of science in policymaking. We have learned about such issues from scientists themselves, having conducted surveys of federal scientists for their views about political pressure on their scientific work during the last three presidential administrations. We have pushed for and participated in congressional oversight related to scientific integrity, and regularly work with reporters to bring abuses of science to light. We developed model good government policies for federal scientific agencies and analyzed and made recommendations about both the content and implementation of federal agency scientific integrity policies since they were developed nearly a decade ago.

I am thrilled to see that legislation to mandate the development of scientific integrity policies, H.R. 1709 the Scientific Integrity Act, is receiving a hearing today. We want to thank Congressman Tonko for leading the way on this legislation, as well as Chairwoman Johnson and Chairwoman Stevens on the Science Committee for their leadership as well. We hope that today will serve as an example to all that there can be a bipartisan commitment to promoting responsible conduct in federal scientific agencies with regard to the development and communication of scientific information.

This testimony can be summarized as follows:
1. Political interference in science happens under all presidential administrations, although the recent level of attacks on science is unprecedented.
2. Scientific integrity standards are essential for government accountability, but current scientific integrity policies are insufficiently written, inadequately implemented, and vulnerable to being ignored or repealed by any administration.
3. The Scientific Integrity Act has support from a wide variety of organizations. With a few improvements, the legislation should make a real bipartisan advance that will broadly impact policymaking for the better. It should be passed and signed into law.
4. There are other steps that must be taken to strengthen the role of science in policymaking that are outside of the scope of this legislation and hearing. The legislation does not address all issues related to science-based policy-making and it should not attempt to do so.
5. This legislation is not directed at the actions of the current or any other administration. It is a good government effort that should transcend partisan politics.

Strong Scientific Integrity Standards Are Essential for Government Accountability

The United States government has long worked to ensure the integrity of the science that is maintained within executive branch agencies. Originally, this meant ensuring that a scientist's research was conducted ethically and in accordance with high scientific standards. Policies were put in place to protect human research subjects, ensure that confidential data is protected against disclosure, promote effective peer review, address scientific misconduct, and more.

In recent years, the definition of scientific integrity has been focused on ensuring that science produced and considered by the federal government is not censored or politically influenced, that this science fully informs public policy decisions, and that the public is more fully aware of the knowledge and data that are produced by federal scientists that pertains to policymaking.

The importance of safeguarding scientific integrity within our federal government cannot be overstated. Science-informed decisions made by executive agencies have direct impacts on all of our lives. Whether those decisions are determining how safe or clean our waters are to drink, or our air to breathe, or whether certain species are deserving of greater protections under law, four fundamental principles should be embraced:

1. Decisions should be fully informed by (but not necessarily proscribed by) science;
2. Scientists working for and advising the government should be unobstructed in providing scientific evidence to inform the decision-making process;
3. The public should have reasonable access to scientific information to be able to understand the evidentiary basis of public policy decisions; and
4. The public and Congress should be able to evaluate whether the above principles are being adhered to.

Clearly, science is not the only factor that goes into many policy decisions. There are often many factors to consider. There are times, however, when determinations must be made *solely* on the best available scientific information. For example, current law requires the Food and Drug Administration to consider only the scientific evidence when determining whether drugs are safe and effective. It is not appropriate or legal to consider how profitable the drug will be. Similarly, when determining what level of air pollution is unsafe for human populations, the Clean Air Act requires the EPA to stick to the science. Economics and other factors can then be taken into account when standards are implemented and enforced.

The Scientific Integrity Act Is Government Accountability Legislation that Prevents Political Interference in Science

The attacks on science described in this testimony—including censorship and self-censorship, misrepresentation of findings, improper interference in scientific methods, and delays in publishing research—all could have been prevented had scientific integrity protections been formalized in statute when the attacks took place. At a minimum, there would have been recourse for federal employees faced with such political interference.

The Scientific Integrity Act is good government legislation. It is agnostic on matters of policy; rather, it aims to ensure that policies are fully informed by science. The legislation contains many of the best practices that have been identified for the development and maintenance of a thriving federal scientific enterprise.

The legislation prohibits any employee from manipulating or misrepresenting scientific findings. On issues from endangered species to toxic chemical contamination to worker safety, political appointees have personally made changes to scientific documents (or ordered that changes be made) in order to justify action or lack of action on public health and environmental threats. The legislation helps ensure that government communication of science is accurate by giving scientists the right of last review over materials that rely primarily on their research. It also gives scientists the right to correct official materials that misrepresent their work. This provision makes it less likely that federal agencies will put out inaccurate information, either intentionally or inadvertently.

The legislation ensures that scientists can carry out their research—and share it with the public—without fear of political pressure or retaliation. It enables scientists to talk about their research in public, with reporters, in scientific journals, and at scientific conferences. The bill empowers federal scientists to share their personal opinions as informed experts, but only in an individual capacity, not as government representatives. This is essential due to the amount of censorship and self-censorship that has been documented on issues from climate change to food safety.

The legislation requires agencies to devote resources to designate scientific integrity officers and provide federal employees with appropriate training to help prevent misconduct. Some agencies have developed policies that have no enforcement mechanisms, rendering them virtually meaningless.

The legislation would *not* empower scientists to speak for their agency on policy matters. It would not enable scientists to circumvent the agency leadership with regard to policy decisions. It would be clearly applied to expressing views with regard to their scientific expertise.

Scientists Should Be Free to Speak Publicly without Asking Permission

Notably, the legislation extends appropriate free speech protections for agency experts by allowing them to speak about their scientific work without political filters. Many current and former agency leaders initially worry that by extending additional rights for scientists that scientists will confuse the public. Policies are already in place however at several agencies that assert this right and there have been no recorded problems.

The National Oceanic and Atmospheric Administration was the first agency to assert that scientists could speak publicly about their scientific work without prior approval when NOAA released its scientific integrity policy in December 2011. Several other agencies and departments have followed suit, including the Department of Commerce (NOAA's parent department), the Department of Energy, the Department of Interior, the Centers for Disease Control and Prevention, and the Environmental Protection Agency. As noted above, this does not mean that scientists feel free to exercise this right, which is one reason that codification should happen.

It is worth noting that this is one area where the 2010 White House memorandum falls significantly short. The memorandum requires "coordination" with supervisors and public affairs, which introduces significant opportunities for censorship. It also implicitly allows these individuals to instruct scientists to refuse interviews; offer alternative spokespeople who would be more likely to provide more "favorable" messages; or delay interviews until deadlines have passed and the information is no longer relevant. The past decade has demonstrated that these guidelines are insufficient.

Notes

1. Bipartisan Outrage as EPA, White House Try to Cover Up Chemical Health Assessment, Michael Halpern, May 16, 2018, https://blog.ucsusa.org/michael-halpern/bipartisan-outrage-as-epa-white-house-try-to-cover-up-chemical-health-assessment.
2. Joshua Tree National Park Superintendent Reprimanded for Climate Change Science, UCS Staff, Jan 5, 2018, https://www.ucsusa.org/center-science-and-democracy/attacks-on-science/joshua-tree-national-park-superintendent-reprimanded.

Print Citations

CMS: Halpern, Michael. "Scientific Integrity in Federal Agencies." Presentation at the U.S. House of Representatives, Washington, DC, July 17, 2019. In *The Reference Shelf: Representative American Speeches, 2018–2019,* edited by Sophie Zyla, 155-159. Amenia, NY: Grey House Publishing, 2019.

MLA: Halpern, Michael. "Scientific Integrity in Federal Agencies." U.S. House of Representatives, 17 July 2019, Washington, DC. Presentation. *The Reference Shelf: Representative American Speeches, 2018–2019,* edited by Sophie Zyla, Grey House Publishing, 2019, pp. 155-159.

APA: Halpern, M. (2019, July 17). Presentation on scientific integrity in federal agencies. U.S. House of Representatives, Washington, DC. In Sophie Zyla (Ed.), *The reference shelf: Representative American speeches, 2018–2019* (pp. 155-159). Amenia, NY: Grey House Publishing.

You Have Stolen My Dreams and My Childhood

By Greta Thunberg

Greta Thunberg is a politically unaffiliated environmental activist from Sweden that has traveled the world as a spokesperson for global warming and other environmental causes. Thunberg was born on January 3, 200,3 and became concerned about global warming when she was eight years old. Thunberg became popular when she organized a school strike and protest outside the Swedish Parliament at 15. She also won an essay writing competition that same year and became affiliated with Fossil Free Dalsland, an environmental group committed to action against climate change. Thunberg has been nominated for the Nobel Peace Prize in 2019 and Time Magazine *named her one of the 100 most influential people of the year.*

My message is that we'll be watching you.

This is all wrong. I shouldn't be up here. I should be back in school on the other side of the ocean. Yet you all come to us young people for hope. How dare you!

You have stolen my dreams and my childhood with your empty words. And yet I'm one of the lucky ones. People are suffering. People are dying. Entire ecosystems are collapsing. We are in the beginning of a mass extinction, and all you can talk about is money and fairy tales of eternal economic growth. How dare you!

For more than 30 years, the science has been crystal clear. How dare you continue to look away and come here saying that you're doing enough, when the politics and solutions needed are still nowhere in sight.

You say you hear us and that you understand the urgency. But no matter how sad and angry I am, I do not want to believe that. Because if you really understood the situation and still kept on failing to act, then you would be evil. And that I refuse to believe.

The popular idea of cutting our emissions in half in 10 years only gives us a 50% chance of staying below 1.5 degrees [Celsius], and the risk of setting off irreversible chain reactions beyond human control.

Fifty percent may be acceptable to you. But those numbers do not include tipping points, most feedback loops, additional warming hidden by toxic air pollution or the aspects of equity and climate justice. They also rely on my generation sucking hundreds of billions of tons of your CO2 out of the air with technologies that barely exist.

Delivered on September 23, 2019, at the United Nations Climate Summit, New York, NY.

So a 50% risk is simply not acceptable to us—we who have to live with the consequences.

To have a 67% chance of staying below a 1.5 degrees global temperature rise—the best odds given by the [Intergovernmental Panel on Climate Change] —the world had 420 gigatons of CO2 left to emit back on Jan. 1st, 2018. Today that figure is already down to less than 350 gigatons.

How dare you pretend that this can be solved with just "business as usual" and some technical solutions? With today's emissions levels, that remaining CO2 budget will be entirely gone within less than 8 1/2 years.

There will not be any solutions or plans presented in line with these figures here today, because these numbers are too uncomfortable. And you are still not mature enough to tell it like it is.

You are failing us. But the young people are starting to understand your betrayal. The eyes of all future generations are upon you. And if you choose to fail us, I say: We will never forgive you.

We will not let you get away with this. Right here, right now is where we draw the line. The world is waking up. And change is coming, whether you like it or not.

Thank you.

Print Citations

CMS: Thunberg, Greta. "You Have Stolen My Dreams and My Childhood." Keynote Address at the United Nations Climate Summit, New York, NY, September 23, 2019. In *The Reference Shelf: Representative American Speeches, 2018–2019*, edited by Sophie Zyla, 160-161. Amenia, NY: Grey House Publishing, 2019.

MLA: Thunberg, Greta. "You Have Stolen My Dreams and My Childhood." United Nations Climate Summit, 23 September 2019, New York, NY. Keynote Address. *The Reference Shelf: Representative American Speeches, 2018–2019*, edited by Sophie Zyla, Grey House Publishing, 2019, pp. 160-161.

APA: Thunberg, G. (2019, September 23). Keynote Address on you have stolen my dreams and my childhood. United Nations Climate Summit, New York, NY. In Sophie Zyla (Ed.), *The reference shelf: Representative American speeches, 2018–2019* (pp. 160-161). Amenia, NY: Grey House Publishing.

Science Activation: How Do We Get Our Science Used by Those in Power? (Excerpt)

By Lucy Jones

Dr. Lucy Jones is a disaster scientist and founder of the Dr. Lucy Jones Center for Science and Society, whose "mission is to foster the understanding and application of scientific information in the creation of more resilient communities." Working with both the public and private sectors, Dr. Jones seeks to increase communities' ability to adapt and be resilient to the dynamic changes of the world around them." She is also a research associate at the Seismological Laboratory of Caltech. Jones is the author of the book The Big One. *She has a bachelor's degree in Chinese language and literature from Brown University and a PhD in Geophysics from MIT.*

Well thank you all and I'm impressed that you're all still here at the end of the conference so thank you for hanging out for this. I'm gonna talk today about what I like to call science activation, looking at the issue of how do we get science really engaged in the community and use it to inform policy decisions.

    I mean I think we all agree that there is a crisis even in our society about how we use science. We all know about climate change denial on one side but there's also all the issues about opposing GMOs or anti-vaccination, and what we are seeing here is there is a significant part of society that doesn't understand how the scientific process works and looks at scientific information as something you get told to believe because the scientist said it's true and then if you're going to believe that authority figure there's several others that you could turn to as well. So obviously this is a problem that goes beyond just the scientists but we have a role within this and ways in which we can address this. I hope that we can look at ways to move forward with it and this is more than science communication.

    Science communication is obviously a very important part of the process but involves a unidirectional approach. The idea that science communication is that I have information and I'm trying to get it to you so that you can accept that information and be able to understand it. Activation, if we put it on the other term, would be rather a bilateral communication process in which we engage with policymakers and actively work with them, and this is exchanging information to understand the problem at hand. Because when you really are trying to find solutions to some of these difficult problems it is not just a scientific issue and you need to really weigh

---

Delivered on February 17, 2019, at the American Association for the Advancement of Science Annual Meeting, Washington, DC.

how the various science results compared with what are the other constraints on what they can be making and what we are trying to do is empowering the use of the information rather than just accepting it.

So what are the challenges to undertaking science activation?

I think we've all seen this as we you know watch the March on Science but there are significant issues that go behind the problem. Why is this a joke? Alright, so I want to start with looking at what the culture of science is and the ways in which that culture interferes with communicating beyond our group. I think that most of you probably know the "xkcd" cartoon, and you know normal people say I'm not going to do this again and the scientist, let's see if it happens over and over.

Right. The point is that the scientist understands that we need, we don't get the right information out of stories. The plural of anecdote is not data. Right. We need to be able to test what we're doing. We need to make sure it is repeatable, and so we avoid stories for a very good reason. You know, I mean as somebody who's been involved in the earthquake prediction research all that time I spent in China in my graduate student days was a time when we still thought earthquake prediction was possible because we would have anecdotes. We would hear that X or Y happened before an earthquake. . . . But you can't predict an earthquake with it. You need to go see if it happens again.

I brought this up, this one I think that the whole thing about electromagnetic radiation pulses, it happened before one earthquake, and millions, tens of millions of dollars have been spent trying to track it down. And at this point, there's still no evidence that it's any more than a story that mislead you. I mean, so we try very hard to avoid stories. And the problem, of course, is that that is how people make decisions.

When you look at what role do stories play in human disease, making you need to think about how we came to have rational thought. We evolved the ability to reason, to protect ourselves, to be able to figure out, you know, make patterns, make theories about what was happening with the predator. But we did it in a hyper socialized setting. So we were rewarded for winning arguments, which does not require being right. It requires emotional connection, and it requires being able to manipulate somebody else's emotions. Hey, and so we have a very strong tendency to believe in things because someone told it to us that we trusted. We have emotional connection to, rather than being right. Right. This is called a confirmation bias. It is a little bit more than this. It is our tendency to be more open to data that supports our current view and more critical of data that opposes our view. Sometimes called an internal yes-man. Right. And that process of that is the reason that we had to develop the scientific method.

Human nature does not do logical reasoning very well. We have to work at it. So how does it work? Let's think about what it is that we do when we undertake experiments. Right. We might notice a coincidence, say, between electromagnetic radiation and that earthquake, and we want to go and figure out whether or not it's actually coincidental. Right. We are human enough that there's a lot of people that stumble at this point. They have to, you know, we really want to believe the patterns there, and accepting the data that says it's not is sometimes a challenge for us. But we hopefully get through that, or at least get caught along the way. We create a model that's consistent with known data to explain the relationship, and we make predictions from that model and test the predictions. Using statistics again, we know that the anecdote alone doesn't tell you what's going on. And we go through statistics to see whether or not the pattern actually exists. We present the results of all of this to our colleagues through meetings and through papers. And our colleagues then rip us to shreds. Right. That's what we do, and it is a necessary part of the scientific process, because the easiest person to fool is yourself.

Every one of us is subject to the confirmation bias, as much as any nonscientist, and, in fact, the fact that we believe in data actually means that we are more susceptible to confirmation bias. If you really don't care about data at all, and you have a different way of reacting to the whole process, so, we then learn to communicate by never giving the answer first. You know that you're going to be torn apart if you do this when you go to tell your colleague about the great new results you had. You first lay out the background, you tell them the approach you took, you give him your data, your error analysis, and show that you properly considered all of the uncertainties. And you do all of that before you give the result, because otherwise the result is going to have triggered him to start opposing it.

All right. So, we naturally communicate in this way, and it's fundamental to what we do. And we actually wonder why would anyone have a problem with this? The reality, of course, is that most of the rest of the world communicates in a very different way. Right. Read any newspaper article. It starts with the main results. It then tells you it matters, and it's only if you read to the end of the article that you actually get to see how that, how the result was being done. Okay. So, why do we worry about the fact that we are communicating in the way we do? They can, you know, so, people have to wait a bit for the result, they should understand it's important. Well, let's go back to these challenges that we're really facing. What happens is, we end up talking about our uncertainties, and when you talk with the larger public, talking to your colleague talking about the uncertainties is critically important to show you've done the work the right way. When you talk with a policymaker, they often hear, rather than an analysis of uncertainties, they hear that you are uncertain. So what's the problem with that? We understand that uncertainty analysis gives you the understanding of whether or not something is true. All right. They hear it as whether it is that we are uncertain, and uncertainty decreases action.

One of the things that's been able to be understood is that when people think it's uncertain, you increase anxiety. Instead of giving an answer, you increase the uncertainty that they're feeling. You increase their anxiety. You basically reduce the actions. Right. So we will often be in a position where we try to sound as certain as we can, and in many ways that is a good thing. But we have be very careful because if we act, if we act more certain than we are, and it comes out that we were wrong, it really can backfire.

People hear that as that you really didn't know what you're talking about, and then they don't hear you in the last time. This is tied to the risk perception, the people, how people perceive risk. Right. If you've never read the book on risk perception by Paul Slovak, it's a really wonderful way to get started into this. People do not analyze risk in a logical way. There are a lot of factors that determine whether we are afraid of something that is not connected to what the risk actually is. It's very clear that we are more afraid on things that we can't see coming. We are more afraid of things that it's uncertain whether they will be there, and if there is a perception that it is unknowable, it greatly increases the fear. Think about the fear people have about radiation, that it feels like unknown or weird science and we don't know when it's coming. Earthquakes also push all of these buttons because when you go back to the older world in which we evolved the unseen predator is a bigger problem. You know if you can see the predator coming, you know how to act to it. But it's that the possibility that it could be coming out from the, and you're gonna be caught by surprise, and that leaves us feeling much more frightened, right? So and this is tied to the idea that we really want to have patterns when we evolved our brains in this uncertain world. I mean we, the ability to make patterns kept us safe, helped protect us from the predators with bigger teeth and stronger muscles. What we had was the ability to make a pattern and figure out where to move to safety, how to deal with that predator coming out after you, so the ability to create patterns is what kept us safe.

And it's often incredibly important. Think about the ability to hypothesize a connection between your gastrointestinal distress and the mushrooms you just ate. That ability to make those connections made us safer, gave us the ability to survive and pass on our genes. The problem is that we make patterns whenever we see them, even if they don't really exist. All right, so we make a lot of patterns and that gets back to that testing of the scientific method. It's the way in which we determine whether or not the pattern that we think we're seeing is actually true.

. . .

Throughout human history we have a great fear of randomness, and that really affects our ability to look at these things and we try to find patterns no matter what happens. So I said that if we're trying to be too certain when in fact we aren't certain this can be a bad thing. This is some data from some social scientists looking at the response to, if you remember, peanut contamination. There was salmonella and peanut products, they [said] yes, we're very ascertain that there was no connection. When they were proved to be wrong, there was a huge return in media coverage and spikes of reports on this showing that when you act as though you're certain and you get proved wrong it undermines your ability to further communicate. I mean I think one other example of this, if you look at what has gone on in public health and the ideas around the food pyramid. In 1992 there was a desire to try and get people to stop having saturated fats, and they thought that people would have a difficult time recognizing the difference between saturated fats and other bad fats. So they just called all fats bad and said that grains were really good because it was really too hard to explain the difference between whole grains and white processed foods. And of course we now recognize that this is not such a good idea, but we have had this public use of this in a way that is actually harmful. I think of the health of our country and when they went to try and change that, they were afraid, and for good reason, of changing it by too much. So now we have this healthy eating pyramid where they've tried to sort of shift things around, and you notice the white breads now up in the top and they put exercise at the bottom and try to shift it because we are afraid of changing the message along the way.

So this provides a lot of challenges for us where we need to try and be as certain as we can be but then we're also faced with the issue about whether or not things have actually changed. And I mean so I sort of jumped on this is not going okay so when we look at these things about the challenges. I said there's too much focus on uncertainty and what has happened is we have been most successful when science reduces the uncertainty rather than when it increases it. One place you can see this is in the response to earthquakes. And we have with countries around the world, you will find that right after the earthquake everybody runs to the scientists and wants us to tell them what is happening. And if you actually think about it, why do people care what fault an earthquake happened on? It will not help them rebuild their house, right? But people, the media comes to us because they are—because providing information reduces fear. We give the earthquake a name we give it a number for the magnitude. We give it a fault and we are saying somebody understands it and this has been over decades a very positive place of interaction. It's led to a lot of my public visibility, because I was the person they turn to, and I find it very astonishing. Because I think of myself being a scientist out there providing them this information, and I have had so many people tell me I feel better when you tell us what's going on, you're a source of comfort.

But what it is, is I am reducing uncertainty. So I think this is this really important issue, that science activation is most successful when it reduces the uncertainty. One thing, however, that increases the uncertainty is the way in which we generally communicate about science results. Because the newest science is not consensus science. When you come to your disciplinary meeting and we give our press conferences, right, you come to give a talk at a meeting . . . and we give a press conference about it and this is on work that has not yet gone through peer-review, right? It's the newest stuff. So you're there and you talk about and you have this great result and your PR department from your university pushes you to go and do this because this is going to get you good coverage, right, but next year there might be another talk that says, you know, that thing last year, that was wrong. We found this, and don't believe those people over at JPL, us over here at Goddard have got a better picture of what's going on. And what the public is hearing is, oh they said this then they say that. We are increasing the uncertainty, presenting a picture that we don't know what we're talking about because we have a fundamental issue that the larger community doesn't really understand the science process. And what we are doing in our conferences is the first chance to vet your ideas with your colleagues and you do it to get the feedback, to find the things you better add to that study before you go to publish it.

It's likely not going to turn out to be the final answer, and yet it's the one that we are promoting to the public. And we don't really have an alternative at a different time to get people that consensus science because when you get to this consensus science, right, we skateboard right? Once everybody agrees it's true, we stop working on it. That's the time when we walk away from it, right? So you look at a policymaker, they're taught something in college that would be . . . you know, recent consensus science there now is twenty years out from college. They've been hearing these news reports going back and forth as people do their cutting-edge research.

But they once it's settled, they haven't heard what that final answer is.

And I think that we need to really focus on how we support scientists working in this realm of communicating consensus science that's not yet, you know, that's not sending everybody back to college because they haven't heard the most recent things. And you know one other aspect of this is when you think about how we talk about the need for STEM education, that is almost always qualified. There are so many STEM jobs we don't talk about it as though everybody really needs to understand how STEM works, right? I think we can actually make an argument that the Internet is playing something of the same role that the printing press played.

Think about Europe a thousand years ago. Nobody knew how to read and write. If you needed to read and write you got a specialist to do it for you. Even the King didn't read and write. I mean we had scribes. What happened with the printing press is that easy access to the written word turned reading from something that only the specialist did to something that everybody needed. I mean, you could still get a job, but you really couldn't participate in that larger social discourse. We are now in the position where the Internet has really changed the way in which we distribute information. Now it doesn't cost anything to go out, so you don't have an editor checking the facts and making sure that it is worth distributing. This information, everything, whether it is true or not, is easy to access, right? And we are watching the consequences of that, as lots of misinformation goes through.

And we have a larger society that has been told believe it because the scientists say it's true rather than saying believe it because you understand for yourself how it works out and how the logical reasoning works. And I would argue that this, the skill of a science researcher, is the skill to analyze the significance of a set of data and determine whether or not it's true and that is a skill that everybody needs to handle the flood of information coming in through the Internet. And I really believe strongly that we have to change the way we think about STEM education for everyone. We shouldn't be accepting that some people just can't do it, right? They probably can, and they haven't. But they've been discouraged out of it, and we have to recognize that maybe not everybody can understand this at this level but we all need to try. And we need it just to keep society functioning, so that's a pretty big list of problems.

Print Citations

CMS: Jones, Lucy. "Science Activation: How Do We Get Our Science Used by Those in Power?" Keynote Address at the American Association for the Advancement of Science Annual Meeting, Washington, DC, February 17, 2019. In *The Reference Shelf: Representative American Speeches, 2018–2019*, edited by Sophie Zyla, 162-168. Amenia, NY: Grey House Publishing, 2019.

MLA: Jones, Lucy. "Science Activation: How Do We Get Our Science Used by Those in Power?" American Association for the Advancement of Science Annual Meeting, 17 February 2019, Washington, DC. Keynote Address. *The Reference Shelf: Representative American Speeches, 2018–2019,* edited by Sophie Zyla, Grey House Publishing, 2019, pp. 162-168.

APA: Jones, L. (2019, February 17). Keynote Address on science activation: How do we get our science used by those in power? American Association for the Advancement of Science Annual Meeting, Washington, DC. In Sophie Zyla (Ed.), *The reference shelf: Representative American speeches, 2018–2019* (pp. 162-168). Amenia, NY: Grey House Publishing.

Speech on the 50th Anniversary of the *Apollo 11* Moon Landing

By Mike Pence

Michael R. Pence is the 48th and current vice president of the United States. He was elected to Congress six times, was the Republican Conference Chairman, and the 50th governor of Indiana. Mike Pence has a bachelor's degree in history from Hanover College and a law degree from Indiana University McKinney School of Law.

Governor Ron DeSantis, First Lady Casey, Administrator Bridenstine, Director Cabana, General Selva, distinguished members of Congress, Marillyn Hewson, the dedicated men and women of NASA, and especially Rick Armstrong and the members of the Neil Armstrong family, and *Apollo 11* astronaut Buzz Aldrin: It is my great honor to be here with all of you today.

It's great to be back here at the John F. Kennedy Space Center, as Vice President and as Chairman of the National Space Council, with my wonderful wife Karen, to celebrate—to celebrate with all of you the 50th Anniversary of the *Apollo 11* Moon Landing a half a century ago that will be remembered forever.

And I've been looking forward to this day, but allow me to bring greetings from another great space enthusiast and a great champion of American leadership in space. I begin today by bringing greetings from the 45th President of the United States of America, President Donald Trump.

Today, our nation pays tribute to the three brave astronauts who sat atop a 360-foot rocket that lifted off from Pad 39A 50 years ago this week—two of whom walked on the moon 50 years ago today.

We also gather to pay tribute to the nearly 400,000 Americans—engineers, technicians, designers—whose sacrifices and dedication made it possible for *Apollo 11* to complete what another president called "the most hazardous and dangerous and greatest adventure upon which mankind has ever embarked." Let's hear it for all those who supported these three brave astronauts 50 years ago.

When President Kennedy challenged the nation in 1961 to put a man on the moon and return him safely to the Earth before the decade was out, it's important to remember that our country was not yet ready to meet that challenge.

We didn't have the rockets or the launch pads, or the spacesuits or the lander. We hadn't even invented many of the materials or tools that we would need. Not only did we not have what we needed, we didn't even know what we needed.

Delivered on July 20, 2019, at the John F. Kennedy Space Center, Cape Canaveral, FL.

But President Kennedy summarized that epic endeavor in one simple sentence: "We choose to go to the moon."

And make no mistake about it: The moon was a choice. An American choice. And like every time the American people make up their mind, once that decision was made, American ingenuity, grit, and determination—the achievement was inevitable.

The only challenges that remained were challenges of engineering and science. The moon didn't come easily, and it didn't come without costs. And it did not come without grave danger or without sacrifice.

To this day, Americans grieve the loss of three brave astronauts of *Apollo 1* who were lost in a fire on the launchpad in January of 1967. And we think of them and their families even today.

The risks for Apollo were so great, the odds were so long, that many feared that even if our astronauts made it to the moon, they might not make it back.

In fact, history records that President Nixon prepared a speech in the event of a tragedy, where he would explain to the nation that the mission had failed.

But, of course, the mission didn't fail. After all—with 400,000 men and women behind the mission at NASA, and with the hearts and prayers of the American people—how could it fail?

For at the controls of the *Apollo 11* Lunar Module, known as *Eagle*, stood two great Americans: Mission Commander Neil Armstrong—and a man who is with us today, Lunar Module pilot Buzz Aldrin.

And circling overhead in lunar orbit was Command Module pilot Michael Collins.

Just picture it: Fifty years ago today, at almost exactly this hour, Neil Armstrong and Buzz Aldrin were about halfway into their powered descent on the final leg of their landing on the moon. There they were, standing beside one another in a capsule not much bigger than a couple of telephone booths, just minutes from touchdown.

They thought they were ready for every contingency. After all, as Buzz told me just a few days ago, they had spent two years intensively training for this moment, and they'd run almost 600 simulated landings all designed to be more difficult than the real thing.

Eagle had just finished its rollover to position itself for final approach, when all of the sudden, Neil Armstrong called out to Houston that *Eagle* had a "1202 Alarm." The problem was nobody on board or in Houston had any idea what a "1202 Alarm" was.

Eagle's flight computer was overloading. Not only could they not see the moon out their windows; they couldn't know for certain how far they were from the surface. Not a good way to fly.

And yet, how calm they were. Working with the team back here on Earth, they quickly resolved the problem without betraying the slightest anxiety. People all over the world were watching, with no idea that anything had gone wrong. That, my friends, is what they used to call "The Right Stuff."

You know, there's a reason Neil Armstrong, as well, was called the "Ice Commander" in his day. When the original landing area turned out to be so full of large boulders that landing there would have doomed the mission and the crew, history records that Neil Armstrong calmly took control of the Lunar Module, skimmed along the top of the surface of the moon in search for a safe place to touch down. And by the time he found a safe spot, known to all of us as "Tranquility Base," Armstrong and Aldrin had only 17 seconds of fuel remaining.

Like every one of my generation, I remember that day. Six hundred million people around the world were watching their TVs and listening to their radios, waiting with admiration, anxiety, and wonder. And I was one of them—a little boy sitting in front of our black-and-white television in the basement of our home in Indiana.

When those first snowy images of Neil Armstrong stepping off the bottom rung of the ladder beamed down to Earth at 10:56 p.m. on Sunday, July 20, 1969, they made an indelible mark—not just on my imagination, but on the imagination of my generation and every generation to come.

It was a moment so rich in meaning that, upon hearing Neil Armstrong's first call from Tranquility Base, even the era's greatest newsman, Walter Cronkite, could only shake his head and utter two words: "Oh, boy."

All at once, the nation held its breath—as through the crackling broadcast we listened to, we heard Neil Armstrong use those immortal words: "That's one small step for man, one giant leap for mankind."

In that moment, the men of *Apollo 11* did more than help expand our understanding of Creation, and they did more than win the Space Race. They brought together our nation. And for one brief moment, all the people of the world were truly one.

Now, true to their creed, astronauts have never liked the idea of being called heroes. Yet for all they did—and for all the risks they took—if Neil Armstrong, Buzz Aldrin, and Mike Collins are not heroes, then there are no heroes.

We honor these men today, and America will always honor our Apollo astronauts. They were heroes all. We honor the men of *Apollo 11* by remembering their epic voyage and telling their story. But we also honor them by continuing the work they so nobly and courageously advanced in American space exploration.

Apollo 11 was followed by five more successful moon missions culminating in the final historic journey of *Apollo 17*—America's last trip to the moon. As we honor our *Apollo 11* astronauts, we are also honored today to be joined by *Apollo 17* astronaut Harrison Schmidt. Thank you for your courageous service.

As Harrison and I have discussed about his mission, while the last words spoken on the moon might not be as well-known as the first words, his fellow astronaut Gene Cernan said more perhaps than anyone could've known at the time. It was a challenge to our time.

As he stepped off the moon on December 17, 1972, Gene—he said these words, and I quote, "As I take man's last steps on the moon for some time to come, history will record...that America's challenge of today has forged man's destiny of tomorrow." And then he ended by saying, "We leave the moon as we came and, God willing…we shall soon return with peace and hope for all mankind." Those were words of challenge in 1972.

And in our time, as President Trump said, this generation of Americans knows that it is "America's destiny to be…the leader amongst nations on our adventure into the great unknown."

And standing before you today, I am proud to report, at the direction of the President of the United States of America, America will return to the moon within the next five years, and the next man and the first woman on the moon will be American astronauts. We're going back.

After more than 45 years, where one Administration after another chose to limit America's space program to low Earth orbit, President Donald Trump has changed all that.

Early in this Administration, the President revived the National Space Council within the White House to coordinate all space-related activities across the government, including matters related to national security. And we've been hard at work.

The Space Council has helped bring together skilled leaders in business and industry to revive and renew America's commitment to human space exploration. And I'm pleased that many members of our Users' Advisory Group for the Space Council are with us today for this historic occasion. Join me in welcoming these dedicated and distinguished Americans.

The President also signed Space Policy Directive 1, "challenging NASA to lead the return of Americans to the moon, send the first Americans to Mars, and enable humans to expand and deepen our reach across the solar system." It is our mission.

And as I speak to you today, I'm proud to report we're investing in new rockets, new spaceships. We're working with private companies around this country to develop the new technologies of the future by unleashing the burgeoning private space industry that dots the landscape of this historic center and this nation.

And within the next year, we will once again send American astronauts into space on American rockets, from American soil.

Already, we've given our human exploration missions a newfound sense of urgency not seen in more than a generation.

And, last year, NASA and American innovators began an accelerated design process for both the lunar orbital gateway and the lunar surface base—all of which we will need to support Americans on the moon and to train and prepare to send Americans to Mars.

And while we've made great strides in advancing the President's bold vision for space—unlike in years past, we will have the budgets to match it. And that's why I'm especially grateful today to be joined by some of the greatest champions of American leadership in space in the Congress of the United States: House Minority Whip Steve Scalise, Congressman Robert Aderholt, Congressman Brian Babin, Congressman Bill Posey, and other distinguished members of Congress. Would you please rise and allow us to express our appreciation for your strong support of renewed American leadership?

With strong bipartisan support, this President has already signed into law the largest NASA budget ever. And on this historic occasion, I'm told that we've also achieved a critical milestone in our effort to go to the moon and beyond.

Today, thanks to the hard work of the men of NASA—men and women of NASA and of American industry, the *Orion* crew vehicle for the Artemis 1 mission is complete and ready to begin preparations for its historic first flight.

In the coming years, American astronauts will return to the moon aboard the *Orion*, and they'll return with new ambitions. We will spend weeks and months, not days and hours, on the lunar surface. This time we're going to the moon to stay— and to explore and develop new technologies. We will extract water from ice in the permanently shadowed craters of the South Pole. We will fly on a new generation of spacecraft that will enable us to reach Mars, not in years but in months.

Americans are leading in space once again. And today we're reminded—we're reminded how American leadership 50 years ago, and the accomplishment of *Apollo 11*, inspired our nation. As the President said, it "ignited our sense of adventure" and "steeled our belief that no dream is impossible, no matter how lofty or challenging."

And as Buzz Aldrin said today, in his words, "Looking back, landing on the moon wasn't just our job, it was a historic opportunity to prove to the world America's can-do spirit."

But as we lead in human space exploration again, we'll carry not only American ingenuity and pride, but most importantly, we'll carry America's ideals into the vast expanse of space—ideals of freedom and liberty.

Apollo 11 is the only event in the 20th century that stands a chance of being widely remembered in the 30th century.

A thousand years from now, July 20, 1969 will likely be a date that will live in the minds and imaginations of men and women, as long as there are men and women to remember—across this world, across this solar system, and beyond.

So, today, we remember the heroes of *Apollo 11* and all the heroes that supported them in their mission—some 400,000 Americans.

But today, we also reaffirm our commitment to "unlock the mysteries of space" and to lead. And as we continue on this American journey, we go with the same resolve and determination of those who have gone before.

And we go with faith.

Faith in the courage of this new generation of astronauts—men and women of the character and caliber of those who have gone before. They're remarkable pioneers who will carry American leadership into space.

Faith in the ingenuity of the men and women of NASA and all of those across the American space enterprise, whose creativity and tireless efforts in the days ahead will match that of their forebears who created and invented new ways to explore and expanded human understanding with American leadership.

And finally, I believe, as we go forward—and as millions of Americans believe in their hearts, and have throughout the generations—that we'll go forward with faith that as those pioneers put on the spacesuits and climb aboard the rockets, that we'll believe that even if they rise on the wings of the dawn, even if they go up to heavens, that even there His hand will guide them, and His right hand will hold them fast. And that'll be our prayer.

Today, we mark the 50th anniversary of *Apollo 11*. We celebrate the heroic astronauts who accomplished that extraordinary feat in human history—and all those who supported them.

And today, we resolve, for the sake of all they accomplished, that America will lead in space once again. And this nation will once again astonish the world with the heights we reach and the wonders we achieve.

So may God bless the crew of *Apollo 11* and all who supported them on their historic journey. May God bless this new generation of pioneers and all who will support them. And may God continue to bless the United States of America.

Thank you.

Print Citations

CMS: Pence, Mike. "Speech on the 50th Anniversary of the *Apollo 11* Moon Landing." Keynote Address at the John F. Kennedy Space Center, Cape Canaveral, FL, July 20, 2019. In *The Reference Shelf: Representative American Speeches, 2018–2019*, edited by Sophie Zyla, 169-174. Amenia, NY: Grey House Publishing, 2019.

MLA: Pence, Mike. "Speech on the 50th Anniversary of the *Apollo 11* Moon Landing." John F. Kennedy Space Center, 20 July 2019, Cape Canaveral, FL. Keynote Address. *The Reference Shelf: Representative American Speeches, 2018–2019*, edited by Sophie Zyla, Grey House Publishing, 2019, pp. 169-174.

APA: Pence, M. (2019, July 19). Speech on the 50th anniversary of the *Apollo 11* moon landing. John F. Kennedy Space Center, Cape Canaveral, FL. In Sophie Zyla (Ed.), *The reference shelf: Representative American speeches, 2018–2019* (pp. 169-174). Amenia, NY: Grey House Publishing.

5
Health Issues

Photo by Pete Marovich/Bloomberg via Getty Images.

CMS Administrator Seema Verma outlined a plan to help states take control of insurance and other medical regulations, supporting decentralized health care decisions.

Remarks on the HEAL Initiative

By Alex M. Azar II

Alex Azar served as general counsel and deputy secretary prior to being sworn in as secretary of the U.S. Department of Health and Human Services (HHS) in January of 2018. In the private sector Azar was vice president of corporate affairs and communications at Eli Lilly and Co. and president of Lilly USA LLC. Azar was an attorney and also clerk for U.S. Supreme Court Justice Antonin Scalia. He has a bachelor's degree in economics and government from Dartmouth College and a law degree from Yale University.

Good morning, everyone, and thank you for joining us on this call.

This morning, it's an honor to be announcing nearly $1 billion in grants as part of NIH's HEAL Initiative, which is by far the largest and most ambitious research effort on pain and addiction ever launched.

I want to put this announcement in context not only of our opioid strategy, but of President Trump's vision for healthcare and our efforts at HHS around impactable public health challenges.

President Trump's vision for healthcare is comprehensive. We are working on three cross-cutting platforms for improving Americans' health: reforming how Americans finance their healthcare, delivering better value from that care, and addressing particular, impactable health challenges.

One of those impactable challenges is the opioid crisis, where, thankfully, the President's leadership and the united efforts of communities across America are already producing results. Provisional estimates of overdose deaths dropped by 5 percent from 2017 to 2018, the first decrease in more than 20 years.

We're making an impact because we're making use of the effective tools we have. During my very first speech on the opioid crisis as HHS Secretary, I made it very clear that our efforts would follow the science. We would expand access to the gold standard for treatment of opioid use disorder, medication-assisted treatment; we would expand access to the life-saving drug naloxone; and we would reduce inappropriate opioid prescribing.

President Trump promised these same steps when he launched his opioid initiative, and we've delivered on them: From 2016 to 2019, we estimate that the number of Americans receiving medication-assisted treatment has increased by 38 percent. The amount of naloxone prescribed monthly has increased 378 percent

---

Delivered on September 26, 2019, at the U.S. Department of Health and Human Services, Washington, DC.

since the President took office, while the total amount of prescription opioids being prescribed monthly has dropped by 31 percent.

So we're making an impact with the tools we have. But NIH, as part of our department-wide strategy for the crisis, has also identified a number of crucial needs or significant opportunities for new tools, improved tools, or better use of the tools we have.

Dr. Collins will explain a bit more about what each of those areas looks like. They encompass every aspect of this crisis: methods and tools for addiction treatment, treatment for neonatal abstinence syndrome, better understanding of chronic pain and better tools for treating it, and more.

As the largest single investment ever made in pain and addiction research, NIH's HEAL Initiative will be a major leap forward for our understanding of the opioid crisis and the very real problem of pain in America.

NIH research has already undergirded our work in so many ways. One of the best data points we have on the effectiveness of medication-assisted treatment came out of an NIH-funded study, which found that treatment of opioid use disorder with methadone or buprenorphine following an overdose is associated with significant reductions in opioid-related mortality—59 percent for methadone and 38 percent for buprenorphine.

And NIH isn't the only game in town on supporting and promoting research: CDC released grants this month to support better data at the state level; SAMHSA has worked to make scientifically based resources more available to practitioners; and CMS's support for state innovation in Medicaid will expand our knowledge of how to support addiction treatment through our financing programs.

Better research is one of the five pillars of the HHS opioid strategy put together by our department under President Trump. But it really undergirds all of the other pillars, too: Better research will support better prevention, treatment, and recovery services; it will support better access to overdose-reversing drugs; it will support better pain management; and it will support better data on the crisis.

So, we look forward to how the sweeping set of grants announced by NIH today will advance our work against opioid addiction and pain on all fronts.

With this research, we will not only develop knowledge to combat this crisis, but also to lay a foundation such that our country will never again see another addiction crisis like this one.

With that, I now want to hand things over to Dr. Collins to talk more about NIH's research agenda.

Print Citations

CMS: Azar II, Alex M. "Remarks on the HEAL Initiative." Speech at the U.S. Department of Health and Human Services, Washington, DC, September 26, 2019. In *The Reference Shelf: Representative American Speeches, 2018–2019,* edited by Sophie Zyla, 177-179. Amenia, NY: Grey House Publishing, 2019.

MLA: Azar II, Alex M. "Remarks on the HEAL Initiative." U.S. Department of Health and Human Services, 26 September 2019, Washington, DC. Speech. *The Reference Shelf: Representative American Speeches, 2018–2019,* edited by Sophie Zyla, Grey House Publishing, 2019, pp. 177-179.

APA: Azar II, A.M. (2019, September 26). Remarks on the HEAL initiative. U.S. Department of Health and Human Services, Washington, DC. In Sophie Zyla (Ed.), *The reference shelf: Representative American speeches, 2018–2019* (pp. 177-179). Amenia, NY: Grey House Publishing.

Remarks on Individual Health Insurance Market Rates

By Alex M. Azar II

Alex Azar served as general counsel and deputy secretary prior to being sworn in as secretary of the U.S. Department of Health and Human Services (HHS) in January of 2018. In the private sector Azar was vice president of corporate affairs and communications at Eli Lilly and Co. and president of Lilly USA LLC. Azar was an attorney and also clerk for U.S. Supreme Court Justice Antonin Scalia. He has a bachelor's degree in economics and government from Dartmouth College and a law degree from Yale University.

Thank you all for joining this call today. We have some important news to share: For the second year under President Trump, benchmark premiums for Affordable Care Act plans on the federal exchange will drop, and the number of options available will increase.

Lower costs and more options for American patients is a key piece of the President's vision for healthcare: an affordable, patient-centric system that puts you in control, and treats you like a person, not a number.

The President's approach to the ACA reflects his overall approach to healthcare, which is to protect what works and fix what's broken.

This administration has made no secret about it: We believe the Affordable Care Act simply doesn't work. It is still unaffordable for far too many.

But until Congress gets around to replacing it, the President will do what he can to fix the problems created by this system for millions of Americans, including the 29 million Americans who remain uninsured.

That's included opening up new, affordable options, such as short-term plans, association health plans, and health reimbursement arrangements.

It's also included his commitment to stabilizing the Affordable Care Act's exchanges and bringing certainty to the market.

Our efforts are bearing fruit, now for the second year in a row. The premium for the average Healthcare.gov state's second lowest cost silver plan, also known as the benchmark plan premium, will decrease by 4 percent for a 27 year-old. This follows a 1 percent decrease from 2018 to 2019.

I said last year that President Trump, the President who was supposedly trying

---

Delivered on October 22, 2019, at the U.S. Department of Health and Human Services, Washington, DC.

to sabotage this law, has been better at running it than the guy who wrote the law—and that has remained the case this year.

In total, 27 out of the 38 states on the federal exchange are seeing decreases in the benchmark premium.

There will be 175 issuers offering plans on the federal exchange, an increase of 20 issuers from 2019. Only two states have a single issuer this coming year, compared with five states last year.

Shoppers on the federal exchange will generally have more options compared with 2019: The average enrollee will have 3.5 issuers available in 2020, compared with 2.8 issuers in 2019.

Now, it must be emphasized that these premiums are still unaffordable for many. For instance, a 27-year-old single person buying the second-lowest cost silver plan in Nebraska is going to pay $583 a month for coverage, down from $687 in 2019. That's real savings. But she's still going to be spending almost $7,000 a year on insurance premiums, when she could be making as little as $48,000 in income—and she will still have a sizeable deductible to spend through.

This is not a workable way for Americans to finance the care they need, and that is why we continue to look for ways to open up new alternatives and replace this broken law.

But we're headed in the right direction. For 2020, Medicare Advantage premiums are down, Part D premiums are down, and now ACA premiums are down. The bottom line under President Trump: Costs are down and choices are up.

That's what it looks like to deliver the affordability you need, the options and control you want, and the quality you deserve.

I now want to hand things over to Administrator Verma, to discuss more about the marketplace and how we're improving the experience as best we can for patients under the ACA.

Print Citations

CMS: Azar II, Alex M. "Remarks on Individual Health Insurance Market Rates." Speech at the U.S. Department of Health and Human Services, Washington, DC, October 22, 2019. In *The Reference Shelf: Representative American Speeches, 2018–2019*, edited by Sophie Zyla, 180-181. Amenia, NY: Grey House Publishing, 2019.

MLA: Azar II, Alex M. "Remarks on Individual Health Insurance Market Rates." U.S. Department of Health and Human Services, 22 October 2019, Washington, DC. Speech. *The Reference Shelf: Representative American Speeches, 2018–2019*, edited by Sophie Zyla, Grey House Publishing, 2019, pp. 180-181.

APA: Azar II, A.M. (2019, October 22). Remarks on individual health insurance market rates. U.S. Department of Health and Human Services, Washington, DC. In Sophie Zyla (Ed.), *The reference shelf: Representative American speeches, 2018–2019* (pp. 180-181). Amenia, NY: Grey House Publishing.

State Relief and Empowerment Waivers: Affordable Care Act

By Seema Verma

Seema Verma was nominated administrator for the Centers for Medicare and Medicaid Services (CMS) by President Trump and confirmed by the Senate on March 13, 2017. Verma was the president, chief executive officer (CEO), and founder of SVC, Inc. a health care consulting company. She has a master's degree in Public Health from Johns Hopkins University and a bachelor's degree in life sciences from the University of Maryland.

It's truly a pleasure to welcome you to the CMS National Forum on State Relief and Empowerment Waivers. It was just six months ago that President Trump stood where I'm standing today to announce the Administration's new direction to lower prescription drug prices, making it very clear that in health care, it is not business as usual on his watch.

It's energizing to be in a room with state officials discussing the opportunities for locally-led reform. I'm glad to hear that we have members of the national press watching our live stream, who I hope take note.

If you spend too much time inside the beltway, it's easy to become disconnected from the innovation happening in state capitols across the country.

Of course, thinking outside the box is what state governments are doing all the time. No wonder states have long been held up as laboratories of democracy—driving innovative policy reforms forward. This isn't surprising to any of us, because all of you certainly know that the Federal government just isn't as nimble and responsive as state governments.

While the ACA imposed massive new regulations and costs on health care, there was at least a recognition that states might want to try different approaches. After all, states have historically been in charge of regulating insurance.

The ACA includes a provision under section 1332 that allows states to waive certain ACA regulations to design and implement new state health care programs.

We're all here today to focus on how states can better take advantage of this flexibility under the law.

I came to this job with a belief that Washington doesn't have all the answers when it comes to our health care needs . . . that states are the testing grounds of innovation and reform . . . and that care decisions centralized in Washington too often

---

Delivered on April 23, 2019, at the Centers for Medicare & Medicaid Services National Forum, Washington, DC.

come at the expense of patients. So, one of our goals here at CMS is to be a strong supporter of states, helping them pursue their vision and their solutions.

The Problem with Federalizing Health Care Policy

This view is quite the contrast to the "Medicare for All" proposals that we're seeing emerge from Congress. These proposals would actually end private insurance and put the wellbeing of every American patient in the hands of Washington officials.

Looking at the short history of the ACA should be proof enough for why it's such a mistake to double down on government solutions.

After the ACA's main requirements were implemented in 2014, it didn't take long at all for premiums to begin to escalate and insurers to begin leaving the market. In the fall of 2015, a number of states began reporting substantial premium increases for the 2016 benefit year, nine states in all saw average premiums on the individual market rise by more than 20 percent in that one year.

The next year, these premium increases spread across the country. Average monthly premiums in the individual market increased by 21 percent for the 2017 benefit year. In all, 27 states saw premiums rise by more than 20 percent that year, which included all nine states that had experienced 20 percent or higher rate hikes the previous year. Yes, that means nine states suffered back-to-back premium hikes exceeding 20 percent.

At the same time premiums increased, enrollment dropped by 10 percent in 2017. Most of this drop in enrollment occurred among the unsubsidized portion of the market, which experienced a 20 percent drop for the year.[1] That represented 1.3 million unsubsidized people leaving the market.

Now these are averages and some states experienced far more substantial premium increases and enrollment declines. For example, premiums in Arizona increased by an astonishing 97 percent while enrollment among the unsubsidized dropped by 73 percent.

At the same time premiums were rising, insurers began fleeing markets across a substantial portion of the country. The number of issuers participating on Healthcare.gov nationwide declined by 28 percent in 2017 and another 21 percent in 2018.[2] As a result, more than half the counties in America had just a single issuer that year.[3]

With no competition, these monopoly issuers have the market power to hike rates. In fact, a recent study found that Exchange premiums were 50 percent higher, on average, in rating areas with a monopolist insurer compared to those with more than two insurers.[4]

Actions to Expand State Authority

On his first day in office, President Trump issued an executive order to agencies to minimize the economic burden of the law and "to provide greater flexibility to States and cooperate with them in implementing healthcare programs."

Within three weeks CMS issued a market stabilization rule, and, building on that rule, CMS then issued the 2019 Payment Notice. Collectively, these rules delivered on a number of policies that industry analysts and state officials, including many of you, recommended to help strengthen the markets. In addition, they gave states new tools and flexibility in regulating their insurance markets to lower premiums and increase choice.

And it worked.

I'm pleased to report that we are starting to see results. For the first time since the ACA's implementation, we've seen average premium rates decline by 1.5 percent for plans selected on HealthCare.gov.[5] While this decline might be modest, it's a substantial departure from the double-digit premium increases the market suffered in recent years. And this is just an average. Some states saw larger drops, including an 18 percent drop in Tennessee and a 16 percent drop in New Hampshire.

We're also seeing a boost in insurer participation. For 2019, there are 23 more issuers participating on HealthCare.gov than 2018. As a result, only five states will have one issuer, compared to ten states last year.

I'm also very pleased to report that, just last week, we finalized a reduction in the user fee on issuers participating in the federal Exchange thanks to the successful efforts to improve the efficiency of Exchange operations. The savings from this reduction will pass directly to consumers in the form of lower premiums.

While this is all positive movement, we recognize the ACA's serious problems remain. Many Americans continue to be priced out of the market and there are 28.5 million uninsured.[6] As a result, enrollment among unsubsidized people continues to decline.[7] The average monthly premium for a family of four on HealthCare.gov is over $1,500, which can easily exceed the family's mortgage.[8] There are areas of the country with far higher premiums. A 60-year-old couple living in Grand Island, Nebraska, making $70,000, will need to pay over $3,000 per month. That's almost $38,000 per year for the lowest cost silver tier plan with an $11,100 deductible. That's over half their income.

It is no wonder Americans are increasingly concerned about health care. The ACA did nothing to address the underlying problems behind rising health care costs in this country. Health care costs continue to be on a trajectory to consume nearly 1 in every 5 dollars of the nation's economy by 2027. At the end of the day, we have to address rising health care costs because that is what is increasing premiums.

So, while the steps outlined above are moving us in the right direction, they were steps to build on, not to rest on.

Given the current constraints on addressing these problems legislatively, we're not going to stand still and wait while millions of Americans are struggling to access affordable coverage. This Administration has taken immediate, appropriate, and necessary administrative actions to promote more choice and affordability. But we also know there are opportunities for states to take action.

As long as we have this unworkable law in place, we simply have to offer states flexibility to work towards real solutions.

Therefore, and this is what we are all here to discuss today, last fall the Administration issued new guidance expanding state flexibility to waive certain ACA requirements through a waiver under section 1332 of the law.

New 1332 Guidance Expands State Flexibility

Under the law, states have significant opportunities to chart a different course. States can seek waivers of certain federal requirements as long as their proposal meets a set of four guardrails.

Unfortunately, guidance issued under the prior administration in December 2015, significantly thwarted the types of creativity and innovation states could pursue. The prior administration imposed a one-size-fits-all approach to these waivers, making it difficult for states to address the specific needs of their citizens.

Before I came to CMS, I can tell you from my experience with states, it was impossible to put forward ideas. I worked with states on 1332 waivers and found the prior guidance to be extremely limiting.

With this unnecessarily restrictive guidance in place, very few states have come forward with innovative new strategies because the guidance tied their hands. To date, we have approved eight waivers. And, all but one of these waivers have been for states to create their own reinsurance programs. While these reinsurance waivers offer states an important tool to reduce premiums, they really represent the first step in stabilizing the market and bringing down premiums. We believe reinsurance waivers barely touch the surface of what may be possible.

In response to numerous state requests to help them address some of the ACA's most onerous and limiting requirements, the new guidance gives states the flexibility they need to increase choices for their citizens, promote market stability, and more affordable coverage.

The guidance increases flexibility with respect to the guardrails. The guidance also provides new functionality for states to leverage components of the federal Exchange platform. Finally, and to be very clear, the new guidance does nothing to change the ACA's pre-existing condition protections. The protections cannot be waived, and a waiver cannot be approved that might otherwise undermine these protections. And, regardless, this administration stands committed to protecting people with pre-existing conditions.

Waiver Templates

We didn't stop with issuing the new guidance. Based on my former work with states, I knew states would benefit from further details on what can be possible through a 1332 waiver. To help stimulate innovation and spur further discussion, last November we also released a series of waiver concepts that illustrate how states might take advantage of these new flexibilities.

Later today, we'll also be going over these concepts in more detail, but I do want to highlight the fact that these concepts offer a real opportunity for states to provide better coverage to people with pre-existing conditions. Today, we know that the

ACA has not delivered on its promise to people with pre-existing conditions. In particular, if you are unsubsidized and have a pre-existing condition, coverage on the individual market has likely become unaffordable to you. If that couple in Grand Island, Nebraska that I mentioned before has a pre-existing condition, they're not going to be able to drop over half their income on a premium. They'll have to find another way or go uninsured.

Furthermore, plans on the individual market generally have high deductibles and cost-sharing requirements that are not designed for people with pre-existing conditions. When you know you'll spend through a $7,000 deductible in just a few months and need access to a particular doctor, the growing number of high-deductible, narrow network plans are just not for you.

Through the risk stabilization waiver concept, states have the flexibility to develop a different approach that can provide better coverage options for people with pre-existing conditions while at the same time reducing premiums for everyone else. So far seven states have implemented reinsurance programs that fund people with high claims costs and, therefore, remove these costs from the individual market risk pool. By removing these costs, reinsurance lowers premiums for everyone in the market. Premium savings ranged from 8 percent in Oregon to 30 percent in Maryland.

Reinsurance is what many states are already doing, but we're here to think about new ideas states can pursue. In addition to the reinsurance concept, the waiver concepts we'll be discussing today highlight a new type of high risk pool approach to provide better coverage for people with pre-existing conditions. This would provide an opportunity to better tailor coverage for people with pre-existing conditions while lowering premiums for everyone else just the same as reinsurance.

Some have criticized the new guidance and waiver concepts because they claim there is an opportunity for states to adopt waivers that undermine the individual market risk pool and, as a result, make the market more expensive for people with pre-existing conditions. These critics claim that giving states the opportunity to offer new options to purchase health plans outside the individual market, such as short-term, limited duration insurance, could pull healthier people out of the market and undermine coverage available to people with pre-existing conditions who remain in the market.

Again, I want to make clear that a waiver cannot undermine coverage for people with pre-existing conditions. While the new guidance creates more flexibility with respect to the guardrails, the guardrails remain in force and continue to provide strong, meaningful protections. Any state waiver will need to carefully account for any impact on the individual market risk pool and guarantee that people with pre-existing conditions continue to have access to coverage that is at least as comprehensive and affordable as before.

So, if a state is to allow subsidies to be used for short term plans, they must have a solution for how to continue to guarantee access to the same level of affordability and comprehensiveness for people who remain in the individual market.

While we're focused on 1332 waivers today, we will also spend a short time identifying some new opportunities for states in the Medicaid program. When the key people working with states on Medicaid waivers are already in the building, it seemed a waste not to invite someone down to provide an update on what we're doing to give states more tools to improve their Medicaid programs.

Next, you will hear from my Senior Counselor Calder Lynch on these opportunities. As states consider possibilities under 1332, we want states to keep in mind how a 1332 waiver can be part of a more comprehensive health care program that provides a continuum of coverage from a Medicaid 1115 waiver to a 1332 waiver. A state does not have to have one coverage model for low-income adults on Medicaid and a completely different one for people with premium subsidies. Income fluctuates, and we want people to strive for financial independence. Recognizing this, a state could design one seamless structure that guarantees people have access to affordable health insurance in the private market while removing barriers to upward mobility.

At CMS we are focused on being a strong partner with states. Whether you are working on a 1332 waiver, 1115 waiver or other options, our staff are here to help you as you work to develop better healthcare programs.

Look, we've given you options and now you have the power to make the individual markets work through innovative policies that best meet the needs of your citizens. We are returning freedom, authority and innovation to you, state leaders.

Since we published our guidance last November, my staff has held regional forums for states across the country in Illinois and Georgia—and the innovative thinking there was impressive. And we have another session coming up next month in Denver.

But today, we are bringing the conversation to Washington. Now with you all here in the Great Hall of HHS—we are ready to talk about great ideas that will accomplish great things. I am looking forward to an inspiring day.

Thank you all for coming today and thank you for your leadership as you pursue innovative solutions to provide more choice and affordability to all Americans.

Notes

1. https://www.cms.gov/CCIIO/Programs-and-Initiatives/Health-Insurance-Marketplaces/Downloads/2018-07-02-Trends-Report-2.pdf.
2. https://aspe.hhs.gov/system/files/pdf/260041/2019LandscapeBrief.pdf.
3. https://www.cms.gov/CCIIO/Programs-and-Initiatives/Health-Insurance-Marketplaces/Downloads/2017-10-20-Issuer-County-Map.pdf.
4. https://www.healthaffairs.org/doi/full/10.1377/hlthaff.2018.0054.
5. https://www.cms.gov/newsroom/press-releases/cms-issues-2019-exchange-open-enrollment-period-final-report.
6. https://www.census.gov/library/publications/2018/demo/p60-264.html.
7. See https://www.cms.gov/CCIIO/Programs-and-Initiatives/Health-Insurance-Marketplaces/Downloads/2018-07-02-Trends-Report-2.pdf; and https://www.kff.org/health-reform/press-release/

enrollment-in-the-individual-insurance-market-continued-to-fall-in-the-first-quarter-of-2018-with-the-12-percent-overall-decline-concentrated-in-off-exchange-plans/.
8. https://aspe.hhs.gov/system/files/pdf/260041/2019LandscapeBrief.pdf.

Print Citations

CMS: Verma, Seema. "State Relief and Empowerment Waivers: Affordable Care Act." Speech at the Centers for Medicare & Medicaid Services National Forum, Washington, DC, April 23, 2019. In *The Reference Shelf: Representative American Speeches, 2018–2019,* edited by Sophie Zyla, 182-188. Amenia, NY: Grey House Publishing, 2019.

MLA: Verma, Seema. "State Relief and Empowerment Waivers: Affordable Care Act." Centers for Medicare & Medicaid Services National Forum, 23 April 2019, Washington, DC. Speech. *The Reference Shelf: Representative American Speeches, 2018–2019,* edited by Sophie Zyla, Grey House Publishing, 2019, pp. 182-188.

APA: Verma, S. (2019, April 23). Speech on state relief and empowerment waivers: Affordable Care Act. Centers for Medicare & Medical Services National Forum, Washington, DC. In Sophie Zyla (Ed.), *The reference shelf: Representative American speeches, 2018–2019* (pp. 182-188). Amenia, NY: Grey House Publishing.

The Cost of Health Care

By Lamar Alexander

Lamar Alexander served as governor of Tennessee from 1979–1987 and as a U.S. senator from 2002 to the present. In 2016 Alexander received the James Madison Award for his work on No Child Left Behind. He is the chair of the Senate Health, Education, Labor and Pensions Committees. Alexander was elected three times to be chairman of the Senate Republican Conference. He has degrees from Vanderbilt University and New York University Law School and is the author of seven books. Alexander covers some of the reasons for high health care costs and also some of the solutions that are possible.

Mr. President, today, I am asking experts at the American Enterprise Institute and the Brookings Institution as well as other leading health care experts, for specific ideas about how Congress and the president can work together to reduce the cost of health care in the United States.

Here is why:

Last July, at the Senate health committee's second in a series of five hearings on reducing health care costs, Dr. Brent James, a member of the National Academy of Medicine, testified that 30 percent, and probably as much as 50 percent, of all the money spent on health care is unnecessary.

That startled me, as I hope it startles you.

So I asked another witness, Dr. David Lanksy, from the Pacific Business Group on Health, if he agreed with Dr. James' estimate, and he said yes.

And then at our next hearing not one witness on our distinguished panel disagreed with Dr. James.

That means we are spending as much as half of all that we spend on health care on unnecessary treatment, tests, and administrative costs.

As a country, we spend a huge amount on health care—$3.5 trillion in 2017 according to the Centers for Medicare and Medicaid Services.

When we use Dr. James' estimates, that means we spent between roughly $1-$1.8 trillion on unnecessary health care in 2017.

That is more money than the gross domestic product of every country in the world except for the top nine.

That is three times as much as we spend on all of our national defense, 60 times as much as we spend on Pell grants for college students, and about 550 times as much as we spend on national parks.

Delivered on December 11, 2018, at the U.S. Senate, Washington, DC.

For the last eight years, most of the debate about health care has not been about this extraordinary fact that we may be spending up to half of what we spend on health care unnecessarily but instead on health insurance, and in fact on six percent of the health insurance market.

The truth is we will never have lower cost health insurance until we have lower cost health care.

Instead of continuing to argue over a small part of the insurance market, what we should be discussing is the high cost of health care that affects every American.

Here is something that we ought to be able to agree on: that we are spending too much on health care and that too much of what we spend is on unnecessary care

And the five hearings we held reminded us of something else we should agree on: one major reason for the unnecessarily high cost of health care is that the health care system does not operate with the discipline and cost saving benefits of a real market.

Too many barriers to innovation drive up costs.

And most Americans have no idea of the true cost of the health care services they buy—which also drives up costs.

As a country—American families, federal and state governments, private companies—we spent $3.5 trillion on health care in 2017 according to the Centers for Medicare and Medicaid Services—almost as much as the $3.98 trillion the entire federal government spent in 2017, according to the Congressional Budget Office.

High health care costs impact everyone:

First, the taxpayer, because the federal government spends about one-third of all federal dollars on health care. According to the Congressional Budget Office, of the $3.98 trillion the federal government spent in 2017, $1.1 trillion of that was mandatory spending for Medicare, Medicaid, and other health care programs.

This federal government runaway spending is the principal cause of the national debt. It squeezes the budget for national parks, national defense, and basic research.

Health care costs also impact states, all of which have to balance their budget.

When I was governor of Tennessee, Medicaid was 8 percent of the state budget; today is it 30 percent of the budget. That means states have less to spend on fixing roads and on higher education.

Second, health care spending adds to the cost of doing business.

And Warren Buffett has called the ballooning costs of health care "a hungry tapeworm on the American economy."

Third, and most important, the rising cost of health care is squeezing the budgets of American families.

According to a Gallup poll released days before the midterms, 80 percent of registered voters rated health care as "extremely" or "very important" to their vote—a higher percentage than every other issue polled, including the economy, immigration, and taxes.

I would imagine that every senator has heard stories from their constituents about struggling to stretch their paychecks to afford a prescription or cover a surprise bill in the mail.

Any one of us who has received a medical bill in the mail has wondered what you're actually paying for.

Here is a story that I heard recently: Todd is a Knoxville father who recently took his son to an emergency room after a bicycle accident. His son was treated, Todd paid a $150 copay because the emergency room was "in-network" for his health insurance, and they headed home.

So, Todd was surprised when he received a bill for $1800—because even though the emergency room was "in-network," the doctor who treated his son was not.

Todd wrote me, trying to figure out why it is so hard to understand what health care really costs and said, "If I'm expected to be a conscientious consumer of my own health care needs, I need a little more help."

The issue of surprise billing is a widely recognized problem—it was highlighted in a report from the White House on health care costs released last Monday.

We want Americans like Todd and his son to be able to access quality care they can afford, so earlier this year, the Senate health committee set out to explore what could be done to lower costs.

We have held five hearings over the last six months to examine why health care costs so much:

In June, at our first hearing, we set out to better understand how much health care actually costs in America.

In July, at our second hearing, we heard from Dr. James that up to half of what we spend on health care is unnecessary.

At our third hearing later in July, we looked at administrative tasks imposed by the federal government—and how those burdens lead to doctors spending more time on paperwork, less time treating patients, and an increase to the cost of care.

In September, we looked at why, when you can check reviews and prices before buying everything from a coffee maker to a car, the cost of health care has remained hidden in a black box.

This is something even the federal government's top health care official knows personally.

Health and Human Services Secretary Alex Azar recently told the story of his doctor ordering a routine echo cardio stress test. He was sent down the street and admitted to the hospital, where, after considerable effort on his part, he learned the test would cost him $3,500. After using a website that compiled typical prices for medical care, he learned the same test would have cost just $550 in a doctor's office. Secretary Azar said that consumers are so in the dark they often feel 'powerless.'

In an age when you can compare different prices and check a dozen reviews when shopping for a new BBQ grill, Americans should be able to more easily understand the cost of their health care.

And last month, at our fifth hearing, we heard about steps the private sector is taking to disrupt the health care system and what kinds of federal barriers are preventing private companies from lowering costs.

As we held these five hearings, two conclusions became clear.

First, as a country, we spend more on health care, but we don't spend it well.

Again, Dr. James told us that 30 percent, and probably over 50 percent, of all the money spent on health care is unnecessary.

That really is astonishing.

It echoes what Dr. Ashisha Jha, a witness from our first hearing and Director of the Harvard Global Health Institute, who said, "The popular belief has been that the reason we spend so much more on health care than other countries is that we just use too much health care. Well, it turns out when you look at the data . . . we are not using more health care. Why is it we are spending twice as much? There are two reasons. One, is administrative complexity. [And second] Every time we use health care in America, we pay a lot more than any other country in the world."

Second, while it would be convenient to have a moonshot to reduce health care costs, this will require people other than the federal government.

First, as the largest purchasers of health insurance, employers are really leading the way in the effort to lower health care costs.

For example, Memphis-based International Paper, uses a service called Best Doctors, that employees can use for a second opinion on health care.

Best Doctors review an employee's records, and then either reaffirm the treatment recommended by a doctor, or recommend a different course of treatment, such as physical therapy.

The use of this voluntary program saved International Paper over half a million dollars in 2017 by preventing unnecessary treatment.

Another way employers reduce health care costs is through wellness programs—which encourage employees to lead healthier lives.

There is a consensus that wellness—lifestyle changes like eating healthier and quitting smoking—can prevent serious illness and reduce health care costs.

And it is hard to think of a better way to make a bigger impact on the health of millions of Americans than to connect the consensus about wellness reducing health costs to the health insurance that 181 million people get on the job.

Second, states are taking an active role in the cost of health care.

In 2017, the state of Maine required health insurers to split the savings with a patient if the patient shops around and chooses a doctor that is less than the average price the insurer pays.

And in Oregon, the state compiles data on insured residents and uses this information to run a tool that allows patients to compare the costs of procedures at different hospitals.

Third, private companies are creating innovative tools to reduce health care costs.

For example, Healthcare Bluebook, a Nashville company and a witness at one of our hearings, is a tool that helps patients find the best price for the highest quality care in their area, using their employer sponsored insurance.

This is useful to lower costs because, for example, the amount a patient pays for cataract surgery in Memphis can range from as little as $2000 to more than $8000.

Fourth, hospitals, doctors, and other health providers have the potential to make a large impact on the cost of health care.

On a smaller scale, one of our witnesses, Dr. Gross, runs a practice under what is called the direct primary care model.

He charges a flat membership rate of $60 per patient in cash for adults under age 65, $25 for one child, and $10 for each additional child.

His practice does not bill anything to an insurance company for direct primary care members—not to Obamacare plans, Medicaid, or Medicare.

In return for this membership fee, members can receive an annual wellness exam, 25 office visits per year including same-day appointments, and some in office testing and chronic disease management without paying anything additional out of pocket.

This gives patients access to a defined level of health care at a predictable price.

On a larger scale, HCA Healthcare, who also testified and has 178 hospitals and 119 freestanding surgery centers located in the U.S. and the United Kingdom, is implementing new techniques to reduce the spread of MRSA [MER-sa], a drug-resistant bacterial infection, in Intensive Care Units (ICUs).

These new techniques have reduced cases of MRSA by 37 percent in HCA hospitals, and have been so effective that the World Health Organization and the Centers for Disease Control and Prevention have added them to their best practices.

According to HCA, this reduction in MRSA infections saves $170,000 for every 1,000 patients. Those savings are shared among the hospital, insurers, and patients.

And finally, information needs to be easily available so patients can find out the cost of their care and take an active role in choosing health care and planning for medical expenses when they can.

The federal government spent $1.1 trillion on Medicare, Medicaid, and other health care programs in 2017—about one third of all health care spending in America—so how we spend federal dollars will obviously make a big difference to the health care system.

There may also be things Washington is doing that are increasing health care costs, or preventing private companies from taking steps to lower those costs.

I want to find what concrete, specific steps the federal government can take to reduce unnecessary health care spending, or at least stop making the problem worse.

For example, after we heard a concern about "gag clauses" that prohibit a pharmacist from telling a patient their prescription would be cheaper if they paid with cash instead of their insurance, Congress was able to act and ban those "gag clauses" earlier this year.

In August, CMS is beginning to require hospitals to post the amount they charge for services online and to keep that information up to date.

These are the types of specific recommendations I'm looking for.

I've had success working with experts to get recommendations and then turning those recommendations into legislation.

In 2005, I stopped by a National Academies of Sciences meeting on American competitiveness, and I said to them, "most ideas fail for the lack of an idea. I believe if you will give Congress ten specific ideas in priority order to improve our competitiveness, I believe Congress will enact them."

The Academies got busy immediately, recruited Norm Augustine, and put together a task force—called the Committee on Prospering in the Global Economy of the 21st Century—of American leaders.

Under Norm's leadership they produced a National Academies report, "Rising Above the Gathering Storm."

The committee came up with 20 new, specific ideas such as:

Doubling funding for basic science research; and

Creating an energy agency modelled after the Department of Defense's highly successful DARPA that would invest in high-potential, high-impact energy technologies—what we now call ARPA-E.

And Congress used most of those ideas and put together a bill called America COMPETES, which we passed in 2007 and reauthorized it in 2010.

So that's an example of how a report, that has specific and precise policy recommendations, can help produce a legislative product.

That is what I am looking for with the letter I am sending today to experts at the American Enterprise Institute and the Brookings Institution.

I also want input from other leading policy experts, including economists, doctors, nurses, patients, hospital administrators, state regulators and legislators, governors, employers, insurers, and health care innovators.

I am asking for as many specific legislative, regulatory, or sub-regulatory solutions as possible, in writing, by March 1, 2019.

I am especially interested in policies that bring to the health care system the discipline and lower-cost benefits of a real functioning market.

One way to do that is to remove the barriers that discourage innovators from coming up with new ways to reduce health care costs.

A second way is to make it easier for consumers of health care to know the cost of what they are buying.

And I would welcome suggestions of how those policy ideas could be implemented—what law to amend, what regulation to change—and any potential downsides to the policy recommendations.

I will be sharing these recommendations with Ranking Member Murray, and other members of our health committee, as well as Senator Grassley and Senator Wyden.

The federal government is not going to lower the cost of health care overnight, but I believe there are steps we can take that would make a real difference to American families.

That might be two or three big steps, or a dozen smaller ones, but we shouldn't let this opportunity to make progress pass us by.

Print Citations

CMS: Alexander, Lamar. "The Cost of Health Care." Speech at the U.S. Senate, Washington, DC, December 11, 2018. In *The Reference Shelf: Representative American Speeches, 2018–2019,* edited by Sophie Zyla, 189-195. Amenia, NY: Grey House Publishing, 2019.

MLA: Alexander, Lamar. "The Cost of Health Care." U.S. Senate, 11 December 2018, Washington, DC. Speech. *The Reference Shelf: Representative American Speeches, 2018–2019,* edited by Sophie Zyla, Grey House Publishing, 2019, pp. 189-195.

APA: Alexander, L. (2018, December 11). Speech on the cost of health care. U.S. Senate, Washington, DC. In Sophie Zyla (Ed.), *The reference shelf: Representative American speeches, 2018–2019* (pp. 189-195). Amenia, NY: Grey House Publishing.

SAMSHSA's 2018 National Survey on Drug Use and Health (Excerpt)

By Elinore F. McCance-Katz

Dr. Elinore "Ellie" F. McCance-Katz was nominated in April 2017 to lead the Department of Health and Human Services Substance Abuse and Mental Health Services Administration (SAMHSA). She has a bachelor's degree in biology from Eastern Connecticut State University and earned an MPhil and PhD from Yale University for studies in infectious disease epidemiology, and an MD from the University of Connecticut. Dr. McCance-Katz feels that there is a shortage of treatment available for people suffering from mental health issues and opioid disorders for a variety of reasons.

Hello, my name is Dr. Elinore McCance-Katz and I'm the assistant secretary for mental health and substance use. I lead the substance abuse and mental health services administration and today I'm pleased to present the 2018 results from the National Survey on Drug Use. The National Survey on Drug Use is done as a household survey that asks Americans about their use of substances, substance use disorders, mental health and the receipt of treatment services for these conditions.

. . .

Interviewers . . . go out and speak to Americans about their mental health and about their use of substances. They ask questions of the civilian population, non-institutionalized populations, and people that are 12 years of age or older. It includes people living in households across the nation, college dormitories, homeless living in shelters, and civilians living on military bases. But it excludes active-duty military people that are long-term hospital residents, prison populations, and homeless who are not in shelters.

The sample includes . . . people from all 50 states and Washington, DC. So how do we use the national survey on drug use and health? Well, it provides a window into the state of substance use and mental health issues in our country and it helps us at a federal level to guide policy directions in terms of problem substances, the prevalence of mental illness, the intersection of substance use and mental health issues. And it provides insights that can be studied in the context of data from other federal agencies that helps in decision-making about what types of resources are needed and where those resources should be directed.

Before I go on to speak about the 2018 survey results let me just go over a few of the highlights of our 2017 *Newsday* survey in terms of the opioid epidemic. We saw

---

Delivered on August 20, 2019, at the U.S. Department of Health and Human Services, Washington, DC.

that new users of heroin significantly decreased relative to 2016. We also saw significant decreases in pain reliever misuse for all age groups. There was a downward trend in heroin users, but an estimated 2.1 million Americans living with opioid use disorder in terms of marijuana. We saw significant increases in use of this drug by young adults 18- to 25-years-old, both for past month and for daily or near daily use, and those increases were driven by significant increases in use by young adult women. We saw pregnant women using substances in greater numbers, including significant increases in daily or near daily marijuana use during pregnancy. We saw frequent marijuana use associated with opioid misuse, heavy alcohol use, and depression in adolescents and in young adults.

We saw young adults with increasing rates of serious mental illness major depression and suicidality and we saw how common co-occurring substance use and mental disorders are in our nation and the major gaps in treatment received by affected individuals. So let's go on now at what SAMHSA's response was to the

NIST findings of 2016 and 2017 in 2018. We launched a new approach to technical assistance and training. Previous efforts at SAMHSA had focused on technical assistance but only to grantees, and the number of grantees is really relatively low compared to the number of practitioners' organizations and community members who need information about mental and substance use disorders.

So we expanded our training and technical assistance to a national approach. We established a clinical support system for serious mental illness. This is a program that focuses on national efforts to train practitioners on serious mental illness assessment, treatment, and recovery. This program focuses on appropriate use and monitoring of psychotropic medications. It focuses on the use of clozapine in treatment refractory schizophrenia, a medication that is underused but is the treatment of choice for treatment of resistant schizophrenia. And this program focuses on assisted outpatient treatment and the provision of wraparound services for those individuals living with the most serious mental illnesses.

We established a regional system of technology transfer centers throughout the United States that include substance abuse prevention technology transfer centers, addiction technology transfer centers, mental health technology transfer centers, with supplements for school-based services to address the needs of our very young, who may have mental health issues. We have training and technical assistance programs that are also focused on Native American and Alaska Native needs as well as Hispanic Latino needs. And we established new national training and technical assistance programs. We put in place the state-targeted response technical assistance training program, and this is a program that puts teams in place in every state to address the needs of that state as they relate to opioids issues. That program has had over a thousand requests already and those requests have all been met to meet the needs of Americans living with opioid issues. We put in place a privacy technology transfer center to address confidentiality and information sharing related to HIPAA and 42 CFR, and we put in place an eating disorders technology transfer center.

We have a program called PCSS-Universities [Provider's Clinical Support System], which embeds the data waiver training in pregraduate education for all healthcare providers who are eligible to get the data waiver that allows them to prescribe buprenorphine for the treatment of opioid use disorder from their office-based practices. This includes physicians, nurse practitioners, and physician assistants. We expanded training and technical assistance on opioids in rural America through supplements to the US Department of Agriculture Cooperative Extension programs. We re-established the drug abuse warning network, a Sentinel program, that tells us about what substances are being used in different parts of the nation and the toxicities that are being seen in urgent care settings. We expanded the Suicide Prevention lifeline network and we have done public-targeted messaging based on areas of concern that are identified in Vista, including public service messaging on marijuana, methamphetamine, and suicide prevention.

So now let's talk about the survey findings for 2018. And this figure is an overview of mental illness and substance use disorders in America. What you see here is that 19 percent of Americans, 47.6 million people over the age of eighteen, had a mental illness in 2018, and among those with a mental illness one in four, 11.4 million, had a serious mental illness that produced an impairment that adversely impacted their day-to-day lives. We saw that 7.8 percent of Americans, 19.3 million people 18 and older, had a substance use disorder. Of those with substance use disorder, the majority, 75 percent, struggled with alcohol use; 38 percent with illicit drugs; and 12.9 percent with both illicit drug use and alcohol use. 3.7 percent of Americans, over 9 million Americans. had both a substance use disorder and a mental illness, so co-occurring disorders are quite common.

These numbers are not very different from those for 2017: 57.8 million Americans had a ental or substance use disorder in 2018. In findings over several years, from 2015 to the present time, 2018, what you see is a modest increase in new users of alcohol in the 12- to 17-year-old age group, essentially no change in young adults in terms of new users of alcohol. If we look at alcohol use at large we see a significant decrease in adolescents that are using alcohol. Similarly, we see a significant decrease in 2018 for 18 to 25- year-olds compared to 2016 results, and we see steady numbers of alcohol users in those 26 and older. If we look at alcohol use disorders we see declining alcohol use disorders in adolescents, and in our 18- to 25-year-olds and we see steady rates of alcohol use disorder in those that are 26 and older. To summarize, regarding alcohol use in 2018, we saw no change in alcohol initiation rate among youth since 2015.

We see lower rates of alcohol use disorder among youth and young adults compared to 2015. These findings are related to SAMHSA's efforts on reductions and alcohol use in children, youth, and transitional age youth. Our center for substance abuse prevention has a drug-free communities program that prioritizes alcohol use and it has reported a 27 percent reduction in use of alcohol by middle school students and a 23 percent reduction in use by high school students.

SAMHSA's prevention technology transfer centers also produce resources and materials that focus on alcohol misuse prevention. The center for substance abuse prevention has a program that focuses on underage drinking and partnerships for success grantees that emphasize underage drinking prevention as well. The center for substance abuse treatment has promoted screening brief intervention and referral for treatment for alcohol use in all programs, including our criminal justice, pregnant postpartum, parenting women programs and adolescent treatment as well as HIV and homeless programs. And the Center for substance abuse treatment has funded expert training in medical residences and other health care practitioner programs that screen for hazardous alcohol use and other substance use disorders as well.

Marijuana continues to be the most used of the illicit drugs and we see a significant increase in marijuana use compared to that for 2017, 43.5 million Americans in 2018 were marijuana users. When we look at psychotherapeutic drugs, which includes prescription opioids, we see a significant decrease from the numbers in 2017. So there was a drop from 6.6 percent to 6.2 percent of those over the age of 12 that were users of psychotherapeutic drugs. The numbers are relatively steady compared to 2017 for cocaine, hallucinogens, methamphetamine, and inhalants, and we see a small decline in heroin use when we look specifically at opioids.

We see some positive findings in 2018. There were 10.3 million people who were opioid misusers, 3.7 percent of the population over the age of 12. This is a significant decrease from that of 2017, where we had 11.4 million opioid misusers. 9.9 million were prescription pain reliever misusers, so again the misuse of opioids. The majority of the misuse of opioids is related to prescription pain reliever misuse. We saw a significant decrease in misuse of hydrocodone, and that is significantly less than what we saw in 2017. This was followed by oxycodone as the second most misused prescription opioid and a relatively smaller number of those were misusing prescribed fentanyl products. Fentanyl is involved in opioid overdose and death and is primarily from illicit opioids obtained on the street. We see 808,000 heroin users and 506,000 people that misuse both prescription pain relievers and heroin. In 18- to 25-year-olds we saw the greatest decline, followed by those 26 and older. And we also see a significant decline in 12- to 17-year-olds misusing opioids.

When we look at pain reliever misuse and heroin use we see again a significant decline in pain reliever misuse relatively steady numbers from 2015 to 2018 for relief pain reliever use disorder and for new users of pain relievers. We see declining numbers for heroin use. We see a nonsignificant increase in the number of new users of heroin, but that number remains below the numbers for 2015 and 2016. When we look more closely at prescription pain reliever misuse by age group and we look at it over the years 2015 to 2018, again positive findings in the form of significant declines for 12- to 17- year-olds, 18- to 25-year-olds and adults 26 and older. When we look at where people are getting those prescription pain relievers that they're misusing as we have seen every year since this question started being asked in 2006, we see that the majority of people are given these medications or they buy them or steal them from friends and relatives.

Another 35 percent get the opioids they must use through prescriptions from one doctor. When we ask people who get these medications free from their friends and relatives, where do your friends and relatives get these medications, over 83 percent say that those medications came from a single doctor, which underscores the need to continue to work with health care providers about appropriate use of opioid medications.

When we look at misuse of prescription opioids we see that buprenorphine and methadone have the highest rates of misuse. We see greater numbers of misuse for those that are prescribed hydrocodone, oxycodone, and tramadol. This is related to the fact that there are greater numbers of prescriptions for these medications. It's quite concerning that we see these high rates of misuse of buprenorphine and methadone and speaks to the need to continue to educate on safe and effective use of these medications. In terms of heroin use we saw the numbers climb from 2002 up to 2016, the numbers are starting to come down and we see heroin use declining specifically in our 18- to 25-year-olds. We also see declines in adolescents, but thankfully the numbers of heroin users that are adolescents are quite low nationwide. The numbers of adults 26 and older using heroin have remained very steady at point 3 percent of that segment of the population in terms of heroin-related opioid use disorder. Again, we see positive findings in our young adults 18 to 25, with a significant drop in the numbers with heroin-related opioid use disorder. And we see treatment gains in the number of people that are receiving pharmacotherapies. For opioid use disorder medication-assisted treatment, we see increases in all three FDA- approved medications for the treatment of opioid use disorder.

Over 450,000 Americans are receiving methadone therapy for their opioid use disorder. Over 648,000 Americans are receiving buprenorphine and over 73,000 are receiving injectable naltrexone. These numbers have been steadily increasing since 2016. So to provide a brief summary of opioid use in the United States in 2018: we saw a significant decrease in prescription opioid misuse across all age groups. But the majority of those who are misusing continue to get their opioids from friends and relatives and from health care providers, which underscores the need for ongoing public education of individuals across the nation so that they understand the risks versus the benefits of opioids. We need to continue our education of practitioners around appropriate pain management and appropriate use of opioids, as well as alternatives to opioids to manage pain. Our partnership with states to monitor opioid analgesic prescribing buprenorphine continues to have a high rate of misuse relative to other prescribed opioids.

We saw a decline in overall heroin use from 2016 to 2018, with some differences among age groups. There was a decline in young adult heroin use and that's responsible for the overall downward trend in heroin use. For heroin use disorders we saw heroin use disorders significantly decrease compared to 2017, while heroin use disorder in adults 26 and older remains steady. The total with opioid use disorder decreased from 2.1 million in 2017 to 2 million in 2018, a modest decline but in the right direction and we see increases in the use of medication-assisted treatment increases in evidence-based treatment for opioid use disorder.

Marijuana use in this country continues to be problematic. We do see a nonsignificant increase in adolescent marijuana use. The rates in 18- to 25-year- olds remain the same as for 2017, but we see a significant increase in marijuana use in adults over the age of 26. When we look at marijuana use among young adults 18 to 25, this is a group that we were quite concerned about last year because in 2017 we saw a significant increase in their use but that has remained stable. It has not increased in 2018 and we see a small but important decrease in past year regarding daily or almost daily use of marijuana in this age group. When we look at marijuana use in young men and young women we see a small decline in marijuana use in men but a continuing increase in women who are using marijuana, and that is a significant increase relative to 2015 and 2016 results. When we look at adults 26 and older we see significant increases in past month use of marijuana and we see significant increases in daily or near daily use of marijuana. When we look at marijuana use disorder we see an increase in our 18- to 25-year-olds. It is significantly higher than for 2015 and 2016, and we see nonsignificant increases in marijuana use disorder in those 26 and older.

When we look at past months substance use among pregnant women, I have to say this is one of the areas of this survey that I'm most pleased about. In 2017 we saw increases in use of all substances by pregnant women: illicit drug use went up, tobacco product use went up, and alcohol use went up. But look at 2018: we see a significant decline in illicit drug use by pregnant women, and this is due to a decrease in marijuana use by pregnant women. We also see declines in the use of tobacco products and alcohol used by pregnant women, and we're quite pleased about that because it's been a special emphasis of this agency to reach pregnant women about the dangers of substance use during pregnancy Over the course of 2018 when we look at marijuana use among women by pregnancy status, again we see the decline from 2017 to 2018, and we don't see that in women who are not pregnant. In fact, we see a significant increase in marijuana use by women who are not pregnant. When we look at daily or almost daily marijuana use among women who are pregnant, again we're very pleased to see a better than 50% drop in the number of women that are daily users of marijuana during pregnancy. But again, we see daily use of marijuana by women who are not pregnant continuing to increase, so we are seeing trends in the right direction related to substance use in pregnancy. As I said, we were quite concerned about the startling increase in substance use, particularly marijuana use in pregnancy, which can be associated with a variety of very adverse effects on the developing fetus in terms of low birth weights, possibly still births or preterm births, and long term problems for the child that can include neurological developmental issues, hyperactivity, and poor cognitive function. SAMHSA made strong efforts to address this situation to improve the health of mothers and their babies through public awareness efforts through the launch of SAMHSA.gov/marijuana.

. . .

I want to move on to cocaine use and I'm pleased to report that we've seen a significant decline in cocaine use among young adults 18- to 25-years old. When we look at methamphetamine use in adults that are 26 and older we see significant increases in use we see a decrease in use by 18- to 25-year-olds, but we're quite concerned about the significant increases in methamphetamine use. When we look at methamphetamine use we have to keep in mind that the states are affected differently. There are a relatively small number of states that have significant issues with methamphetamine. . . . When we look at prescription stimulants, again we see a decline in misuse of these drugs by adolescents and a significant decline in misuse of prescription stimulants by young adults 18 to 25. And when we look at hallucinogens, again we see a decline in adolescent hallucinogen use and a decline in young adult hallucinogen use, but we see significant increases in hallucinogen use by adults.

So the summary for substance use in the United States and 2018 for marijuana: we saw no changes in youth use but we saw significant increases in adults over age 26. We see a significant increase in marijuana use disorder in 18- to 25-year-olds and it's likely that we'll continue to see increases in marijuana use disorder as states liberalize their marijuana laws and people use more marijuana. We see marked declines in illicit drug use by pregnant women, particularly marijuana; declines in cocaine use in adolescents; in young adults, declines in methamphetamine use but increases in adults 26 and older. We see a significant decline in prescription stimulant abuse in 18- to 25-year-olds and a decline in hallucinogen use in adolescents and young adults.

The message, I think, is that prevention works. And I want to take just a moment to thank all the preventionists that are working so hard across this nation to get the information to our people about the risks associated with substance misuse. Your work is reflected in our survey data. Thank you for everything you do and please keep doing it.

I'm going to turn to mental health, and I want to show you the results for serious mental illness. What you see is that we are observing significant increases in serious mental illness for young adults 18 to 25 and adults 26 to 49 years old, and many of them are not getting treatment. Over 46 percent of young adults, and over 36 percent of those 26 to 49 years old, with serious mental illness that adversely impacts day-to-day living. These folks got no treatment services. When we look at major depressive episodes by age group over the years 2015 to 2018, we see significant increases for adolescents, young adults, and adults from ages 26 to 49. When we look at major depressive episodes with severe impairment among adolescents—again relative to 2015 and 2016—we're seeing significant increases in severe impairment.

Major depression is a serious illness. It can be associated with many adverse effects, up to and including death. It's very important that we address major depression in all Americans that experience it. When we look at major depressive episodes with severe impairment in 18- to 25-year-olds, again we are seeing significant increases in that severe form of major depression, both in men and women. When we look at suicidality, we see significant increases relative to 2008. So we went back 10 years and looked at suicidal thoughts, plans, and attempts and compared that to our 2018 data, and we see significant increases in all aspects of suicidality. This is a very serious issue and one that we must continue to focus on.

I want to take a couple of minutes to speak about co-occurring disorders. Co-occurring issues are quite common in the United States. Data for adults over the age of 18 indicates that substance use is more frequent in individuals who have mental illness, and it's a dose-effect response. Any mental illness confers greater risk for use of other substances, and that increases with severity of the mental illness. When we look at illicit drugs, marijuana opioid misuse, prescription pain reliever misuse, and heroin misuse, we see again significant increases in those with any mental illness and serious mental illness relative to those who do not have a mental illness in terms of drug use.

I'm going to take just a couple of minutes to talk to you about the relationship of specific substances to other substance use and serious mental illnesses. I think it's important to make the point that the use of these substances confers risk for other substance use and serious mental health conditions. So alcohol use by past month or heavy alcohol use is defined as four or more binges a month, and a binge is defined for men as five or more drinks in a two-hour sitting or for women four or more drinks in that approximate time frame. So when you look at alcohol use you see that, relative to those who do not use alcohol, there are greater rates of marijuana use, opioid misuse, cocaine use, and methamphetamine use and greater rates of major depressive episodes and serious mental illness.

When we look at marijuana use, we see similar findings compared to those who do not use marijuana versus any past year marijuana use or daily or near daily use. Again, we see increasing opioid misuse, past month heavy alcohol use, cocaine use, methamphetamine use, major depression, and serious mental illness. And again, the more marijuana you use the greater the likelihood that you will engage in other substance use or experience a serious mental health condition.

I want to make this point very clear: these numbers for marijuana use are higher than those for alcohol use, even heavy alcohol use. Too often I'm still hearing that marijuana is safer than alcohol. I believe that this data proves that to be a false statement. Marijuana is not safer than alcohol and it confers very serious risks for polysubstance use and for serious mental disorders. When we look at opioid misuse again, any past year opioid misuse is associated with greater use of marijuana, heavy alcohol use, cocaine, methamphetamine, and mental disorders. Similarly, the stimulant cocaine is associated with the use of other substances and serious mental health conditions. . . . When we look at methamphetamine we see very high rates of marijuana use, high rates of opioid misuse, high rates of heavy alcohol use, substantial rates of past year cocaine use, and we see significant rates of major depression and serious mental illness.

We also know that co-occurring substance use disorder is associated with suicidality compared to people who do not have a substance use disorder. We see much higher rates of serious thoughts of suicide, plans for suicide, and suicide attempts in substance users. And despite all of the consequences, despite the disease burden, we see that the treatment gaps remain vast and are very similar to those that I told you about in 2017. Nearly 90% of those with substance use disorders get no treatment; nearly 57 percent of those with mental illnesses get no treatment; 36 percent with serious mental illness get no treatment; over 90 percent with co-occurring disorders get no treatment; and over 58 percent of our adolescents with major depression will get no treatment.

So, to summarize mental health issues in the United States in 2018, we see serious mental illness increases in adults 18 and older. We saw significant increases in major depression and severe impairment associated with this illness in adolescents and young adults, and these findings for our young people were higher than for adults 26 and older. We see significant increases in suicidality, particularly in 18- to 25-year-olds. We see co-occurring substance use and mental disorders are quite common, and the use of one substance, be it alcohol or other illicit substances, is strongly correlated with polysubstance use and with serious mental health conditions, major depression, and serious mental illness.

This underscores the need to screen for all substances as well as mental disorders when evaluating a person, identifying either a substance problem or a mental health issue. These disorders co-occur commonly. As practitioners we really must screen for all of the issues and treat those co-occurring disorders. A person cannot have a full and sustained recovery without getting treatment of all of their mental and substance use disorders. Substance use disorders increase risk for suicidality, and we continue to see the large gap in treatment.

So 2018 was a year of some progress but clearly there are ongoing needs for Americans living with substance use and mental health conditions. The data has shown us areas where we need to focus our resources. We need to continue to address the opioids epidemic. We need to address rising rates of marijuana use and methamphetamine use, particularly in adults who are over the age of 26. We see rising rates of major depression in adolescents and adults that really must be attended to. Substance use and mental disorders are closely linked. Our data tells us that illicit substance use increases risk for other hazardous substance use and for mental illness. We see mental illness is a risk factor for illicit substance use.

This underscores the need for ongoing efforts in prevention of substance use disorders, and SAMHSA will make a response to these data. We will focus on workforce issues and continue to address the need for clinicians to be prepared to assess and treat mental health issues and substance issues through our national training and technical assistance programs. In terms of opioids, we'll continue to work with states to address their opioid crisis needs in terms of prevention treatment and community recovery resources through our state opioid response grants. Our tribal opioid response grants are discretionary grant programs that focus on pregnant, postpartum, and parenting women; children and families; drug court grants; and first responder and prevention grants.

Through collaboration with our partners and HHS and other federal departments to expand resources to communities in terms of other substances, we're going to continue to encourage states to use their block grant funds to address prevention and treatment needs. We're going to continue to provide training and technical assistance on evidence-based therapies, including psychosocial therapies for stimulants, cocaine, methamphetamine, and marijuana. We do not have FDA-approved medication treatments. Psychosocial therapies are going to be extremely important to helping Americans address these issues, and so SAMHSA will be focusing on training around the use of psychosocial interventions and therapies to assist Americans living with these types of substance use problems. We'll continue to connect with the public and get the message out on the importance of prevention treatment and community supports. We will continue our public service messaging on substance use and mental health issues with a focus on prevention. I've given you the website for our technology transfer centers. You can find our public service messages there, they are free to download and use as you wish.

If you believe that public service messaging would be helpful in your community please take a look at these messages and make use of them. We will continue to monitor outcomes through . . . the drug abuse warning network and through our SAMHSA grant program evaluations, and we will make policy modifications as needed. I want to thank you for taking the time to listen to the results of the National Survey on Drug Use and Health for 2018. It's our sincere hope at SAMHSA that these results will help to inform Americans so that they can better understand the risks presented by substance use, the risks associated with mental health conditions, and the importance of treatment and recovery services. SAMHSA will be your partner in helping to address mental and substance use disorders going forward. Thank you very much.

Print Citations

CMS: McCance-Katz, Elinore F. "SAMHSA's 2018 National Survey on Drug Use and Health." Presentation at the U.S. Department of Health and Human Services, Washington, DC, August 20, 2019. In *The Reference Shelf: Representative American Speeches, 2018–2019,* edited by Sophie Zyla, 196-205. Amenia, NY: Grey House Publishing, 2019.

MLA: McCance-Katz, Elinore F. "SAMHSA's 2018 National Survey on Drug Use and Health." U.S. Department of Health and Human Services 20 August 2019, Washington, DC. Presentation. *The Reference Shelf: Representative American Speeches, 2018–2019,* edited by Sophie Zyla, Grey House Publishing, 2019, pp. 196-205.

APA: McCance-Katz, E.F. (2019, August 20). Presentation on SAMHSA's 2018 national survey on drug use and health. U.S. Department of Health and Human Services, Washington, DC. In Sophie Zyla (Ed.), *The reference shelf: Representative American speeches, 2018–2019* (pp. 196-205). Amenia, NY: Grey House Publishing.

Time for Physicians to Create History Together

By Patrice A. Harris

Patrice Harris became the first African American woman and the 174th president of the American Medical Association in June 2019. She the chair of the Opioid Task Force and she is a psychiatrist. Harris has a bachelor's degree in psychology, a master's degree in counseling psychology, and a medical degree from West Virginia University.

Good evening. Tonight is very special for me and I honored that each of you is here to share it. The poet Maya Angelou once said if one is lucky a solitary fantasy, and I would add dream, can totally transform 1 million realties. Now you didn't think you'd sit through an address from a psychiatrist and not hear something about fantasies and dreams, did you?

But the great thing about psychiatrists is that we can talk about dreams as well as the hippocampus and the cytochrome p 450 system. It's truly a dream come true to stand before you tonight, a dream my ancestors, parents, my extended family and supported before it even entered my imagination. A dream my West Virginia Georgia psychiatry and AMA helped me achieve and I know in my heart tonight that I am my ancestors' wildest dreams.

I would like to thank my parents Barbara and Titus Harris, my fierce protector Anthony, the Harrison Smith families, the Baron Singley Williams families and Clark Brody family, my sorority sisters of Alpha Kappa Alpha Sorority, my WVU and West Virginia friends, my 80 aliens and Georgians who are here tonight and all my management and staff. Please join me in thanking.

I'd also like to recognize two other who broke barriers in our organization: Dr. Lonnie Bristow, the first African American to lead the AMA, and Dr. Nancy Dickey, the first woman to lead the AMA.

So if you'd hadn't guessed already I've chosen as the theme of my inauguration from many families, one now each of our families, whether composed of relatives, friends, or colleagues has something to teach us and mine have been no different. A common thread of my lessons is the importance of standing together. From my Aunt Betty who when confronted with a challenging situation would remind me we Harris's stick together. From my Georgia family who taught me that physicians are at our best in advocacy when we work together, and you, my AMA family, remind me daily that there is strength in our collective voice.

Delivered on June 11, 2019, to the American Medical Association Annual Meeting, Chicago, IL. © American Medical Association. All rights reserved/Courtesy of AMA Archives.

Now my personal journey has also taught me many valuable lessons. First, medicine involves a community. I learned this from *Marcus Welby MD*—I know the younger folks are gonna have to google that but a fictional television doctor from the 1970s who actually inspired me to become a physician doctor. Welby not only cared for his patients inside the exam room but he cared about their lives, their families, and their communities. Another lesson, medicine relies on teamwork, I learned this as a medical student in the emergency department holding a woman's hand in my heart, holding a woman's heart in my hand as a member of the on-call trauma team and we were working to keep her heart beating after a motor vehicle accident.

Medicine needs a broad perspective. From my work with patients who've been abused, neglected, diagnosed with a mental illness, subjected to childhood trauma, my patients who are homeless or unemployed, I learned that I often overlooked health determinants that have an effect on one's health over a lifetime.

Medicine needs allies. I've learned the critical importance of partnerships with legislators, community-based organizations and the business community, and the impact of those partnerships on patient health. And finally, medicine's future needs leadership. It needs us, the AMA, to lead the way. Last month I gave the commencement address at the Morehouse School of Medicine, and there I saw the future. I saw our brilliant and highly motivated future colleagues who cannot wait to stand where we are and who are counting on us to lead before we pass the baton.

Our personal journeys inform the people we become, and just as I am the sum of my parts—an African American, a psychiatrist, a child from the heart of coal country—so each of you is the sum of your parts, where you came from, your specialty, and your experiences. Our diversity is the source of our strength as we face medicine's most daunting challenges. From geography to age and gender, our uniquely lived experiences shape who we are as people and as physicians. Now while we have many differences at the AMA we have this common goal through this great organization: we believe we can uplift our profession, we believe we can improve care for all of our 300-plus million fellow Americans and we believe we can stand as leaders in health care across the globe.

So lead we must, and lead we will. But our core values—access to health care for all, diversity and inclusion, the primacy of the patient-physician relationship, the advancement of science and public health—these core values will not be a part of a healthcare landscape unless ensure that they are. Over our 172-year history as an organization we have faced many challenges and we are all too well aware of what we face today.

While the Affordable Care Act brought coverage to millions of Americans, millions still lack coverage and we know there are those who want to roll back the gains we've made. Far too many people—one in two adults—struggle with chronic conditions like diabetes and heart disease. Though we've made progress the face of medicine still fails to match the faces of our patients. People living in rural areas too often have to drive hundreds of miles to the nearest physician or hospital. Overdoses continue to outpace other causes of premature death and wreak havoc on our communities. Our young people are subject to the dangers of e-cigarette use at epidemic levels and pharmaceutical prices continue to soar. But I see these not as intractable problems but as intractable opportunities. Opportunities that we as physicians fully embrace because we don't run away from problems.

Physicians run towards them, and that is our role, our responsibility and our AMA mission. We can make a difference and we do make a difference. Our formula for success? Community, teamwork, a broad perspective, professional allies, and a willingness to lead. Well, as Barbara said, a year is not a long time. Like all who came before me, I too hope to leave a mark on the AMA, both as a child and a lesson psychiatrist and as the first African American woman to hold this position. And so when I look back on my time as president I hope to say we turned the promise of parity for mental health into reality.

We moved the needle on health equity. We reformed prior authorization so that more patients could get the right care at the right time. And we saw the end to the opioid epidemic on the horizon and furthered alliances in Washington and across every state to remove barriers treatment for those diagnosed with substance use disorders.

One of my favorite poems about leadership was written by Mary Lou Anderson and she wrote leaders are called to stand in that lonely place between the no longer and the not yet and intentionally make decisions that will bind, forge, move, and create history. When it comes to health equity, to mental health and too many other issues, medicine is in that lonely place between the no longer and the not yet, and we must act intentionally to move forward. We are no longer at a place where those with mental illness and addiction are hidden and ignored but we are not yet at a place where mental disorders are viewed without stigma and truly integrated into healthcare. We are no longer at a place where we can tolerate the disparities that plague communities of colored women and the LGBTQ community but we are not yet at a place where health equity is achieved in those communities and not yet at a place where women can live with confidence that we are firmly in charge of our own medical decisions. We are no longer at a place where underrepresented groups are unwelcome in medicine but we are not yet at a place where African American men are entering or graduating from medical schools at the rates of their peers. We are no longer at a place where we can tolerate bureaucratic government and PARE requirements that add to the cost of care without increasing value but not yet at a place where we have eliminated unnecessary regulations and can truly focus on care. We are no longer at a place where we can turn a blind eye to the chronic conditions that plague half of American adults but not yet at a place where everyone has access to affordable health care.

So colleagues, as medicine's leaders we all need to stand in those sometimes lonely places and make decisions now that will move us forward to a future we helped create. So I asked you to join me in taking the next step of leadership and intentionally make decisions that will bind, forge, move, and create history. The AMA has led the way on numerous public health advances throughout our history. So let us commit tonight to move medicine forward again this year. And we state emphatically that health in all its dimensions is a basic human right.

AMA family, friends, colleagues, partners, we can do this because when we all join together bringing our differing perspectives, backgrounds, experiences, and resources to bear, that's when we can truly move medicine forward for the good of our patients, the nation and the world.

So I'll close with one more quote from Maya Angelou, who said life is not measured by the number of breaths we take but by the moments that take our breath away. And for me tonight is one of those moments. I am honored that each of you is here to share it with me and by the trust you have placed in me. I can promise you that the legacy of the AMA will be in good hands as we work together to transform 1 million realities.

Print Citations

CMS: Harris, Patrice A. "Time for Physicians to Create History Together." Keynote Address at the American Medical Association Annual Meeting, Chicago, IL, June 11, 2019. In *The Reference Shelf: Representative American Speeches, 2018–2019*, edited by Sophie Zyla, 206-209. Amenia, NY: Grey House Publishing, 2019.

MLA: Harris, Patrice A. "Time for Physicians to Create History Together." American Medical Association Annual Meeting, 11 June 2019, Chicago, IL. Keynote Address. *The Reference Shelf: Representative American Speeches, 2018–2019*, edited by Sophie Zyla, Grey House Publishing, 2019, pp. 206-209.

APA: Harris, P.A. (2019, June 11). Keynote Address on time for physicians to create history together. American Medical Association Annual Meeting, Chicago, IL. In Sophie Zyla (Ed.), *The reference shelf: Representative American speeches, 2018–2019* (pp. 206-209). Amenia, NY: Grey House Publishing.

Advancing Health Care through the Lens of History: Health Equity

By James L. Madara

James L. Madara, MD, is the chief executive officer (CEO) and executive vice president of the American Medical Association. Madara is the adjunct professor of pathology at Northwestern University, and he spent 22 years at Harvard Medical School for clinical and research training as a tenured professor and director of the Harvard Digestive Diseases Center. Dr. Madara served as dean of the medical school and CEO of the hospitals at the University of Chicago. Dr. Madara covers some of the inequalities and barriers to health in Chicago and rural areas of the country: food and housing insecurity, income inequality, and limited health care access.

Madam Speaker, Madam President, members of the Board, delegates, and guests:

Welcome to Chicago . . . a city known for its architecture, museums, restaurants and rich music scene.

Chicago is a place where anything is possible . . . even time travel.

Here in downtown Chicago, it's 2019, and life expectancy for those living here is 82 years.

But if we hop on the train and ride just 20 minutes south to Fuller Park . . . life expectancy is only 65 years—that's less by 17 years.

That's right . . . just a few miles south, a person loses 17 years of life.

How far back in time would we have to travel for the average American to lose this much life expectancy—to expect to die at age 65?

The answer is from the 1930s to the 1940s . . . a period overlapping with the Great Depression . . . Prohibition . . . the infamous Chicago Stockyards.

All it takes to revist that distant era—from a health standpoint—is a short trip south. Or a short drive west for that matter, as life expectancy in a number of Chicago neighborhoods is far below the national average.

How can that be?

How . . . in a country and in a city as dynamic, rich in educational assets, and affluent as ours . . . can there be such an enormous difference in life expectancy from one neighborhood to the next?

A difference akin to time-traveling back the major part of a century?

One answer is found in what we now refer to as the social determinants of health.

Food insecurity, housing insecurity, income inequality, limited access to health

---

Delivered on June 8, 2019, at the American Medical Association, Chicago, IL. © American Medical Association. All rights reserved/Courtesy of AMA Archives.

care and transportation, and other circumstances . . . all conspire to erode a person's prospects for a healthy life. The're determinants of health and life.

Here in Chicago and, indeed, in much of the country—including rural America—these inequities are barriers to optimal health.

That's to say, there is an absence of health equity.

I'm sure all of you can recite the three arcs of our long-range strategic plan. A plan that rests upon the policy portfolio created by this House.

The first strategic arc is reimagining medical education and lifelong learning. This began with our consortium of medical schools, now numbering 37, and has produced a number of innovations such as the creation of the third medical science—health system science—as well as a shift to measured competancies.

Our second arc . . . confronting the challenge of chronic disease. This includes our focused work on pre-diabetes and better control of hypertension; with the latter, for example, now targeting 22 million hypertensive Americans in our program by the end of 2021. It also includes our work to end the opioid epidemic.

Ambitious aspirations.

And the third strategic arc is attacking the dysfunction in health care . . . by improving the environment of the patient-physician setting. Work here includes our web-based StepsForward practice improvement modules, our work to right-size prior authorization . . . and work which promises to improve the flow of clinical data, using the product of the first company spun out of Health2047 in Silicon Valley.

That new company is Akiri (A-K-I-R-I) —whose product is a clinical data liquidity solution. Check it out at Akiri.com.

As indicated by those examples, we've gained considerable traction in each of our strategic arcs . . . garnering national attention and expanding the AMA's reputation in leadership and innovation.

But what has become clear is that the inequities that persist throughout health care are obstacles to achieving our goals in each of our strategic areas.

That's to say, while we can be proud of our progress in the three arcs over the last seven years, we now have yet another call to action.

As a nation, and as an association, we need to ensure that when solutions to improve healtcare are identified, that positive impacts are recognized by all . . . that one shared characteristic of such solutions is that they also bend toward health equity.

Addressing inequities will require an enormous cooperative effort by our nation . . . the AMA will be a leader, positioned at the tip of this effort.

Not surprisingly, this House has recognized the importance of work toward health equity.

So, let me briefly touch on our emerging work in this area.

First, we're in the early launch phase of the AMA Center for Health Equity. Our founding Chief Health Equity Officer is now on board.

Dr. Aletha Maybank, a prominent national figure in health equity, has joined us from the New York City Department of Health. Aletha's first task is to lead the planning phase for our work on health equity . . . which will critically impact the breadth of our work at the AMA.

A springboard for this effort was our Health Equity Task Force chaired by Dr. Willarda Edwards, a long-standing member of this House and a current AMA Board member. Thanks Willarda and thanks to all members of that Task Force.

Improving health equity will take time . . . it will take patience . . . and it will take perseverance. It will also require new technological tools to facilitate rigorous analyses of underlying factors.

For example, currently there is a lack of a structured hierarchy to capture social determinants in a normalized and exacting fashion.

Lacking such tools impedes progress in understanding how social determinants impact health, and thus without these tools our ability to study, modify, and improve health equity is compromised.

In previous presentations, I have discussed a tool and approach that will aid the work of our three strategic arcs by improving the organization of, and extracting better meaning from, clinical data.

That tool—the Integrated Health Model Initiative, or IHMI—fills gaps in the current health data models to create better and more useful clinical data objects. This is an effort that was birthed in AMA Health Solutions and has now been launched as a unit led by Dr. Tom Giannulli, who I briefly introduced last fall.

Tom is a physician, an engineer, and a seasoned entrepreneur in the health data space.

Let me give an example of recent work of IHMI and you will see how it can carry over to work on social determinants.

Over the past year, the IHMI team created a software-based approach allowing a previous gap to be filled—in this instance it's the ability to capture accurate remote blood pressure measurements . . . and to both incorporate and organize those measurements in the medical record without paper shuffling by physicians.

Remotely monitored blood pressures . . . captured and coded in an organized electronic fashion . . . filling a critical gap in our work on chronic disease.

Similarly, and related to today's theme, this approach also provides a blueprint to more precisely capture, define and code for social determinants of health.

In collaboration with others, our IHMI team has begun work toward filling this need in social determinants . . . another example of how health equity penetrates all of our work, including cutting-edge innovation and technology.

At the Interim, I'll provide a more thorough update on our strategic arcs . . . and there's lots to say. I am compelled to at least provide you a taste.

Earlier this week we announced the eight medical schools, residency programs and health systems that will launch our 15 million dollar "Reimagining Residency" initiative.

Three of these eight institutions have innovative projects that relate to health equity or social determinants of health, better training our physicians of tomorrow to deliver more effective and equitable health care.

This initiative will bridge our work of reinventing medical school to the residency programs. The goal is to make a more seamless handoff from med school to residency while also placing GME on a 21st century footing.

Another taste: in coordination with our work on pre-diabetes, Health2047 has spun out a second company. FirstMileCare creates a new path to the prevention of chronic disease by taking a personal care approach and harnessing the gig economy—check it out FirstMileCare.com.

There're so many exciting things happening across the three arcs that I find myself verging on a tangent.

So, let me return to where we began—time travel.

This nation can't afford to travel backward when it comes to health care and life expectancy.

We need to work creatively, and collaboratively, to move forward; to create a health care system that deserves a place in the 21st century.

But how can we accomplish this considering the current contentious national health care debate?

How do we improve conditions for patients and physicians today, while also working to create the health system for the mid-21st century?

Our approach, as discussed in a prior address, is to focus on what I call pre-competitive needs . . . needs that are vast and unmet, but have to be filled for any health system to function optimally . . . regardless of its structure.

For example, any future health system will have these needs:

The need for better organized clinical data . . . true interoperability as a physician would define it, clinical data liquidity, and data technology that, overall, takes less time and expense—not more.

Also needed: physicians trained for the 21st century . . . not the 20th; for team-based care, analytics, population health, defined competencies including cultural competencies, and . . . the need to define new solutions to handle the tsunami of chronic disease.

Collectively, these are the needs addressed by our strategic arcs . . . and related to each of them are the challenges that come from system inequities related to social determinants of health.

To reach our ambitious goals, we need a mixed portfolio of activity . . . a balance between the needs of today, and the long-term pre-competitive needs that will make health care much better in the future.

Until then, let's focus on time-travel . . . but time-travel that is forward-looking.

Is a future with a well-sculpted health system an aspiration that seems too distant?

As was once said about time-travel: "Nothing is as far away as one minute ago."

Our future can, and should be, more accessible than our past.

Thank you.

Print Citations

CMS: Madara, James L. "Advancing Health Care through the Lens of History: Health Equity." Keynote Address at the American Medical Association, Chicago, IL, June 8, 2019. In *The Reference Shelf: Representative American Speeches, 2018–2019*, edited by Sophie Zyla, 210-214. Amenia, NY: Grey House Publishing, 2019.

MLA: Madara, James L. "Advancing Health Care through the Lens of History: Health Equity." American Medical Association, 8 June 2019, Hyatt Regency, Chicago, IL. Keynote Address. *The Reference Shelf: Representative American Speeches, 2018–2019*, edited by Sophie Zyla, Grey House Publishing, 2019, pp. 210-214.

APA: Madara, J.L. (2019, June 8). Keynote Address on advancing health care through the lens of history: Health equity. American Medical Association, Hyatt Regency Hotel, Chicago, IL. In Sophie Zyla (Ed.), *The reference shelf: Representative American speeches, 2018–2019* (pp. 210-214). Amenia, NY: Grey House Publishing.

Index

9/11, 57
311 calling system, 23
#MeToo movement, 100

Abdelal, Rawi, 23
abortion rights, 96
Abrams, Stacey, ix, 1, 11
addiction, ix, 109, 122, 177, 178, 197, 208
Aderholt, Robert, 172
Affordable Care Act (ACA), xiii, 95, 124, 180, 182, 188, 207
air pollution, 75, 80, 81, 157, 160
alcohol, 50, 197, 198, 199, 201, 203, 204
Aldrin, Buzz, 169, 170, 171, 173
Alexander, Lamar, 189
Alito, Samuel, 95
American Association for the Advancement of Science (AAAS), 147, 153, 162, 167, 168
American Bar Association (ABA), 98
American Dream, xi, 66, 108, 109, 112
American Enterprise Institute, 189, 194
American Institute of Aeronautics and Astronautics (AIAA), 147
American Medical Association (AMA), xiii, 206, 207, 208, 209, 211, 212
Anderson, Mary Lou, 208
Angelou, Maya, 206, 209
anti-Semitism, 109
Apollo 11, xiii, 169, 170, 171, 173, 174
Armstrong, Neil, 169, 170, 171
Armstrong, Rick, 169
artificial intelligence, 125
Assange, Julian, 129, 131
assault rifle, 63
astronaut, xiii, 147, 148, 149, 150, 151, 152, 153, 169, 170, 171, 172, 173, 174

Astronaut Corps, 150
asylum, 49, 51
Auñón-Chancellor, Serena, 148
authoritarianism, 109
authoritarian leaders, 122
Azar, Alex II, xiii, 73, 177, 180, 191

Babin, Brian, 172
background checks, x, 64, 65
Bacow, Larry, 36
Baird, James, 155
Bakaj, Andrew, 136
Barrasso, John, 74
Berlin Wall, 36, 37, 39
Bernhardt, David, 73, 82
Beyond Carbon, 23
Biaggi, Alessandra, 113
Biden, Hunter, 137, 138
Biden, Joe, 136, 137, 138, 140
bigotry, xi
bin Laden, Osama, 96
bipartisan, 74, 78, 156, 159, 173
birth control, 96
Bishop, Dan, 139, 140
Blatt, Lisa, 98
Bloomberg, Michael, 23
Booker, Cory, x, 62, 87
border enforcement, 49
Border Patrol agents, 43
border security, 44, 45, 46, 108
border wall, x, 43, 44
Brett, Jim, 122
Breyer, Stephen, 96
Bridenstine, Jim, 169
Bristow, Lonnie, 206
Brookings Institution, 189, 194
Brooks, David, xi
Brown v. the Board of Education, 96, 97
Bryant, Phil, 57
buprenorphine, 178, 198, 200
Burwell, Sylvia, 11

Bush, George H. W., 122
Bush, George W., 95, 96

Cabana, Robert, 169
capitalism, 26, 27, 28, 29
carbon dioxide, 31
Cato Institute, 123
censorship, 156, 157, 158, 159
census, 17, 187
Centers for Disease Control and Prevention (CDC), x, xiv, 155, 178
Cernan, Gene, 171
Chao, Elaine, 74
checks and balances, 69
child labor, 120
chronic conditions, 207, 208
citizenship, 111, 125
Citizens United, 117
civil rights, 106, 110, 111, 117, 150
civil rights movement, 71, 106, 120, 150
Civil War, 141
Clean Air Act, 157
clean energy, 23
clean water, 32, 73, 74
Clifford, Stephanie, 132
climate change, ix, xii, 13, 23, 28, 30, 32, 113, 115, 122, 125, 155, 158, 160, 162
Clinton, Bill, 96
Clinton, Hillary, 131, 133
Close, Glenn, ix, 18
Close, Jessie, 20
Clustered Regularly Interspaced Short Palindromic Repeats (CRISPR), 33
coal mining, 136, 141
cocaine, 43, 137, 199, 201, 202, 203, 204
codebreakers, 31
Cohen, Jonathan, 142
Cohen, Michael, xi, 128
Cold War, 36
Collins, Michael, 170, 171
Collins, Susan, xii, 94

confirmation bias, 163, 164
confirmation hearings, 92
confirmation process, xii, 94, 98, 99
consensus science, 166, 167
conservation, 78, 80, 82, 83, 125
conservative, ix, 12, 98, 123, 125
Constitutional Convention, 69
co-occurring substance use, 197, 203, 204
Copernicus, 33
corruption, xi, 4, 9, 60, 115, 116, 117, 119
cosmonaut, 147
Craft, Joe, 140
Craft, Kelly, 136, 140
Cramer, Kevin, 74
criminal gangs, 44, 56
criminal justice, 12, 13, 106, 107, 109, 118, 124, 199
Cronkite, Walter, 171
Cruz, Ted, 57
Cummings, Elijah, 69, 128, 134, 135
cutting-edge innovation, 212
cybersecurity, 111
cytochrome p 450 system, 206

Daines, Steve, 74
Darwin, Charles, 33
Declaration of Independence, 64
DeMint, Jim, 55
democracy, xi, 16, 37, 39, 60, 61, 69, 71, 72, 108, 111, 114, 115, 116, 117, 123, 126, 156, 159, 182
Democratic National Committee, 129, 131
Democrats, x, xi, 26, 44, 54, 60, 76, 78, 120
Department of Interior (DOI), 155
deportation, 57
depression, xiv, 197, 202, 203, 204
DeSantis, Casey, 169
DeSantis, Ron, 76, 169
Deutsche Bank, 129, 131
Dickey, Nancy, 206

dictatorship, 36
discrimination, 26, 27, 118, 119
disease, 38, 106, 136, 141, 163, 193, 196, 203, 207, 211, 212, 213
diversity, 147, 154, 207
Douglass, Fredrick, 110
Dreamers, 108
drug abuse, 198, 205
drug addiction, 109
drug dealers, 56
drug prices, 182
drug smugglers, 44
Durbin, Dick, 137

economy, xi, 25, 44, 49, 73, 74, 75, 76, 79, 80, 85, 108, 109, 110, 115, 117, 119, 123, 125, 184, 190, 213
education, x, 3, 19, 27, 28, 34, 39, 89, 110, 118, 125, 126, 148, 153, 167, 190, 197, 200, 211
Edwards, Willarda, 212
Eisenhower, Dwight D., 126
election, xi, 53, 54, 57, 60, 61, 68, 71, 75, 111, 120, 126, 131, 137, 139
Electoral College, 54
electoral integrity, 16
electricity, 32, 74
emissions levels, 161
Engel, Eliot, 69
Environmental Protection Agency (EPA), 76, 80, 155, 157, 158, 159
equal justice, 117
Eshoo, Anna, 91
ethics, 23, 25, 26, 71, 104, 116
Europa, 33

Facebook, 19, 62
Fair Fight Action, 11, 16
"fake news", xiv
farmers, 33, 58, 80
Federal Bureau of Investigation (FBI), 100
Federalist Society, 98
Feinstein, Dianne, 100

fentanyl, 43, 199
filibuster, 62, 67
First Amendment, ix
First Step legislation, 124
Fisk, Robert, 96
Flynn, Karen Hobert, 103, 104
Food and Drug Administration (FDA), 155, 157, 200, 204
forced migration, x, 38, 39
Ford, Christine Blasey, xii, 89, 93, 94, 98, 99
Fossil Free Dalsland, 160
fossil fuel, 103, 114
Founding Fathers, 34
Franklin, Benjamin, 69
Franklin, Bobby, 13
freedom of speech, 13, 65
free speech, ix, x, 158
Frost, Robert, xiv

Garland, Merrick, 98
Gates, Robert, 18
Giannulli, Tom, 212
Ginsburg, Ruth Bader, 96, 98
global warming, ix, 39, 160
Gorsuch, Neil, 55, 95
government accountability, 156
government regulation, 53
Grassley, Chuck, 89, 100, 101, 194
Great Depression, xiii, 26, 120, 125, 210
Great Recession, 107
Green New Deal, 76, 117
Greenwood, Lee, 53
Gregg, Judd, 122
Griswold v. Connecticut, 97
Gross, Al, 193
gross domestic product, 189
guest worker programs, 49
gun control, x, 60
gun lobby, 61
gun owners, 55, 56, 63, 65, 66
guns, x, 49, 56, 60, 66, 106, 107, 115
gun safety, 113, 114

gunshow loophole, x
gun violence, x, 28, 61, 63, 66
Guterres, António, 142
Gutfreund, John, 24

Haley, Nikki, 142
hallucinogens, 199, 202
Halpern, Michael, xii, 155, 159
Hamdan v. the United States, 96
Hamilton, Alexander, 95
Handel, Karen, 53
Harris, Kamala, xi, 106, 107
Harris, Patrice A., xiii, 206
Hawley, Willis, 125
HEAL Initiative, 177, 178, 179
healthcare, ix, xiii, 25, 53, 103, 108, 110, 113, 114, 115, 122, 124, 175, 177, 180, 182, 183, 184, 187, 189, 190, 191, 192, 193, 194, 198, 199, 200, 207, 208, 210, 211, 212, 213
health equity, xiii, 208, 211, 212
health insurance, 115, 181, 187, 190, 191, 192
health system science, 211
Helmut Kohl, 36
heroin, 43, 197, 199, 200, 203
Hesse, Hermann, 36
Heston, Charlton, 53
Hewson, Marillyn, 169
Hogg, David, x, 60
Holocaust, 37, 130
homeless, 16, 196, 199, 207
homicides, 50, 51
homophobia, 109
housing, 25, 118, 210
Hrobak, Bruce, 73, 77
Hughes, Langston, 66
humanitarian crisis, 44
human rights abuse, 108
human traffickers, 44
hunger, ix, 39, 48
hydrocodone, 199, 200

illegal immigrants, x, 43
illegal migration, 43
immigration, ix, x, 44, 45, 46, 49, 51, 52, 56, 57, 125, 190
Immigration & Customs Enforcement (ICE), 43
impeachment, x, xi, xiv, 41, 68, 69, 70, 72
income inequality, 28, 210
Independents, 26
individual freedoms, 39, 122
Industrial Revolution, 31
inhalants, 199
Instagram, 19
insurance costs, xiii
insurance premiums, 181
Integrated Health Model Initiative, 212
International Space Station, 147, 148, 151, 152
intolerance, 128

James, Brent, 189
Jha, Ashisha, 192
Johnson, Eddie, 156
Johnson Space Center, xii, 145, 147, 148, 150, 151, 152, 153
Jones, Lucy, xii, 162
Jordan, Jim, 128
journalism, ix, 3, 6, 9
Judge, Mark, 90, 91, 99
judicial Independence, 98
Jupiter, 33

Kagan, Elena, 95
Kaiser, Leland, 99
Kasich, John, xi, xiv
Kavanaugh, Brett, xii, 89, 90, 91, 92, 93, 94, 95, 96, 97, 98, 99, 100, 101, 102
Kelly, John, 56
Kennedy, Anthony, 97
Kennedy, John F., 11, 169, 174
King, Angus, 63
King, Martin Luther, Jr., 64

Lanksy, David, 189
LaPierre, Wayne, 53
law enforcement, 4, 44, 56, 107, 129
Leahy, Patrick, 137
Letter from the Birmingham Jail, 64
Lewis, John, x, 71
LGBTQ activists, 120
LGBTQ community, 208
life expectancy, xiii, 210, 213
lifelong learning, 211
Lincoln, Abraham, 127, 138
Lincoln Memorial, 73
Littel, John, 18
Lynch, Calder, 187
Lysiak, Hilde Kate, ix, 3

Madara, James L., xiii, 210
Maher, Bill, 143
Marbury v. Madison, 96
March for Our Lives, x, 60, 61
marijuana, 197, 198, 199, 200, 201, 202, 203, 204
Marjory Stoneman Douglas High School, x, 60
Marjory Stoneman Douglas High School shooting, x
Mars, Bruno, 34
Marshall, George, 37
mass shootings, x
Maybank, Aletha, 211
McCain, John, 133
McCance-Katz, Elinore, xiv, 196
McCready, Dan, 139
media bias, xiv
Medicaid, xiii, 178, 182, 187, 188, 189, 190, 193
Medicare, xiii, 110, 117, 181, 182, 183, 188, 189, 190, 193
Mehrbani, Rudy, 104
Menendez, Robert, 137
mental health, xiv, 21, 196, 197, 202, 203, 204, 205, 208
mental illness, xiv, 20, 21, 196, 197, 198, 202, 203, 204, 207, 208

Merkel, Angela, ix, 36, 40
methadone, 178, 200
methamphetamine, 198, 199, 201, 202, 203, 204
Meyers, Daniel, 12
middle class, 28, 106, 107, 110, 113, 126
midterm elections, 60, 61
minimum wage, 120
Mnuchin, Steve, 73
moral leadership, 25, 111, 112
Moynihan, Daniel Patrick, 26
MS-13 gang, 45, 50, 56
Mueller report, 117
Mueller, Robert, 117
Murphy, Greg, 139

Nadler, Jerry, 69
National Academy of Medicine, 189
National Aeronautics and Space Administration (NASA), xiii, 145, 147, 148, 150, 151, 153, 169, 170, 172, 173
National Association of Counties (NACo), 79
National Fish Passage Program, 83
National Instututes of Health (NIH), 177, 178
nationalism, 126
National Oceanic and Atmospheric Administration (NOAA), 158
National Rifle Association (NRA), x, 53, 54, 55, 56, 57, 58, 60, 61
National Science Board (NSB), 153
National Science Foundation (NSF), 153
national security, 45, 57, 69, 172
National Space Council, 169, 172
National Survey on Drug Use, xiv, 196, 205
nativism, 126
natural gas, 75, 84
Nazario, Sonia, x, 47
Neal, Richie, 69

Neumayr, Mary, 73, 74, 81
Never Again MSD, x, 60
New Deal, 26, 76, 117, 120
Newton, Isaac, 33
New York Times, xi, xiv, 47, 155
Nielsen, Kirstjen, xi, 87
Nobel Peace Prize, 160
North American Wildlife Conservation Model, 83
nuclear power, 33, 84
nuclear weapons, 33, 122
Nye, Bill, 30

Obama, Barack, xiii, 95, 131, 133
Obamacare, 193
Ocasio-Cortez, Alexandria, xi, 103
Ochoa, Ellen, xii, 145, 147
O'Connor, Sandra Day, 97
open borders, 49, 53
opioid addiction, ix, 178
opioid crisis, ix, xiii, xiv, 109, 177, 178, 204
opioid disorders, 196
opioid epidemic, xiii, 196, 208, 211
opioids, 178, 197, 198, 199, 200, 204
Opportunity Zones, 81
optimal health, 211
oxycodone, 199, 200
ozone hole, 151

Paris Climate Accords, 23, 75, 125
partisanship, x, 26, 63
Payne, Thomas, 69
peer review, 157
Pelosi, Nancy, x, 41, 68, 70, 135
Pence, Mike, xiii, 169
Perdue, David, 57
Perkins, Francis, 119, 120
Perry, Rick, 73, 84
philanthropy, 27
Pick, Calen, 20
Planned Parenthood v. Casey, 97
political opinions, 8
Posey, Bill, 172

pregnancy, 197, 201
Preston, Levi, 58
Prohibition, xiii, 210
protectionism, 38

racism, 109, 122
Reed, Maryanne, 3
refugees, 49, 111
religion, 38, 60, 71, 110
Republicans, x, 26, 53, 54, 60, 65, 66, 123, 135
Revere, Paul, 58
Rice, Condoleezza, 95
Ride, Sally, 150
right to bear arms, x, 65
risk perception, 164
Roberts, Colleen, 73, 79
Roberts, John, 95
Rodriguez, Kevin, 49
Roe v. Wade, 96, 97
Roosevelt, Franklin D., 26, 28, 119
Roosevelt, Theodore, 26, 28, 80, 125
Ross, Wilbur, 73
Rowe, Katherine, 18
Rubio, Marco, x, 60, 76
rule of law, 26, 56, 117, 122, 126
Russian Space Agency, 151

Sacks, Oliver, xiv
Salomon, Billy, 25, 27
Sandia National Labs, 150
Save Our Seas Act, 78, 82
Scalia, Antonin, 55, 177, 180
Scalise, Steve, 172
Scammon, Howard, 19
Schiff, Adam, 69, 135, 141
schizophrenia, 20, 21, 197
Schmidt, Harrison, 171
Schumer, Chuck, 44
Schwarzman, Steve, 138
science communication, 162
science, technology, engineering, and mathematics (STEM), xiii, 145, 147, 153, 154, 167

Scientific Integrity Act, 156, 157
scientific method, xii, 163, 165
scientific misconduct, 157
Second Amendment, ix, x, 53, 54, 55, 56, 57, 58
Seeing Voices, xiv
Selva, Paul, 169
Sessions, Jeff, 56
Seven-Sky v. Holder, 95
sexism, 109
sexual assault, xii, 91, 92, 93, 98, 99, 100, 107
Shaub, Walter, 104, 105
Sherrill, Mikie, 155
Slovak, Paul, 165
Smoot, Reed, 125
Smyth, P.J., 90
social determinants, 210, 212, 213
social media, xiv, 5, 19, 62, 67, 94
social security, 124
Society for Advancement of Chicanos/Hispanics and Native Americans in Science (SACNAS), xiii, 145, 147, 154
Society of Professional Journalists, 3
Sotomayor, Sonia, 95
Souter, David, 97, 98
space exploration, 148, 151, 171, 172, 173
Stevens, Haley, 155, 156
Stockholm Syndrome, 123
Stone, Roger, 129, 131
student debt, 109, 115, 118, 126
substance abuse, xiv, 196, 197, 198, 199
Substance Abuse and Mental Health Services Administration (SAMHSA), 178, 196, 197, 198, 201, 204, 205
suicide, ix, 197, 198, 202, 203, 204
suicide prevention, 198

tariffs, 125
taxes, 13, 53, 123, 124, 131, 190
technology, xiii, 31, 33, 38, 43, 44, 81, 82, 84, 141, 197, 198, 205, 212, 213
terrorism, 38, 57, 63, 64
Thomas, Allen, 139
Thunberg, Greta, ix, xii, 160
Tonko, Paul, 156
trade, 28, 38, 44, 119, 125
trafficking, 57, 106
tramadol, 200
Tranquility Base, 171
transportation, 30, 117, 211
treason, 136, 140, 141
Triangle Factory fire, 120
Triangle Shirtwaist Factory, 113
Triangle Women, 119
Trump, Donald, ix, x, xi, 41, 43, 53, 54, 59, 68, 73, 78, 79, 80, 81, 82, 83, 87, 94, 95, 96, 97, 115, 122, 127, 128, 129, 130, 131, 132, 133, 134, 135, 136, 169, 172, 177, 178, 180, 181, 182, 183
Trump, Donald, Jr., 132, 133, 134
Trump Foundation, 132
Tubman, Harriet, 110
Twenty-Second Amendment, 143
Twitter, 8, 12, 19, 62, 140, 148

uncertainty analysis, 164
unemployment, 75, 120, 123
Union of Concerned Scientists, 155, 156
uniqueness, ix, 18, 19
United Nations, ix, xii, 136, 137, 142, 160, 161
United States v. Nixon, 96
U.S. Constitution, 34
U.S. Department of Agriculture Cooperative Extension, 198
U.S. Department of Education, 126
U.S. Department of Energy, 78, 84, 158
U.S. Department of Health and Human Services (HHS), 177, 180
U.S. Department of Justice, 126

U.S.-Mexico-Canada Agreement (USMCA), 75
U.S. Supreme Court, 55, 91, 94, 177, 180

Verma, Seema, xiii, 175, 182
veterans, 54, 111, 125
Veterans Administration (VA), 54
Vietnam War, 43, 133
violent crime, 53
volunteer, 27, 120
voter rights, 16
voter suppression, 11, 16

waivers, 185, 186, 187, 188
Wall Street, 24, 107, 123
Wall Street Journal, 123
Warren, Elizabeth, xi, 113
Washington Monument, 73
Washington Post, 91, 92, 103, 155
Water Infrastructure Act, 76
Water Security Grand Challenge, 78, 84
Waters, Maxine, 69

Watt, James, 31
Weisselberg, Allen, 132
Weld, Bill, 122, 127
Westerman, Bruce, 74
Wheeler, Andrew, 74, 80
whistle-blower, 68, 69, 136, 140, 143
white supremacist, 108, 131
WikiLeaks, 129, 131
wildfires, xi, 78, 109, 115
Williams, Robin, 20
Wilson, Edward O., 21
women's rights, 92, 111
Working Families Party, 113
workplace ethics, 23
World Health Organization, 23, 193
World War II, 31, 37, 47, 125
Wright Brothers, 31, 33
Wyden, Ronald, 194

Youngstown Steel v. Sawyer, 96
Zaid, Mark, 136
Zelenskiy, Volodymyr, 136, 137
Zinke, Ryan, 56